Mon Cher Papa

Mon Cher Papa
Franklin and the Ladies of Paris
by Claude-Anne Lopez

With a New Preface by the Author

New Haven and London
Yale University Press

First published in 1966 by Yale University Press.
New edition copyright © 1990 by Yale University.

Designed by Alvin Eisenman and Sheila de Bretteville.
Set in Fournier type.

Printed in the United States of America by
Thomson-Shore, Inc., Dexter, Michigan.

Library of Congress Cataloging-in-Publication Data
Lopez, Claude-Anne.
    Mon cher papa : Franklin and the ladies of Paris / Claude-Anne
Lopez.
        p.   cm.
    Includes bibliographical references.
    ISBN 0-300-04800-9. — ISBN 0-300-04758-4 (pbk.)
    1. Franklin, Benjamin, 1706-1790—Relations with women.
2. Franklin, Benjamin, 1706-1790—Homes and haunts—France—
Paris. 3. Women—France—Paris—History—18th century. 4. Paris
(France)—Social life and customs—18th century. I. Title.
E302.6.F8L8   1990
973.3'092—dc20
[B]
                                                      89-28455
                                                      CIP

10   9   8   7   6   5   4   3   2   1

Le docteur Franklin couronné par la Liberté,
aquatint by the Abbé de Saint Non, 1778

To Lynn, my future and my joy

Preface to the New Edition

In the twenty-three years that have elapsed since the first edition of this book, I have had the opportunity to read the balance of Benjamin Franklin's correspondence during his mission to France and to discover what he was doing when not occupied with the ladies. This has given me a deeper and somewhat darker perspective on his life during these years, when he was in his seventies. The aches and pains he tried to make light of when writing to women friends were revealed as being much harder to bear when seen in his everyday writings or poignantly revealed in fragments of his diaries. The United States Congress's relentless tendency to overspend, the merchants' complaints, the ship captains' quarrels, both with the French and among themselves, the flood of letters too great to be answered one by one, the money to be wheedled out of the French, the diplomatic tensions to be eased, the wounded prides to be soothed: all these problems, discovered in the thousands of documents of the Franklin Collection, must have been sources of anguish to the minister plenipotentiary—a minister who had to function entirely on his own, with a measure of responsibility unimaginable to present-day ambassadors. Above all, the hostility of John Adams, of the Lee brothers, Arthur and William, of Ralph Izard, and of a number of other fellow Americans were revealed to be more vociferous, longer lasting, and more hurtful than I had imagined. Through it all, Franklin fought back with humor. While confined by a severe episode of gout, he wrote in a letter to Montaudoüin that "there seems however some Incongruity in a *Pleni-potentiary* who can neither stand nor go."*

These trials illustrate the importance of some joy in Frank-

* Franklin to Jean-Gabriel Montaudoüin de La Touche, 17 March 1779, copy, Library of Congress.

lin's life, some warmth and comfort, maybe even some un-
warranted adulation. Of course, he cannot have been as
saintly, as perfect as the French imagined him, but by giving him their wholehearted approval at such a crucial and
dangerous moment in both his life and that of his country,
they played a role in the American Revolution that ex-
ceeded in its impact even the sending of supplies and an expeditionary corps. In other words, the topic of this book is
not trivial, as I sometimes feared while writing it twenty-
five years ago.

I was able, in those intervening years, to learn more
about Franklin's life before and after Paris. Stimulated by
the many questions I was asked about his home life, I
joined forces with my friend Eugenia Herbert, and in the
course of writing *The Private Franklin: The Man and His Family* (Norton, 1976) we delved into his English roots and his
love affair with England, his difficult start in life, his extraordinary drive, and his occasional harshness toward his
relatives. The difference between that Franklin and "Mon
Cher Papa" shows how immensely adaptable he was, knowing how best to bend his personality to each time and place.
The prelude with which this new edition opens briefly
evokes the Boston of Franklin's youth, a Boston in striking
contrast with the Paris in which the rest of the book takes
place. Of the huge Franklin family depicted, only two siblings were still alive at the time of "Mon Cher Papa"—
Benjamin, the fifteenth child, and his favorite sister, Jane, the
seventeenth and last of the brood. In a return to his roots, he
would ask Jane to send cakes of the family's Crown soap to
the fancy ladies of Paris.

What would I change in *Mon Cher Papa* if I could? I
would note that, though she wrote in English, Countess
Conway was French. Born Françoise-Antoinette Langlois

du Bouchet, this shy young woman was deeply in love with her impetuous Irish husband, Thomas Conway, who sailed for America in 1777 along with the countess's brother. She began to study English right away, for she planned to join Conway in America after victory, "to live under the Laws of venerable goodman richard," her way of rendering Poor Richard, in French *Le Bonhomme Richard.* From Burgundy, where she lived, many messages were sent to her "dear father américain" by his "truly tenderly daugheter." These letters were always pleas for news, for the countess was full of dark foreboding. She must have known her husband's hot temper only too well. Made a brigadier general in the Continental army, Conway soon found himself in conflict with George Washington and by the end of 1777 had sent a compromising letter to Gen. Horatio Gates about the commander in chief. "Conway's Cabal" led to the resignation of his commission in the spring of 1778 and to a duel with Gen. John Cadwalader on July 4, during which Conway was seriously wounded. When rumors of these events reached his wife, she became frantic, not quite believing Franklin's vaguely reassuring messages, and would not calm down until her husband returned to France in March 1779. Her last letter to Franklin reveals that Conway had berated her for some faux pas. Conway eventually became governor-general of the French possessions in India. He remained a royalist during the French Revolution and died in exile. One can only hope that at some time Françoise knew a little happiness in life.

I owe apologies to the Monsieur Pierre who appears on page 234 as a nobody, prevented by the Fourniers from receiving the Franklin portrait he coveted. Au contraire! Philippe-Denis Pierres (1741–1808) was quite a somebody: printer to the king, typographical innovator, member of various academies, and, best of all, the man to whom Franklin entrusted, in 1783, the job of printing *American Constitutions,* a book Franklin distributed lavishly among his acquaintances. Madame Pierres once declared that she would like to spend the rest of her life with Franklin. Whether the couple ever received their own portrait of the great man, however, is a moot point.

It was an optimistic statement, back in 1965, to say that the publication of Franklin's papers in the ongoing Yale edition would reach the French period within ten years: it took seventeen. But now, for the past five volumes (XXIII–XXVII), Franklin has been in Paris and documents written by or to him from December 1776 through October 1778 can be found in print.

New biographies of Franklin have appeared in the past few years, but only two books deal specifically with his years in France: in *Triumph in Paris: The Exploits of Benjamin Franklin* (Harper & Row, 1976), David Schoenbrun asks questions from a journalist's perspective and comes up with fresh insights; in *Yankees at the Court: The First Americans in Paris* (Doubleday, 1982), Susan Mary Alsop draws a lively collective portrait of the American colony in Paris.**

To reread a preface one wrote almost a quarter of a century ago is a bittersweet experience. That faraway Claude-Anne Lopez speaks in a tentative, apologetic voice that is no longer mine. She sounds a little quaint, more like a grand-

---

** Other references of note: Ronald W. Clark, *Benjamin Franklin: A Biography* (New York: Random, 1983); Thomas Fleming, *The Man Who Dared the Lightning: A New Look at Benjamin Franklin* (New York: Morrow, 1971); Benjamin Franklin, *The Bagatelles from Passy,* Facsimile edition (New York: Eakins Press, 1967); Esmond Wright, *Franklin of Philadelphia* (Cambridge: Harvard Univ. Press, Belknap Press, 1986).

mother than a younger self, and it takes an effort to remember that such was the way we expressed ourselves then.

Several of the people I thanked are no longer alive. The husband to whom I dedicated the book will never know that it has been reissued or that its publication in France, which he desired so much, is about to happen. Our sons still lend their support, though they have long since moved to distant states.

But Franklin will always be there. He has moved closer to the center of my work, and I am glad that Yale University Press has decided to give *Mon Cher Papa* a new chance to honor a life that ended just two centuries ago. My thanks go to John Ryden, director of the Press, to Mary Alice Galligan, editions editor, and to Leslie Nelson, reprints editor, as well as to all the friends who sustained me during the hard times of these past years.

New Haven
October 1989

CLAUDE-ANNE LOPEZ

Another book on Franklin? Has not everything been said about the man, the scientist, the diplomat, the writer, everything about every facet of this American who could be at the same time so thoroughly Anglo-Saxon and so fully cosmopolitan? Why should a woman, not even born in America, whose upbringing and tradition are French, turn the spotlight on him once more?

Everything has not really been said, not from all possible points of view. Just as Robert Benchley remarked about the Vatican that, splendid as it was, it lacked a woman's touch, it does not seem inappropriate to study Franklin once again, from a feminine angle. Women, they say, have no special gift for synthesis but patience enough to ferret out countless details; well, let us try an intimate close-up of a man's leisure hours, after he has been using his gift for synthesis throughout the working day. Women, they contend, are more oriented to personalities than to ideas; well, let us write about people and the thousand ways they react to each other, while ideas take shape. French women, they claim, are endowed with a feeling for the many nuances of tenderness. Here, then, is a book about the facets of love, the tormented yearning of a young woman, the boisterous fondness of an aging widow, the somewhat patronizing affection of a dowager duchess, the shy longing of a printer's wife, and, of course, the ever-changing response of the man with whom all of France was infatuated.

Frivolous? Less than one might believe. Legends die hard; fed by musicals and magazines, drawing both from sensationalism and a lingering puritanical sense of shock, the myth that Franklin in Paris behaved like an old lecher having a jolly time is still with us. The truth is far less titillating. He was, simply, the greatest ambassador that America ever sent to France. So few Americans seem aware of the magnitude of Franklin's role in Paris and of his impact on French thought. And yet, he was the strongest bridge that ever existed between the cultures, one of those rare people who knew how to temper an American seriousness of purpose with a French irony of manner.

As I was working, month after month, at the Franklin Papers at Yale, preparing for a distant publication date the material on Franklin's eight years in Paris (1777–85), there emerged from the thousands of documents assembled in our files a story so human and so fresh that it seemed a pity to wait the ten years or more it will take the Yale edition to reach 1777. While my colleagues were discussing Franklin-the-inventor, Franklin-the-printer, Franklin-the-postmaster, I could not help feeling that my Franklin, the spry and mellow septuagenarian, the indomitable revolutionary, the tireless peacemaker, my French Franklin was indeed the best of them all, the sum total of the man.

Professor Leonard W. Labaree, our editor, was willing to let me bring out this book long before the documents of the French period are published; he consulted the authorities in charge at the American Philosophical Society, sponsors of the Franklin Papers, and brought back their blessing. He also read the various chapters as they were ready and gave me the benefit of his vast Franklinian knowledge; may his time and confidence have been well placed. My colleague Helen Boatfield, too, generously opened to me the elaborate files of background material she has on tap at the Franklin collection. Even though he no longer worked as associate editor at the Franklin Papers, Whitfield J. Bell had become so conditioned to answering my various cries for help that from his new post in Philadelphia he kept me supplied with sprightly bits of Frankliniana and useful leads for illustrations. Working along with him at the Library of the American Philosophical Society, Mrs. Gertrude D. Hess offered prompt and indispensable assistance in the search for pictures.

As soon as one has decided to write a book, help pours in from many sides. Your brooding teen-ager offers to read a chapter and give you his honest opinion. You submit it with trepidation. "Too long," he says, "but show me another." Your eleven-year old volunteers for your notes a "sacred shelf" to be set apart from the battlefield of his room, and stoically leaves it alone. Your friend Florence Kiper Frank, bringing to the task a lifetime of literary achievement, takes a look at your first draft, has the courage to tell you that it will not do at all, why it will not do, and to point out new paths. Caught in the same web of PTA, household, and chauffeuring as you – plus her teaching at Yale – your friend Alice Miskimin finds time for a number of lunches during which, editorial pencil in hand, she removes the gallicisms from your third draft, tones down your metaphors to a proper Anglo-Saxon level, and, by her sheer presence, imparts to your working habits some of her own inexhaustible drive. Then come Anne Bittker to read and polish, and Margaret Tuttle, to listen to large chunks of the manuscript, encourage you, and by her pertinent and impertinent questions force you to clarify your views. Finally, how does one thank Jane Isay, of the Yale Press, with whom it was so much fun to work on the manuscript while she was racing the stork, and on galleys against the background of young David's benevolent gurgling? And how does one thank a husband who prodded, suggested, discussed at every step, made himself unpopular by insisting on rigorous historical standards, and finally committed you to complete the work by doubting loudly that you would?

At this point, I know, I ought to claim total responsibility for the errors in this book, but, in all fairness, I think that those ladies of Franklin's acquaintance who did not date or sign their letters and those who wrote illegibly should partly bear the brunt. I have spent months in their company, attempting to re-create their thoughts, their personalities, their famous *sensibilités*, recognizing facets of them in my own friends, trying to dream their dreams and see myself in their dresses. This book has been conceived as a tribute to them, to their role in Franklin's life. In our modern culture, which pays so much attention to sex and so little to women, it was to be an exercise in nostalgia, a pageant where ladies had the best lines and the leading parts.

But the men would not be kept out. As husbands, lovers, protégés, priests, sons, friends, exponents of thought in the exquisite setting provided for them, as the doers and the movers, they were still clamoring for time, space, and attention, just as they had scrambled, in their day, for a few hours with Franklin. And isn't that, after all, as it should be? It would be a sad society, indeed, if women could be studied apart from men; and the eighteenth century knew better than any other than only when those immensely unequal partners reach out toward each other in an immense complexity of ways do they savor the meaning, the joy, and the glory of life.

New Haven
October 17, 1965   CLAUDE-ANNE LOPEZ

Contents

Preface to the New Edition vii
Preface xiii
List of Illustrations xix
Prelude xxiii

1 *The Toast of Paris* 1
2 *Madame Brillon's Suitor* 29
3 *Madame Brillon's Papa* 55
4 *Madame Brillon's Genius* 89
5 *Friends and Neighbors in Passy* 123
6 *La Comtesse d'Houdetot* 151
7 *From Queen to Countess* 179
8 *From Bourgeoise to Beggar* 207
9 *Notre Dame d'Auteuil* 243
10 *L'Académie d'Auteuil* 273
11 *The Parting of the Ways* 303

Chronology of Franklin's Dealings with France 335
Bibliographical Note to Franklin's Years in Paris 341
Notes 357
Index 379

List of Illustrations

Le Docteur Franklin couronné par la Liberté, aquatint by the Abbé de Saint Non, 1778: courtesy of American Philosophical Society, Philadelphia.   iii

Franklin surrounded by the ladies at court, engraved by W. O. Geller, c. 1830, painted by Baron Jolly, Bruxelles: courtesy of the Papers of Benjamin Franklin, Yale University.   xxvi

The Apotheosis of Franklin, a cotton panel, England c. 1790: courtesy of the Cooper Union Museum, New York, N.Y.   24

Moulin Joli, drawn by Daubigny, engraved by Denis Née, c. 1790: *Voyage pittoresque de la France*; courtesy of the New York Public Library.   28

"Marche des Insurgents," by Madame Brillon: courtesy of American Philosophical Society, Philadelphia.   37

View of Passy, aquatint by Madame Brillon: courtesy of the Papers of Benjamin Franklin, Yale University.   54

Manuscript of the *Dialogue between Dr. Franklin and the Gout*, with Madame Brillon's corrections: courtesy of American Philosophical Society, Philadelphia.   76

Franklin's sketch of a garden in Passy: courtesy of American Philosophical Society, Philadelphia.   86

William Temple Franklin: P. L. Ford, *The Many-Sided Franklin* (New York, Century, 1899), p. 300.   88

Madame Chaumont, a medallion by J.-B. Nini: A. Storelli, *Jean-Baptiste Nini* (Tours, A. Mame et Fils, 1896), p. 121.   122

Franklin, a medallion by J.-B. Nini: ibid., p. 95.   125

Miniature of Louis XVI, his parting gift to Franklin: American Philosophical Society, Philadelphia, courtesy of Mr. Richard B. Duane.   136

Jacques-Donatien Leray de Chaumont, a medallion by J.-B. Nini: Storelli, *Jean-Baptiste Nini*, p. 97.   148

Madame d'Houdetot, 1786: Robert de Crèvecoeur, *Saint John de Crèvecoeur* (Paris, Librairie des Bibliophiles, 1883), facing p. 116.   150

Le Baquet de Mesmer, a cartoon: Bibliothèque Nationale, Paris; courtesy of Librairie Hachette, Paris.   163

An American Eagle: John T. White, *Specimen of Printint Types and Ornaments* (New York, 1843).   176

Coiffure à l'Indépendance, 1778: courtesy of Musée de Blérancourt, Aisne, France.   178

Invitation to dinner from Marquis de Lafayette: courtesy of New-York Historical Society, New York.   201

A royal banquet, January 23, 1782, drawn by J. M. Moreau the younger: Pierre de Nolhac, *Marie-Antoinette* (Paris, Goupil, n.d.), facing p. 72.   204

Ascension of Montgolfier balloon, September 19, 1783: Comte de la Vaulx, Paul Tissandier, and Charles Dollfus, *L'Aéronautique: des origines à 1922* (Paris, Floury, 1922), ill. 6.   206

Lavoisier and his wife in their laboratory: E. Grimaux, *Lavoisier* (Paris, Alcan, 1888), p. 128.   209

Observing the Ephemera by Night: René-Antoine Ferchault de Réaumur, *Mémoires pour servir à l'histoire des insectes* (6 vols., Paris, 1734–1742), VI, p. 1. Courtesy of the Yale University Library.   217

Portrait of Franklin, by Rosalie Filleul: courtesy of American Philosophical Society, Philadelphia.   230

Rosalie Filleul's Self-Portrait: courtesy of American Philosophical Society, Philadelphia.   231

Portrait of Madame Helvétius, by Louis-Michel Vanloo: courtesy of Caisse Nationale des Monuments Historiques, Paris.   242

An eighteenth-century salon: H. W. Lawrence and B. L. Dighton, *French Line Engravings of the Late XVIII Century* (London, Lawrence and Jellicoe, 1910).   261

Portrait of Turgot, from the portrait in pastels by J. N. Ducreux: Nolhac, *Marie-Antoinette*, facing p. 20.   269

Portrait of Franklin, by Philippe Amédée Vanloo: courtesy of American Philosophical Society, Philadelphia.   272

Three Positions of the Elbow, illustration to Franklin's letter in praise of wine, drawn by Temple: courtesy of American Philosophical Society, Philadelphia.   293

Opening of the *Etats Généraux*, 1789: Nolhac, *Marie-Antoinette* (Paris, Plon, 1936), p. 209.   302

Prelude

January 1706. Boston is seventy-six years old. Harvard, its glory, is seventy. New England shivers and the worst of winter is yet to come. Painted in vivid colors, perhaps to defy the gloom, the town's little houses, about a thousand of them, send toward the sky the smoke of their defective stoves. Indoors it is always dark: windows are tiny because of the climate and because glass is so expensive. Sometimes there is not enough wood to go around; sometimes drinking water is in short supply. One baby in four does not make it beyond the first week of life.

And yet the population keeps growing. It has reached almost six thousand. Helped perhaps by an adequate supply of homemade cider and imported rum and wine, the Bostonians think themselves lucky to be breathing an air purer than that of London, and to be freer, too—lucky to live in a society where it is possible to climb to the top.

In narrow Milk Street, near the harbor, Abiah Franklin feels that the time is drawing close for the birth of her eighth child—*her* eighth, but the fifteenth for her husband, Josiah. When she married Josiah seventeen years ago, she took the place of his first wife, Anne, who had died in labor. The transition happened so smoothly that the addition of new babies to the family was not slowed.

Anne had arrived from England with her husband and their three children when she was still quite young; but transplantation, the harsh climate in Massachusetts, and too many pregnancies, perhaps, had exhausted her. Though her first five children thrived, her sixth, little Joseph, lived only a few days. As was the custom, she tried right away to replace him with another Joseph, who was born the following year but died within two weeks, preceded to the grave by his mother. Abiah Folger, a strong girl from Nantucket, took charge of the five older children and soon gave them a string of siblings.

The house and shop, at the sign of The Blue Ball, smell of hot wax. Josiah, whose craft in England had been silk dyeing, had quickly discovered that there was no future in Boston for such a specialty and had converted to the making and selling of such staples as soap and candles.

By January 1706, some of the older children have left home. The family prays at night for the safety of Josiah, Jr., who has gone to sea and from whom they have not heard in a long time. Sorrow seems to be overtaking Abiah's life, as it had Anne's. On his shaky but intrepid little legs, her toddler, Ebenezer, has ventured too close to the vat for melting soap and suffered a dreadful death. Her newest infant, Thomas, struggles to stay alive. She is almost forty.

In spite of such misfortune, Abiah is well aware that, compared with the two generations that preceded her, she has an easy life. Of the eighteen women who landed in Massachusetts in 1628, only four survived their first winter in the New World. Things are better now, for there has been a sort of peace with the Indians for the past thirty years, the witch trials are fading from memory, the stark days of Puritan orthodoxy are almost over, Boston Harbor is sometimes filled with high masts from all over the world. . . . There is little ground for complaint.

The new baby, a healthy boy, makes his appearance on January 6. Josiah names him Benjamin and, as a good Puritan should, has him baptized within twenty-four hours. He also declares that this one, the tenth of his sons, shall be consecrated to the church.

It did not go that way, though. When the moment comes, Benjamin does not offer his life to God but to his fellowman.

He shall, he hopes, win his salvation not through prayer but through deeds. He will apply his genius and his drive to the betterment of life on earth. He will invent a wood stove so ingenious that people will be warmer while expending less. He will invent the double-focused lenses that will allow aging eyes to enjoy for a little longer the beauty of the world. To delight the soul he will perfect a musical instrument endowed with ethereal sound. He will invent the lightning rod, savior of lives and homes. He will endeavor to free people from fear—fear of nature's dreadful whims and fear of tyrants. He will try to educate people, to give them the self-confidence that leads to emancipation and dignity. In his old age he will fight against slavery. He will be one of the creators of an independent America and its first ambassador abroad. He will be bold enough to adopt an easy, natural manner; in a stiff society he will dare to be witty and ironic.

Though Josiah engendered ten sons, the Franklin family did not count a single male member one hundred years later. But thanks to this fifteenth child, the Franklin name, given to streets and squares, to towns and schools, to banks, bridges, foundations, scholarships, prizes, and highways, remains as alive as ever.

The Toast of Paris

America is the hope of the human race   TURGOT

Auray has hardly changed. If Benjamin Franklin were to land there once again, as he did on December 3, 1776, he would recognize the quaint bridge on the quiet river and the steep gables overlooking the wharf. No delegation was waiting on the pier that night. Franklin's ship, the *Reprisal*, had been hovering for a few days along the windswept coast of Brittany before seeking a safe anchorage in the little port.

Still shaken by an illness and by more than four weeks of rough winter navigation under the constant threat of capture by the British and being hanged for treason, the seventy-year-old philosopher stepped on the soil of France. He was so weak, we are told, that he could hardly stand. There was no woman at his side – Deborah, his wife, had died two years earlier – no son, no aide, only two grandchildren, seven-year-old Benjamin Bache and sixteen-year-old William Temple Franklin. Benjamin Bache, known as Benny, the firstborn of Franklin's only daughter, Sarah, was leaving behind in Philadelphia the warmth of his home, the hustle and bustle of his young brother and sister. For William Temple Franklin, generally called Temple, this was the third stage of a chaotic life. The illegitimate son of Franklin's own illegitimate son, he had been raised first in England by his grandfather, then in America by his father, the Royal Governor of New Jersey. His mother's identity has remained a mystery. Now, after a dramatic break between his grandfather, a leader of the Revolution, and his father, a faithful subject of England (put in jail for his Tory stand), Temple was about to make a fresh start, this time in France.

Franklin surrounded by the ladies at court, engraved by W. O. Geller, c. 1830, painted by Baron Jolly, Bruxelles

An exhausted old man and two bewildered youngsters – a most unlikely trio, one would think, to be entrusted with the support of a revolution. Yet, Franklin's very age, combined with his immense prestige, lent respectability to what might have seemed a shady mission, and certainly was a hushed-up one. The boys, helpless as they appeared, were his strength. Together, the three hastened toward Paris by way of Nantes.

The beginning of the trip was gloomy, as Franklin noted with wry detachment.

The carriage was a miserable one with tired horses . . . the evening dark, scarce a traveller but ourselves on the road; and, to make it more comfortable, the driver stopped near a wood we were to pass through, to tell us that a gang of eighteen robbers infested that wood who but two weeks ago had murdered some travellers on that very spot.

Still, vitality must have been flowing back into him, for on the very next day he remarked: "On the road we met six or seven country women in company, on horseback and astride; they were all of fair white and red complexions, but among them was the fairest woman I ever beheld."[1]

Fair women, fair ladies were soon to be a daily occurrence. The news of his arrival traveled faster than he did, and by the time he got to Nantes, a huge ball had been organized in his honor. He did not tarry, this time, as he had on a previous visit ten years earlier, to marvel at the way French ladies applied their rouge (in bright round patches, three inches wide) or did their hair (more than a foot high). Nor did he take time, as before, to deck himself out as a Frenchman "in a little bag-wig and naked ears." Still wearing his own un-powdered grey hair, and the fur cap that had kept him warm on the boat, dressed in the unadorned suit that his admirers mistook for a Quaker outfit, he proceeded from town to town, benign, smiling, evading questions. If that other trip had been for pleasure, this one was undertaken solely to carry out a difficult and delicate mission.

Together with the other two American commissioners awaiting him in Paris, Franklin was to represent in France a government which France was in no position to recognize, and to obtain help from her against a government with which she was not at war. Congress, as a body, had appointed Franklin to this post, but most of its members were not even informed that France, though not ready to form an alliance, had secretly promised to ship a large cargo of arms and ammunition to a port in the West Indies. It would have been too dangerous to apprise all congressmen of such a sensitive piece of news; Robert Morris, of the Committee of Secret Correspondence, had merely whispered it to Franklin on the eve of departure. Now it was up to Franklin to obtain whatever else he could: more supplies, more gifts, more trade, some highly skilled officers, and, as soon as feasible, formal recognition and alliance at war.

The moment was one of extreme peril. By issuing the Declaration of Independence while still uncertain of the future, the American revolutionists had cut all possible ways of retreat. The colonies had no money, no system of taxation, very little credit, and scarce unity of purpose. The campaign of 1776 had been a failure. Benedict Arnold was driven from Canada, George Washington from Long Island; the British were in possession of New York, their well-equipped forces outnumbering Washington's ragged army two to one. Back in England, many thought that the debacle on Long Island had decided the outcome of the contest. In France, Comte de Vergennes, the Foreign Minister, was postponing indefinitely his intention of declaring war on England. He had toyed with the idea after the Declaration of Independence but was now in no hurry to come to the aid of a loser.

Franklin himself had reservations about the propriety of his mission. He had declared in Congress that "a virgin state should preserve the virgin character, and not go about suitoring for alliances, but wait with decent dignity for the applications of others."[2] He had accepted, nevertheless, the role of matchmaker, and was determined to "suitor" France with every resource at his disposal.

What he accomplished over the eight and one-half years he was to remain in Paris, from December 20, 1776, to July 12, 1785, is history. The Treaty of Amity and Commerce with France, the Treaty of Alliance with France (1778), the exchanges of prisoners with England, the shipment of war material, the securing of loans, the Treaty of Peace with Britain (1783), the Treaties of Amity and Commerce with Sweden (1783) and with Prussia (1785) are only the highlights of a rich and complex chapter in economic, diplomatic, and psychological maneuvering.

But how he accomplished it, under what pressures, amid what doubts and squabbling, against what odds, with what help and comfort, will never be known fully. There are clues, however. A glimpse at what Franklin did after hours may explain how he recovered from what must have been during hours a desperate strain. Some insight into his social relationships may illuminate the intensely personal way in which he conducted affairs of state, forever mixing business and friendship. A look at the pleasure he and the French men and women of his day found in each other's company may bring into sharper focus one brief moment in history when it seemed that people from different countries, culture, religion, language, and outlook, might really reach out and touch hands.

Franklin's early days in Paris were full of paradoxes. People of all classes flocked to see him, in a rare display of mass adulation, but the Court, worried by the British Ambassador's protests, kept him uneasily at arm's length. He professed to adore everything French, but after a few months sent Benny to a boarding school in Geneva "so that he might become a Republican and a Protestant which in the French schools would not have been possible."[3] Most of the French grew ecstatic over this foreigner who embodied their avowed dreams and gave focus and clarity to their secret gropings, but his fellow Americans in France eyed him with various degrees of suspicion – one of them with actual hatred.

For if one tends now, in the euphory of subsequent victory, to view the three American commissioners as a somewhat disgruntled team, nevertheless putting their shoulders to the wheel, close scrutiny of the sources reveals a distressing amount of backbiting, pettiness, jealousy, and downright sabotage of one another's efforts. The most aggressive member of the trio was Arthur Lee. His hostility toward Franklin, a matter of long standing, went back to the London days when he had coveted Franklin's post as agent for Massachusetts. Now, in Paris, Lee found himself both superseded by his colleague Silas Deane – who was engaged in the spectacular enterprise of obtaining supplies through the offices of playwright Caron de Beaumarchais – and eclipsed by

Franklin. He managed to convince Congress that the former was an embezzler, thus provoking Deane's recall and eventual ruin. Though Lee was less successful in harming Franklin, he harassed him by conducting a war of attrition. His perpetual dissenting and loud denouncing once provoked the generally serene and humorous old man to burst out:

If I have often received and borne your magisterial snubbings and rebukes without reply, ascribe it to the right causes: my concern for the honour and success of our mission which would be hurt by our quarreling, my love of peace, my respect for your good qualities and my pity of your sick mind which is forever tormenting itself with its jealousies, suspicions, and fancies that others mean you ill, wrong you, or fail in respect for you. If you do not cure yourself of this temper, it will end in insanity.[4]

If Franklin had hoped to find an ally in the person of John Adams, who came to replace Deane in April 1778, he was mistaken. He greeted Adams warmly, took him to meet all his friends, tried to win him to his side, but Adams was, at best, critical of both commissioners. He found the accounts of the Commission confused, its methods disorderly, its manner of living extravagant. Although on occasion he could not suppress a grudging admiration for Franklin, Adams never liked him. Throughout the years they worked together, first as fellow commissioners, later, when the Commission had been dissolved and Franklin remained sole Minister Plenipotentiary, as fellow negotiators of the Peace Treaty with England, Adams' abundant comments on his senior colleague maintain a consistently acidulous tone. They form a sharp and amusing contrast with the mellifluous way in which the French – most of them, at least – wrote and spoke about *le bon Docteur*. At times it is hard to believe that French and Americans were talking about the same person.

Adams' objections to Franklin went much deeper than mere irritation with a geniality of speech and manner so foreign to his own unbending nature. Franklin tended to view countries as people – his comparison of America with a virgin is but one of many such images in his writings – people to be understood, befriended, and wooed. But the future President of the United States belonged to that school of thought, still strong in American foreign policy, that judges the ambassador who seeks identification of any kind with the host country as an automatic betrayer of his own country's interest. Thus, while acknowledging the magnitude of Franklin's popularity in France – "his reputation was more universal than that of Leibnitz or Newton, Frederick or Voltaire, and his character more beloved and esteemed than any or all of them"[5] – Adams implied more than once that the aging man was selling out to the foreign power, not for money, to be sure, but to gratify his vanity.

He dealt harshly not only with Franklin's views of office, but with his manner of carrying them out. Few indictments could be more sweeping than the one Adams wrote soon after his arrival in France:

I found out that the Business of our Commission would never be done, unless I did it. . . . The Life of Dr. Franklin was a Scene of continual discipation. I could never obtain the favour of his Company in a Morning before Breakfast which would have been the most convenient time to read over the Letters and papers, deliberate on their contents, and decide upon the Substance of the Answers. It was late when he breakfasted, and as soon as

Breakfast was over, a crowd of Carriages came to his Levee or if you like the term better, to his Lodgings, with all sorts of People; some Phylosophers, Accademicians and Economists ... but by far the greater part were Women and Children, come to have the honour to see the great Franklin, and to have the pleasure of telling Stories about his Simplicity, his bald head and scattering strait hairs, among their Acquaintances.

So much for mornings, spent in idleness and vanity. Did Franklin, at least, redeem himself in the afternoon?

He was invited to dine abroad every day and never declined unless when We had invited Company to dine with Us. I was always invited with him, till I found it necessary to send Apologies, that I might have some time to study the french Language and do the Business of the mission. Mr. Franklin kept a horn book always in his Pockett in which he minuted all his invitations to dinner, and Mr. Lee said it was the only thing in which he was punctual. ... Mr. Lee came daily to my Appartment to attend to Business, but we could rarely obtain the Company of Dr. Franklin for a few minutes, and often when I had drawn the Papers and had them fairly copied for Signature, and Mr. Lee and I had signed them, I was frequently obliged to wait several days, before I could procure the signature of Dr. Franklin to them.

But why this dilatoriness? Was Franklin sick, enfeebled, overwhelmed with problems? No, he was having a good time! Worse still, he was having it with women.

He went to his Invitation to his Dinner and after that went sometimes to the Play, sometimes to the Philosophers but most commonly to visit those Ladies who were complaisant enough to *depart from the custom of France so far as to procure Setts of Tea Gear as it is called and make Tea for him. Some of these Ladies I knew as Madam Hellvetius,* Madam Brillon, Madam Chaumont, Madam Le Roy, etc., and others whom I never knew and never enquired for. After Tea the Evening was spent, in hearing the Ladies sing and play upon their Piano Fortes and other instruments of Musick, and in various Games as Cards, Chess, Backgammon, etc., etc. Mr. Franklin I believe never play'd at any Thing but Chess or Checquers. In these Agreable and important Occupations and Amusements, the Afternoon and Evening was spent, and he came home at all hours from Nine to twelve O Clock at night.*[6]

And yet, these very methods, in their apparent effortlessness, provoked the admiration of the French. Pierre-Georges Cabanis, a physician who became over the years one of Franklin's intimates, raved:

Franklin's most original trait, the one that would have made him unique no matter in what century he lived, was his art of living in the best fashion for himself and for others, making the most effective use of all the tools nature has placed at the disposal of man . . . He would eat, sleep, work whenever he saw fit, according to his needs, so that there never was a more leisurely man, though he certainly handled a tremendous amount of business. No matter when one asked for him, he was always available. His house in Passy, where he had chosen to live because he loved the country and fresh air, was always open for all visitors; he always had an hour for you.

Let it not be said that he unloaded his work on his secretaries; for he had only one secretary, his own grandson, to whom he

---

*   Note the interesting misspelling: Hellvetius for Helvétius.

allowed as much free time for amusement as he himself took off for conversation; besides, he and his grandson occasionally used the help of an ordinary transcriber. Such was the staff of the Minister Plenipotentiary of the United States. It was sufficient for him to correspond with his government, with all the other American agents throughout Europe, whose operations he was expected to supervise, and with the French Government, which he certainly could not afford to slight.[7]

It might be argued that this divergence of opinion between Adams and Cabanis reflects a divergent point of view on work, as well as on Franklin. The American tradition has always looked upon idleness with horror, demanding that it be veiled by work. The continental tradition has always demanded that work be disguised by outward nonchalance, and in that respect, as in many others, Franklin, while in France, was very French.

Did this make him less American when dealing with his fellow countrymen back home, less uncompromising in his patriotism, less stern when he felt it his duty to be so? A letter written to his daughter Sarah Bache throws some light on a facet of Franklin's character that the French never saw. A little more than two years after her father had arrived in Paris, Sarah, back in Philadelphia, was invited to a ball at which Washington was to be present. In true feminine tradition, she had nothing to wear, and wrote to her father stressing that anything he saw fit to send her from Paris would be most welcome and certainly admired. He replied:

I was charmed with the account you gave me of your industry, the table-cloths of your own spinning, etc. ... but your sending for long black pins, and lace, and feathers*! disgusted me as much as if you had put salt into my strawberries. The spinning, I see, is laid aside, and you are to be dressed for the ball! You seem not to know, my dear daughter, that of all the dear things in this world, idleness is the dearest, except mischief.*

More reproaches followed, in which the black pins and feathers from France were underlined each time with scorn and anger, and the letter wound up in a fresh outburst against luxury, coupled with a paternal scolding:

The war indeed may in some degree raise the price of goods, and the high taxes which are necessary to support the war may make our frugality necessary; and as I am always preaching that doctrine, I cannot in conscience or in decency encourage the contrary, by my example, in furnishing my children with foolish modes and luxuries. I therefore send all the articles you desire that are useful and necessary, and omit the rest; for as you say you should "have great pride in wearing any thing I send, and showing it as your father's taste." *I must avoid an opportunity of doing that with either lace or feathers. If you wear your cambric ruffles as I do, and take care not to mend the holes, they will come in time to be lace; and feathers, my dear girl, may be had in America from every cock's tail.*[8]

America is America, and France is France. What was unbecoming in puritan Philadelphia at war might be unobjectionable in Paris; Franklin was tolerant enough not to condemn a foreign nation because of superficial differences in custom. In a letter to an American friend, while deploring his countrymen's expenses "for Superfluities," he summed up his opinion of the French:

I think the French have no national Vice ascrib'd to them. They have some Frivolities, but they are harmless. To dress their Heads so that a Hat cannot be put on them, and then wear their Hats under their Arms, and to fill their Noses with Tobacco, may be called Follies, perhaps, but they are not Vices. They are only the effects of the tyranny of Custom. In short, there is nothing wanting in the Character of a Frenchman, that belongs to that of an agreable and worthy Man.[9]

After two months at the Hôtel d'Hambourg, rue de l'Université, Franklin had moved out of Paris and settled in Passy, "a neat village on a high ground, half a mile from Paris, with a large garden to walk in." This is how he described the quiet suburb which was later to become, along with Auteuil and Chaillot, the *seizième arrondissement*, now the most elegant part of town. Before being sent to Switzerland, Benny attended boarding school in the village and spent Sundays with his grandfather. Temple acted as Franklin's secretary. A grandnephew, Jonathan Williams, who had come from London, shared his time between Passy and Nantes, overseeing shipments to America.

A grandson as secretary, a grandnephew as assistant: disregarding the advantages of choosing relatives as the cheapest and most reliable helpers, Lee promptly accused Franklin of nepotism. He did not know, of course, that his own secretary was a spy, or that the Commission's secretary, Edward Bancroft, one of the cleverest spies of all time, managed to remain, throughout the Revolution, on both the English and the American payrolls. The progress of negotiation with France and Spain, the means of obtaining credit, letters to Congress, ship departures, names of captains, privateers, and prizes, all this and more was duly reported by Bancroft in invisible ink on the white spaces of letters otherwise devoted to gallantry, sealed in a bottle and deposited every week in the hole of a tree near the Tuileries.

A spy to report his daily doings, a mortal enemy as a colleague, painful attacks of gout and stone, a desperately weak bargaining position – did Franklin not have a single factor working for him? He had one, a tremendous one, which he knew well and never lost sight of: French public opinion.

First of all, he was adored personally as an answer to everyone's particular prayer. By Adams' admission (long after Franklin had died),

his name was familiar to government and people, to kings, courtiers, nobility, clergy, and philosophers, as well as plebeians, to such a degree that there was scarcely a peasant or a citizen, a valet de chambre, *coachman or footman, a lady's chambermaid or a scullion in the kitchen who was not familiar with it and who did not consider him a friend to human kind. . . . When they spoke of him, they seemed to think that he was to restore the golden age. . . . His plans and his example were to abolish monarchy, aristocracy, and hierarchy throughout the world.*[10]

Admittedly, you can not please everyone. There were a few discordant voices, mostly anonymous, in the great choir of praise. In his diary, Adams was happy to note a long and pleasant conversation he had on board ship, while going back to America in 1779, with the newly appointed secretary to the French Legation in New York, François Barbé-Marbois. The diplomat was quoted as saying that Franklin had wit and "charlatagnerie," but was not a statesman after all. (Since a whole section of Marbois' later memoirs on the United States was to be devoted to the docility and submissiveness of American women, the depth of his insights may be questioned.) A scandal book (*Le Vicomte de Barjac*, possibly by a Marquis de Luchet) called Franklin "a very poor statesman," "a mediocre physicist," and "a dotard" (*radoteur*). The forged *Memoirs of the Marquise de Créquy* chided him for his table manners: he bit off the heads of the asparagus, instead of using a fork, and broke his eggs in a cup, making a "philosophical ragoût" with eggs, butter, mustard, pepper, and salt, like the "kind of savage" he was.[11] But these sour comments are mere drops of lemon juice in a bucket of molasses.

In the second place, Franklin's personality served as focus for an admiration that did not confine itself to him but encompassed the whole American experiment. Dissatisfied with the restrictions, the inequities, and the inefficiency of the old order, the liberal circles of France were yearning for a new rational start, released from feudal traditions, frozen hierarchies, and closed frontiers. Such a utopia could be found, if anywhere on earth, in the young country across the ocean.

To be sure, these feelings were not universally shared; above all, they were relatively new. In the 1750s and '60s, the Americans had aroused little interest, and that sparse attention was rather contemptuous. It was said that America, this new continent recently emerged from the sea, was bound to suffer from a moist, unfavorable climate. The proof? Plants, animals, and people degenerated and became smaller than in the Old World: the elephant became a tapir, the lion became a cougar, men became as short as the puniest Indian. Preposterous as they were, such notions were endorsed by the father of natural science, Georges Buffon, and enjoyed a wide and persistent vogue.

At the same time, though, pro-American voices had been raised from three different sources and became progressively louder during the early stages of the break between England and her colonies. Franklin, in 1777, made it his task to detect these voices and gather them into an irresistible chorus.

The political voice was Voltaire's. In his *Lettres philoso-phiques*, he had launched the legend of the Good Quaker, extolled Pennsylvania for its spirit of religious toleration, its peace and prosperity, its virtue, and, in his later works, had made it the symbol of all that was desirable for France. Franklin and Voltaire met melodramatically on a few occasions, once at the Academy of Sciences, where they embraced *à la française* to the delighted howls of the public, once at the Masonic Lodge of the Nine Sisters, and once more or less in private, when the moribund Voltaire, eager to display his English, blessed Benny Bache with the words "God and Liberty."

The economic voice was that of the articulate, powerful group of the physiocrats. Led by François Quesnay and Pierre Samuel du Pont de Nemours (father of a famous immigrant to the United States), the physiocrats held that the soil is the only true source of national wealth, that in an ideal state the population should live mostly on farms (albeit under paternalistic landowners), and that grain trade should be totally free. Even though he did not quite espouse those ideals himself, Franklin, who had met prominent members of the school on his 1767 trip to France, contributed frequently to their *Journal* and let it be known that these very conditions were to be found more in America than anywhere else in the world. The physiocrats, in turn, were vocal in their support of America. Not really one of them, but their

cobelligerent in regard to freedom of trade, Anne-Robert
Turgot had been at the head of French finances until a few
months before Franklin's arrival. As a financial expert, he
thought (with reason) that an alliance with the Americans
would have disastrous effects on the French treasury; as a
philosophe, however, as a friend of America in general, and
Franklin in particular, he could not deny them his moral
support. "America is the hope of the human race," he wrote
to a friend, "and may well become its model."

The idealistic voice which in its broad resonance moved
more hearts than any other, was Rousseau's. He, too (if for
other reasons), wanted a return to the soil, to what he
thought was the purity of primitive man, the innate nobility
of the good savage. Just as the Voltaire group had tried to
push Franklin into the Quaker mold, as the physiocrats had
made him more agrarian than he really was, the followers of
Rousseau tried to ascribe to the "backwoods philosopher
from America" some primitivistic views that he had never
held. The closest Franklin had ever come to extolling the
state of nature – and it was not very close – had been in
1770, when he had scribbled in the margin of a British pamphlet: "Happiness is more generally and equally diffus'd
among Savages than in our Societies."[12]

Though Franklin and Rousseau never met and did not
have much in common, in the French mind they were
almost mystically linked. Apart from both being Protestant
and foreign, they shared a human warmth that endeared
them to many, and especially to women. They appealed to
the romantic strain in the feminine heart that was to set the
literary mood of the following age for men and women
alike.

There is no better example of this state of mind than a hitherto unnoticed, unsigned letter published in the columns of the *Journal de Paris*, and the reply it received. A lady wrote on December 8, 1778, that she had been riding in her carriage with her husband, two friends, and her little son. The conversation had turned on Rousseau, who had died the previous July; her soul was full of his memory when all of a sudden, as her husband and friends were taking leave, she saw a very simple carriage come to a stop, and a very simple man, white-haired, modestly dressed, unescorted, disappear into a house. "C'est Monsieur Franklin!" exclaimed the crowd. The lady burst into tears and cried unashamedly, in full view of the passersby, while her child wondered anxiously what was ailing her. She herself did not know. It had to do with Rousseau, with virtue, with Franklin, but could a "profound Moralist" help her analyze her feelings?

Somebody tried. Another woman? A man? We shall never know. In a lengthy poem, carefully penned on flowery paper, and now buried in the mass of undated Franklin documents, somebody suggested that the lady's emotion had been sparked by one virtue contemplating another. Ordinary people would have been too insensitive to react at the mere sight of a virtuous man; not so the lady, who had been electrified. Then, seized by the belated suspicion that callous readers might make fun of that sacred emotion, the poet concluded defiantly:

Plaisantez, cœurs de fer, j'abjure vos erreurs,
*Moi-même en écrivant et je pleure et j'admire.**

* *You may joke, hearts of iron, I forswear your wrongs,*
  Myself, as I write, I both cry and admire.

Let us not be callous either. Hyperbolic, embarrassing as these effusions sound today, they show the kind of adulation Franklin encountered – and altogether enjoyed. This era, which we tend to dismiss as cynical, frivolous, and gaily impudent, had its sentimental, moralistic side. Cynicism, of course, flourished in the idle, pampered circles where everybody just took for granted that love and marriage were two quite different things. "I allow you any lover," a gentleman was said to have told his bride, "except a prince or a lackey." But the circles Franklin moved in were much more sedate.

His friends were not, as Adams once remarked in conversation, "all atheists, deists, and libertines."[13] Many were clergymen, some were economists, some were fellow scientists, several had no other claim than being simply his neighbors in Passy: middle-of-the-road people, liberal enough to greet the fall of the Bastille with joy, too liberal to survive the Revolution's tyrannical convulsions. These friends gave Franklin what he needed: warmth, devotion, a sense of belonging, a family. In return, he gave them not only Voltaire and Rousseau wrapped in one, but his sharp and humorous outlook on the world, his success story, and the lessons of a long and active life. His acquaintances called him Excellence, his friends called him Docteur, his intimates, men and women, called him Papa.

His company was eagerly sought. As one of his ecclesiastical friends, Abbé Martin Lefebvre de la Roche, wrote in his *Memoirs*,

it was fashionable to entertain Franklin for dinner, to give parties in his honor. Women, especially, flocked to see him, to speak to him for hours on end, without realizing that he did not understand much of what they said, because of his scant knowledge of our language. In spite of the time they wasted, he greeted each one of them with a kind of amiable coquettishness that they loved. When one particular lady, eager for his preference, asked him if he did not care for her more than for the others, he would answer: "Yes, when you are closest to me, because of the force of attraction." [14]

They came quite close, it seems. We hear of a celebration where the prettiest among three hundred ladies was chosen to crown the philosopher with laurel and kiss him on both cheeks. Franklin himself told his stepniece in 1779:

Somebody gave it out that I lov'd Ladies; and then every body presented me their Ladies (or the Ladies presented themselves) to be embrac'd, that is to have their Necks kissed. For as to kissing of Lips or Cheeks it is not the Mode here, the first is reckon'd rude, and the other may rub off the Paint. The French Ladies have however 1000 other ways of rendering themselves agreeable. [15]

Franklin and women. So much has been written on the sensuous storms of his early years, on the outward placidity of his common law marriage with Deborah, on his many-leveled intellectual friendships with younger women – the Cathy Rays of America, the Polly Hewsons, the Georgiana Shipleys of England – on the truly continental lightheartedness of his flirtations with the women of Paris. But if, as it has been said, he lived out his life in one unchanging springtime, it is also true that he never experienced the full-fledged passion of summer. Franklin somehow never committed himself wholly in love; a part of him was always holding back and watching the proceedings with irony.

Women, young and old, loved him because he took a keen interest in them, not merely as objects of desire, but as people with a different outlook, with their own contribution to make. He listened to them, he was not afraid of them – obvious principles of courtsmanship too often lost sight of. Many of his best pages – literary pieces or private correspondence – were inspired by women. They were flirtatious, those pages, in the original sense of the word: *fleuretter*, *conter fleurette*, to tell little flowers, to toss bouquets of gallantry, part of a very old game that had to be played according to the rules, rules no less stringent for being unwritten. That Franklin, at the age of seventy, was able to master those rules and play the game with the elegance, the wit, the detachment it required, is proof of his agile mind and extraordinary adaptability.

Such a quality, which to John Adams seemed another regrettable symptom of Franklin's senility, was, in the social structure of prerevolutionary France, a very real asset. Diplomats have always stressed that winning the women to one's side is a good part of the battle. In the age of the salon, with its delicate network of influence, intrigue, and innuendo, their importance was crucial.

Reared by governesses, convent-bred, trained from infancy for the role she would be called on to perform in society, the late eighteenth-century gentlewoman, a perfectly attuned instrument, was at one with her era as few women, before or after her, have been. She was a new woman with a new ideal of elegance and beauty. No longer the Olympian goddess of the reign of Louis XIV, or the provocative hussy of the days of Louis XV – with her tremendous hoops, her false beauty spots, her incredible hairdos – she wanted to be somewhat closer to nature, more pastoral, tender and soulful. She liked to dress in pastels, still better in white. She had the age-old talent of France to absorb and humanize current events, good or bad, into her own frivolity. Just as her descendants were to convert the ominous dawn of the atomic age into the flippant bikini, she gaily wore dresses *à la Jean-Jacques*, fur bonnets *à la Franklin*, wavy ribbons *au passage du Rhin*, or, when Marie-Antoinette finally had a baby, she sported an unmistakable shade of brown called *caca Dauphin*.

She knew, of course, how to sing and paint, how to turn out witty verse, how to entertain, how to thrust and parry in courtship, how to give a man his best possible chance of shining, how to pull the strings behind the scenes. Best of all, she knew how to make her salon a center for the diffusion of lights, those *lumières* so dear to the philosophic heart: and when she had captured such a gem as Franklin, she spared no effort to keep him entertained.

How was it done? Above all, by brilliant conversation; but in this field, Franklin was at first handicapped both by the confidential nature of his mission and by his lack of fluency in French. He never felt at ease with the continental habit of plunging into an animated conversation instead of waiting patiently for the first speaker to have finished, as was (and still is) the American custom. "If you Frenchmen would only talk no more than four at a time, I might understand you, and would not come out of an interesting party without knowing what they were talking about," he sighed to Abbé de la Roche, and John Adams wrote: "He conversed only with individuals, and freely only with confidential friends.

In company, he was usually silent." [16] To the very end of his stay in France, he was known to be as silent in large company as he was witty in tête-à-tête.

There were other channels of communication in a large gathering: music, for instance. Franklin's love of music was very real. He tried to remain neutral in the raging controversy between the partisans of Gluck, the German, and those of Piccinni, the Italian (most of Franklin's friends in Passy were for Piccinni, himself an inhabitant of the village), but his personal preference, soon widely known and catered to, ran to the simple, traditional airs of Scotland and Ireland. In those tunes, he reflected, each note tends to linger in the ear and to merge with the following one, so that the melody, though sung by a single voice, is really a kind of harmony made up of various sounds.

Franklin also had a positive contribution to offer: his own musical instrument, the armonica, so named by him some fifteen years earlier in honor of Italy, to whose music it seemed particularly adapted, "especially to that of the soft and plaintive kind." [17] The armonica was based on the principle of the *Glasspiel* which had been invented earlier in Germany and was used by Gluck, among others: a number of beer glasses of various sizes fixed in a row to a table, tuned by being filled with different amounts of water, and played by passing a moistened finger around their brim. Even in the improved version he had occasion to see and hear in London, this contrivance seemed clumsy to Franklin. His armonica, which was completed by 1761, consisted of several special glasses blown in the shape of hemispheres, ranging in diameter from three to nine inches, with an iron spindle passing through holes in the middle of each glass. The player, sitting before the instrument, revolved the spindle with a treadle like that on a spinning wheel and touched the edges of the moving glasses with his fingers.

Franklin gave elaborate instructions on the proper use of his armonica: how the instrumentalist's fingers should be soaped and rinsed before playing, and then not only wet but soaked; how the water for wetting both fingers and glasses should be rainwater, lest the tone be too harsh; how a little "fine scrap'd Chalk, free from Grit" should be used on the fingers to restore the smoothness of tone after an evening's playing; how "one Wetting with the Spunge will serve for a Piece of Music twice as long as Handel's Water piece," etc. The results, he promised, were well worth such care:

When these Particulars are all attended to and the Directions observed, the Tone comes forth finely with the slightest Pressure of the Finger imaginable, and you swell it at pleasure by adding a little more Pressure, no instrument affords more Shades, if one may so speak, of the Forte and Piano.[18]

Suddenly, the armonica was all the vogue. Public performances were given in England, Marie-Antoinette, still a princess in Vienna, learned to play it, Mozart and Beethoven composed for it, Metastasio wrote an ode to be accompanied by it. Its popularity, still strong at the time of Franklin's arrival in Paris, was to wane only around 1800. Armonica lovers kept in touch with each other. In the bustle of his last week in France, Franklin found time to discuss Abbé Perno's idea of playing it with keys, and even though he refers loyally to experiments carried on by a duchess in Paris, a baron in Versailles, and a musician in London, he cannot quite conceal his preference for "my manner of playing on my

The Apotheosis of Franklin

instrument."[19] He seems to have derived more pride from his armonica than from many of his other inventions.

Apart from the armonica, Franklin knew somewhat how to play the harp, the guitar, and the violin. This made him all the more appreciative of the endeavors on the part of the ladies, young and old, to satisfy his craving for good music.

But more than music was required in the way of social graces. A woman had to know how to pen a graceful, winged letter, a man how to express his deepest thoughts in nonchalant words, for "the letter," as Chauncey Tinker remarked, "was the chosen medium of the day, as the periodic essay was of the earlier period."[20] Franklin was far from insensitive to the elegance, the polish of the letters he received, and it was an endless source of frustration to him not to be able to answer in kind. As long as he was living in France, he affected to take this shortcoming lightheartedly:

You have accepted with such good grace my poorly written Epistles, that I make bold to send you one I drafted two weeks ago, but did not finish because I did not have the time to look up all those masculines and feminines* in the Dictionary, nor the modes and tenses in the Grammar.

For sixty years, now, masculine and feminine things – and I am not talking about modes and tenses – have been giving me a lot of trouble. I used to hope that at the age of 80 I would be free of all that. But here I am, four times 19, which is mighty close to 80, and those French feminines are still bothering me. It will make me all the happier to go to Paradise where, they say, all such distinctions will be abolished.[21]

* Franklin disarmingly put "masculines" in the feminine and "féminins" in the masculine.

But when he had gone back to Philadelphia and experienced the relief of speaking his own language once more, he admitted, somewhat bitterly, "if a Man desires to be useful by the Exercise of his mental Faculties, he loses half their Force when in a foreign Country." [22]

Here, as usual, the opinion of John Adams was in direct contradiction to that of Franklin's French friends. A few days after his own arrival in Paris, Adams noted smugly:

Dr. F. is reported to speak French very well, but I find upon attending to him critically that he does not speak it grammatically, and indeed upon my asking him sometimes whether a Phrase he had was correct, he acknowledged to me that he was wholly inattentive to the Grammar. His Pronunciation, too, upon which the French Gentlemen and Ladies complimented him very highly, and which he seemed to think pretty well, I soon found out was very inaccurate.[23]

Whereas Adams, bent on learning French the proper way, went to the competent authorities and was sternly directed to Bossuet's *Funeral Orations*, Franklin turned his handicap into an asset by displaying his helplessness and enrolling the enthusiastic collaboration of a number of literate gentlemen and charming ladies. And, in the privacy of his study, he worked at improving his French. Many sheets among his papers are covered with exercises, and some of the drafts in his letterbook attest to his labors in search of *le mot juste*.

Most of Franklin's famed *Bagatelles* (trifles, little bits of fluff) are by-products of his apprenticeship in France under the direction of his Parisian friends. From the accumulated store of anecdotes and moralities in his memory, he would pick out a half-serious, half-facetious theme and jot it down in his awkward French. The draft would then go back and forth between him and his assistants until it was fit for printing. Eventually, he did print it, sometimes in English as he had conceived it originally, sometimes in French as he had worked it out, sometimes in both. The small private press he had set up in Passy was one of his most cherished hobbies, and brought him back to the never-forgotten profession he had exercised as a youth.

Such was one aspect – the social one – of Franklin's life in France. To some it may have looked like one facet of a life generally given to dissipation, to others like the well-earned moments of rest in a time of hard work and high achievement. In the eyes of one contemporary American freshly arrived in Paris, young Elkanah Watson, it needed no justification. It had its own dreamlike quality of sheer elegance and beauty:

We entered a spacious room; I following the Doctor, where several well-dressed persons (to my unsophisticated eyes, gentlemen) bowed to us profoundly. These were servants. A folding-door opened at our approach, and presented to my view a brilliant assembly, who all greeted the wise old man, in the most cordial and affectionate manner. He introduced me as a young American, just arrived. One of the young ladies approached him with the familiarity of a daughter, tapped him kindly on the cheek, and called him "Papa Franklin." I was enraptured, with the ease and freedom exhibited in the table intercourse in France . . . Some were waltzing; and others gathered in little groups in conversation. At the table, the ladies and gentlemen were joined together, and joined in cheerful conversation, each selecting the delicacies of various courses, and drinking of delicious light wines, but with neither toasts nor healths." [24]

Always love God, America,
and me above all ✺ MADAME BRILLON

One hundred three letters from her to him; twenty-nine letters from him to her, at least as many letters as for all the other French ladies taken together, to say nothing of poems and *Bagatelles*; the verb *aimer* flying back and forth between them more than a thousand times in all its modes and tenses. No wonder people in the know have a twinkle in their eye when they speak about Madame Brillon de Jouy, née Anne-Louise d'Hardancourt. Didn't she herself complain to Franklin that gossips criticized "the sweet habit I have of sitting on your lap"? Didn't Franklin himself allude to a game of chess played in her bathroom, while she soaked in the tub? Didn't Monsieur Brillon, the husband, end one of his letters by charging: "I am certain that you have just been kissing my wife"?

And yet – Monsieur Brillon went on to say: "My dear Doctor, allow me to kiss you back in return." Bathtubs in those days were covered with a wooden plank. To murder Marat in his tub, Charlotte Corday had to lose her life, not her modesty. Finally, if Madame Brillon mentioned some unfavorable comments about sitting on Franklin's lap, it was, as we shall see, for her own purposes: in order to steer the relationship exactly along the course *she* wanted – a course spiritually intense, physically chaste.

No doubt, when Franklin met Madame Brillon in 1777, she struck him as the embodiment of glamour and success. Here was a beautiful woman in her early thirties, married to a rich man, the mother of two little girls endowed with

Moulin Joli, drawn by Daubigny, engraved by Denis Née c. 1790 pretty singing voices, living in a handsome house surrounded by terraced gardens. Moreover, she was an artist – not just a dilettante in painting or the harp, as were most society women of the age – but an accomplished, recognized musician. At the time when the piano was just being perfected and made fit to displace the harpsichord, she owned more than one of these novel instruments (including, perhaps, one of the very first Erards?) and had mastered its technique. The famous English music critic, Charles Burney, traveling through France in 1770, had been enchanted:

Madame Brillon is a great musician, one of the greatest lady-players on the harpsichord in Europe, and is regarded here as the best performer on the pianoforte, but just brought to Paris ... This lady not only plays the most difficult pieces with great precision, taste, and feeling, but is an excellent sight's woman; of which I was convinced by her manner of executing some of my own music, that I had the honor of presenting to her. She likewise composes; and was so obliging as to play several of her own sonatas, both on the harpsichord and pianoforte, accompanied on the violin by M. Pagin ... a pupil of Tartini ... regarded here as his best scholar.

Nor is this all, Burney goes on to say, for

she plays on several instruments; knows the genius of all that are in common use, which she said it was necessary for her to do, in order to avoid composing for them such things as were either impractical or unnatural; she likewise draws well and engraves, and is a most accomplished and agreeable woman. To this lady many of the famous composers of Italy and Germany, who have resided in France any time, have dedicated their works: among them are Schobert and Boccherini.[1]

Schobert (not Schubert, but almost as sentimental as his better-known colleague) had been Madame Brillon's teacher. One year after his death in 1768, she met Luigi Boccherini. He was twenty-six, at the start of a career that would know triumph and destitution; she was twenty-five, on the threshold of an affluent life that was to be troubled only by emotional storms. His "Sei sonate ... dedicate a Madama Brillon de Jouy" are still famous, though few people have noted that Beethoven himself borrowed one of their themes in his First Symphony. Madame Brillon did not seek fame; she composed "only for her friends." Her friends were numerous, but it was not until the 250th anniversary of Franklin's birth, in 1956, that some of her pieces were performed before a public audience.

A good-looking woman, still young in 1777, pampered, talented; and yet, as Franklin was soon to find out, she considered herself a poignant figure, endowed with an exceptional capacity for love, hence doomed to suffer. She was indeed wealthy, and her husband held the enviable position of receiver-general of trusts of Parliament; but he was also twenty-four years her senior, and, in her eyes, coarse – the typical partner parents selected for their daughters by matching financial rather than spiritual assets. (That, in addition, he was unfaithful, she had not discovered yet.) She was indeed an artist, but she had to pay the price of the artistic temperament: a high-strung personality, easily upset nerves (a few gusts of wind were enough to send her into despondency), a moody disposition, with rare outbursts of joy and frequent fits of despair. A child of her age, too, Madame Brillon embodied the type of woman that novels, mostly epistolary novels written by women, were then bringing into fashion: frustrated, self-centered, self-pitying. The late eighteenth-century climate, it has been said, was not as cold as it was "wet"; while there was great faith in unlimited human progress, many tears fell on individual destinies. Another century, and Madame Brillon might have become an Anna Karenina; still another, and she would be spending long hours on the analyst's couch. While she had surprisingly modern insights into her troubles, her doctor had to go by the lights of his age: when her balance was threatened, he advised – not without success – a special diet, a prolonged rest, and a change of scenery.

She tried all these remedies but also followed her instinct, which told her to look for that we would call today a father figure: a man not only older than herself, as her husband was, but revered as a sage. And Franklin, who knew no more than the doctor about the deep roots of neurosis, who had furthermore been married for more than forty years to a down-to-earth, energetic, half-illiterate woman, never tired of wooing, comforting, and sustaining this intelligent, sophisticated, narcissistic French lady. He might be wracked by the stone or the gout, overburdened with work, saddened by tragic reports from home; but somehow he managed to summon – at her every cry of distress – the infinite resources of his warmth and wit, offering them half in reckless gallantry, half in paternal tenderness. The noises, conflicts, and ideas of the outside world were strangely muffled in this exchange between the two. Only occasionally did a piece of good news from the battlefield break through the cocoon they built for themselves. Everything else was bathed in that rare atmosphere which is more than close friendship and less than love of the flesh – what the French call *amitié amoureuse*.

Their correspondence, lasting over twelve years (eight in France, four across the ocean), is a biographer's despair. For if Madame Brillon carefully dates her letters by the day of the week and the state of her soul, the month and the year are almost always omitted. As for Franklin's messages, they are mostly undated drafts or posthumously published pieces. In the face of this amorphous mass of writings – dealing with moods rather than events, alluding to whispered confessions, forgotten people, vanished crises – no serious attempt at chronology has ever been made. Madame Brillon, èven though she gets the lion's share in all accounts of Franklin's social life in France, has remained, up to now, an elusive figure. From the unwieldy bulk of her letters, Franklin's biographers have quoted over and again a few sparkling samples. They have marveled at the spell she held over the old statesman, wondering how far that spell carried him, whether he was really in love, whether there really could have been an affair. Reality, as it emerges from *all* the letters, is both sadder and more complex, the profile of a strange communion between an old philosopher and a romantic woman. And especially, as all human relations do, it changed from day to day.

Their story began in the spring of 1777, shortly after Franklin had settled down in Passy. It opened under the auspices of music, but with little fanfare. Another resident of Passy, who happened to be a next door neighbor and close friend of Madame Brillon, Louis-Guillaume Le Veillard, brought Franklin to pay a call on her. The lady felt acutely self-conscious, and, as soon as her visitors had left, wanted to make up for the poor impression she thought she had made. On a "Monday," not otherwise designated, remembering that Franklin had mentioned his fondness for Scottish tunes, she seized the opportunity to try to arrange a second meeting, again through Le Veillard.

You would do me a real favor, my neighbor, if you could procure for me the Scottish melodies Mr. Franklin kindly promised to give me; I would try to play them and compose some in the same style! I should be happy if my musical talent could please Mr. Franklin. Vanity does not prompt me. I have no vanity about playing the clavichord better than some other people, but I do wish to provide the great man with some moments of relaxation from his occupations, and also to have the pleasure of seeing him. If Monsieur Brillon were not indisposed, he would have gone to pay back his call and invite him, if it should prove convenient, to have dinner with us any day he feels like telling me whether I play them well or ill, those Scottish tunes. You must do us the favor of making this proposal to him; it would be important for me to know which day he can come, so that we can have Pagin [the violinist] whom he will certainly be glad to hear! Farewell, kind neighbor; if it were possible to arrange it for the end of this week, it would suit Pagin.

I am also planning to beg you to bring me along with you to visit Mr. Franklin. I want to go with you because, should I turn out to be as shy as the day he did me the honor to come to my house, you, who know my feelings, will interpret them, and I shall not be the loser! [2]

A coy, but adroit beginning. She could not have struck closer to home. Franklin, as we have seen, had always loved Scottish songs; he often reminisced about a night he had spent in a frontiersman's house near the Alleghenies, when a young girl had sung "Such merry as we have been" so movingly that his eyes filled with tears. Thirty years later, in Paris, the tune still rang in his ears.

Le Veillard, who was a good friend of Madame Brillon (a *very* good friend, according to gossips, but to this we return later), hastened to oblige. On that same "Monday," he forwarded her letter to Franklin, adding only a couple of lines: "I need not support a request made attractive enough by the attractiveness of she who formulates it." Thus, Le Veillard found himself cast from the start in his future role of common friend, common neighbor, and liaison man, to be referred to henceforth as *le voisin*, or *le grand voisin*.

Properly brought together again, Franklin and Madame Brillon started circling each other with the gracious formality of a minuet. Just as the ladies at court hid their eyes and smiles behind a fan, so she hid her eagerness behind the stiffness of the third person. In her round, somewhat immature, hand-writing, with a multitude of unnecessary *accents aigus* on the e's (a handwriting which, later, Franklin would occasionally enjoy imitating), she sent him at first a spate of formal little notes: "Madame Brillon presents her compliments to Mr. Franklin and asks him whether he is free Tuesday or Thursday of next week," [3] and then, more expansive messages:

Madame Brillon has the honor of presenting a thousand compliments to Mr. Franklin and of sending him the little tune he seemed to enjoy yesterday; she copied it this morning upon awakening; it is a real source of joy for her to think that she can sometimes amuse Mr. Franklin whom she loves and esteems as he deserves; still, she is a little miffed about the six games of chess he won so inhumanly and she warns him that she will spare nothing to get her revenge![4]

They played chess together, they drank tea together, the little girls (thirteen and ten) sang, their mother glided from "Monsieur Franklin" to "papa," while still closing with the traditional "your most humble and most obedient servant," followed by her maiden and married name, D'Hardancourt-Brillon, but, according to the French custom of the time, never by her given name. Little by little, Franklin slipped into the habit of spending first one, then two evenings a week at the Brillons. Some years later, he would evoke the handsome flight of a hundred steps leading from their terrace to the lawn and praise the view, as he had enjoyed it from that terrace during the long summer twilights, between the hours of six and nine. Whenever outsiders were present, he kept very quiet and listened. A female visitor remarked somewhat huffily that it looked as if the famous Doctor had taken a vow of silence.

By December 1777, the news of General Burgoyne's defeat at Saratoga reached Passy. There was tremendous rejoicing among the friends of the *insurgents*, as they were called. Beaumarchais, riding posthaste to be the first in Paris with the news (as befitted the father of Figaro), was thrown into a ditch and dislocated his shoulder. Madame Brillon, in a style far from stilted now, exclaimed:

My dear papa, my heart is too full, too moved to control itself; I yield to my overwhelming desire to write you a word; that word is that we share your joy as fully as we love you . . . Farewell, I am about to compose a triumphal march to enliven the way of General Burgoin [sic] and his men, wherever they may be heading.[5]

No wonder Franklin used to say of his soirées at the Brillons:[6]

"I call this *my Opera*, for I rarely go to the Opera at Paris."*

All surviving letters of the first year of their acquaintance are from her to him. As she would confess later, she had wanted this friendship very much and had taken most of the initial steps in fostering it. Franklin, however, after a number of months of tea, chess, music, and the view from the terrace, became restless and more demanding. He may have observed that the Brillon ménage was rather ill-assorted and thought that his chances were good; and he knew enough of French ways now to feel that nothing was to be lost by indulging in some overstatement and bantering, those basic ploys of gallantry. But as the woman he planned to conquer was obviously a virtuous one, the opening guns of his campaign sounded more like church bells – the bells of Voltaire's France, not of Cotton Mather's America.

By March 6, 1778, Franklin had entrusted Madame Brillon with no less a task than saving his soul. The pleasures and tribulations of the afterlife were indeed one of his favorite themes, a convenient device for the expression of a great variety of fantasies, ranging from lofty visions of universal brotherhood to jolly daydreams of private fraternization. Given a free scope, wishful thinking would blot out age

"Marche des Insurgents," by Madame Brillon

* If Madame Brillon's "Marche des Insurgents" (to be performed *vivement et fièrement*) did not make the Opera at Paris, at least it was given a rousing performance in Philadelphia, at the Franklin commemorative concert in 1956.

differences, language barriers, social conventions, and there would be no impropriety in a request for the forbidden fruit of paradise – on the outside chance that it might not really take eternity to be allowed to savor it.

Franklin broached the subject of his "salvation" in an unrecorded conversation. Madame Brillon eagerly fell into step the following day:

You were kind enough, yesterday, my dear brother, to entrust me with your conversion; a director, a minister usually arranges matters with a view to his own glory and profit; such is my hope in undertaking this task ... I will not be stern, I know my penitent's weak spot, I shall tolerate it! As long as he loves God, America, and me above all things, I absolve him of all his sins, present, past and future; and I promise him Paradise where I shall lead him along a path strewn with roses.

The first six capital sins were easily disposed of. In fact, each of them supplied the confessor with a pretext for lavish praise of a facet of the penitent's character:

The first is pride – when a sage has always done good, solely for the love of God and the happiness of his fellowmen, if there happens to be glory at the outcome of this conduct, it is not its motivation; hence, you are not proud.

The second is envy – mediocre men envy the reputation, the merits, the success of superior men: it is impossible for you to be envious.

The third is avarice – moderate desires, simplicity, tidiness place you above all suspicion.

The fourth is gluttony – it does seem to me that you are fond enough of good things, but that it would be no great sacrifice for you to live like a savage chief, so you are not a glutton.

The fifth is anger — your calm soul, ever guided by reason, is flawless on this point.
The sixth is sloth — America, nay the very thunderbolt, if one could summon it as a witness, will testify that if all men resembled you, sloth would be unknown . . .

The seventh sin was the real stumbling block, but extenuating circumstances came readily to mind:

The seventh — I shall not name it. All great men are tainted with it: it is called their weakness. I dare say this weakness removed the roughness, the austerity that unalloyed philosophy might have left with them. You have loved, my dear brother; you have been kind and lovable; you have been loved in return! What is so damnable about that? Go on doing great things and loving pretty women; provided that, pretty and lovable though they may be, you never lose sight of my principle: always love God, America, and me above all . . .[7]

Franklin argued back at length. With typical thrift, he was endeavoring to improve both his soul and his French. Madame Brillon knew no English, and all of Franklin's letters to her are in French. Hence the various corrections, supplied probably by irreplaceable Le Veillard, on a manuscript whose original language, while ungrammatical, was forceful and picturesque. After thanking his friend for her leniency, especially since it stretched to cover future sinning, Franklin deftly switched from the seven sins to the Ten Commandments. He had been brought up to believe, he said, that there were not only ten, but twelve Commandments:

the first is: increase, multiply and fill the earth; the twelfth (a commandment I enjoin you to obey): love one another. Come to think of it, they are a bit misplaced, and shouldn't the last one be first? . . . But please tell me, my dear casuist, whether to have observed those two commandments religiously (even though they are not in the Decalogue) could not compensate for my having so often failed to respect one of the ten? I mean the one which forbids us to covet our neighbor's wife. A commandment which (I confess) I have consistently violated (may God forgive me) every time I have seen or thought of my kind confessor; and I fear that I shall never be capable of repenting of this sin, should I even obtain full possession of my confessor's person . . . But then, why should I be so scrupulous, when you have promised to absolve me even of future sins? [8]

The catch was too obvious. Madame Brillon immediately initiated one of those teasing retreats at which she was incomparably adept. Theology, she replied on March 16, was admittedly not her forte; had she tried to build a case on it, she would have lost herself in a maze. Instead, she appealed to Natural Law and suggested coming down to earth:

Let us start from where we are. You are a man, I am a woman, and while we might think along the same lines, we must speak and act differently. Perhaps there is no great harm in a man having desires and yielding to them; a woman may have desires, but she must not yield. You have kept two very pleasant commandments religiously; you have broken another, one easily violated.

No matter how offhandedly, she did hint at her best line of defense: her husband.

My friendship, and a touch of vanity, perhaps, prompt me strongly to pardon you; but I dare not decide the question without consulting that neighbor whose wife you covet, because he is a far better casuist than I am. And then, too, as Poor Richard would say, In weighty matters, two heads are better than one.

Then, as people in love will do, she recalled those early days when feelings were still unexpressed and no choices had to be made:

Before closing, I want to confess to you in all humility that in the matter of desire, I am as great a sinner as yourself. I have desired to see you, desired to know you, desired your esteem, desired your friendship. I have even given you mine at the very outset, in the hope of receiving a little of yours.

Finally, her view of the situation: it should escape forever the realm of reality, remain a dream.

And now, I desire that you may love me forever; this desire grows day by day in my heart and it will last all my life. But such is the compassion of God, it is said, that I have not the slightest doubt that all our desires will eventually lead us to Paradise! [9]

So absorbed was Madame Brillon in her glimpses of paradise that she seemed unaware of what was going on under her very roof. But outsiders took note. Among them, that distinguished visitor from America, John Adams.

Dipping his pen in the venom reserved for Franklin and his French friends, Adams wrote in his diary two days after he arrived in Paris:

It so happened or had been so contrived, that We Were invited to dine at Monsieur Brillons, a Family in which Mr. Franklin was very intimate, and in which he spent much of his Time. Here We met a large Company of both Sexes and among them

Monsieur Le Vaillant [obviously Le Veillard] and his Lady. Madame Brillon was one of the most beautiful Women in France, a great Mistress of Musick, as were her two little Daughters. The Dinner was Luxury, as was usual in that Country. A Large Cake was brought in with three flags flying. On one of them " Pride subdued" : on another " Haec dies, in qua fit Congressus, exultemus et potemus in ea."

Mr. Brillon was a rough kind of Country Squire. His Lady all softness, sweetness and politeness. I saw a Woman in Company, as a Companion of Madam Brillon who dined with her at Table, and was considered one of the Family. She was very plain and clumzy.

When I afterwards learned both from Dr. Franklin and his Grandson, and from many other persons, that this Woman was the Amie of Mr. Brillon and that Madam Brillon consoled herself by the Amitie of Mr. Le Vaillant, I was astonished that these People could live together in such apparent Friendship and indeed without cutting each others throats. But I do not know the World. I soon saw and heard so much of these Things in other Families and among allmost all the great People of the Kingdom that I found it was a thing of course. It was universally understood and Nobody lost any reputation by it.[10]

Madame Brillon would have been very surprised to read the censorious thoughts running through her illustrious visitor's head while he was dining on her flag-bedecked cake. Adams' information was correct on one point: the "plain and clumzy" woman he saw at the table was indeed Brillon's "amie," although Madame Brillon did not suspect it yet. She was the governess of the "little Daughters," a Mademoiselle Jupin, and continued another full year to enjoy the benefit not of her mistress's cynicism, as Adams imagined, but of her mistress's blind trust. If the Brillon family was, at least, a *ménage à trois*, was it really a *ménage à quatre?* And, whatever the truth, did Franklin really believe that Le Veillard was Madame Brillon's lover?

Though one cannot exclude the possibility that Franklin, at first, may have picked up such a rumor and been emboldened by it in his own risqué suggestions to Madame, he certainly did not entertain the suspicion for long. A month after the dinner with Adams, he described her to an American friend, William Carmichael, as "a lady of most respectable character"[11]; and when writing to her, henceforth, his perennial complaint was that she was too demure. The lady herself (as would one whose conscience is clear) never concealed her warm affection for Le Veillard, but there is not a scrap of evidence to support Adams' hasty conclusion.

Far from worrying about irregularities in her own ménage, Madame Brillon, at that time, affected some jealousy on account of Franklin's philandering:

You ask me for the list of your sins, my dear papa; it would be so long that I dare not undertake such a great work. And yet, you commit only one, but it has so many branches, it is repeated so often that it would take infinite calculations to assess its magnitude. And after all that, you would like me to forgive you – me, the director of your soul! . . . The dangerous system you are forever trying to demonstrate, my dear papa – that the friendship a man has for women can be divided ad infinitum – *this is something I shall never put up with. My heart, while capable of great love, has chosen few objects on which to bestow it; it has chosen them well, you are at the head of the list. When you scatter your friendship, as you have done, my friendship does not diminish, but from now on I shall try to be somewhat sterner toward your faults.*[12]

Franklin was well aware that he had been broadening his social circle and paying compliments to ladies somewhat less prim, but he offered no apologies. On the contrary, he retorted at length:

What a difference, my dear friend, between you and me! You find innumerable faults in me, whereas I see only one fault in you (but perhaps it is the fault of my glasses). I mean this kind of avarice which leads you to seek a monopoly on all my affections, and not to allow me any for the agreeable ladies of your country. Do you imagine that it is impossible for my affection (or my tenderness) to be divided without being diminished? You deceive yourself, and you forget the playful manner with which you stopped me. You renounce and totally exclude all that might be of the flesh in our affection, allowing me only some kisses, civil and honest, such as you might grant your little cousins. What am I receiving that is so special as to prevent me from giving the same to others, without taking from what belongs to you? ... The sweet sounds brought forth from the pianoforte by your clever hands can be enjoyed by twenty people simultaneously without diminishing at all the pleasure you so obligingly mean for me, and I could, with as little reason, demand from your affection that no other ears but mine be allowed to be charmed by those sweet sounds.

Then, after the gentle scolding, an unusually mannered tableau in the precious style of some eighteenth-century painting – perhaps one of Madame Brillon's own making:

My poor little love, which you should have cherished, it seems to me, instead of being fat and lively (like those of your elegant paintings), is thin and ready to die of hunger for want of the substantial nourishment that his mother inhumanly refuses! And now, also, she wants to cut his little wings, so that he cannot go to seek it elsewhere.

Finally, back to himself and statesmanship, a peace treaty, distant echo of those he drafted with the Indians when he was a younger man:

I imagine that neither of us can gain anything in this war. Consequently, feeling myself to be the weaker, I shall do what ought, in fact, to be done by the wiser: make proposals of peace . . .

ARTICLE I *There must be peace, friendship, and eternal love between Madam B. and Mr. Frank.*

ARTICLE II *In order to maintain this inviolable peace, Madam B. on her side stipulates and agrees that Mr. F. shall come and see her every time she asks him to.*

ARTICLE III *That he shall stay at her house as much and as long as it shall please her.*

ARTICLE IV *That when he is with her, he shall be obliged to take tea, play chess, listen to music or do anything that she may ask him.**

ARTICLE V *And that he shall love no other woman than her.*

ARTICLE VI *And the said Mr. F. on his side stipulates and agrees that he shall go to Madam B's as much as he pleases.*

ARTICLE VII *That he shall stay there as long as he pleases.*

* A footnote prudently adds: "All that he is able to do, of course."

ARTICLE VIII   *That when he is with her he shall do anything he pleases.*

ARTICLE IX   *And that he shall love no other woman as long as he finds her agreeable.**

How do you like these preliminaries? Don't they seem to express the true way of thinking and the real intentions of both parties more clearly than most treaties? I am planning to insist heavily on ARTICLE VIII, *although without much hope of your consenting to its execution, and also on* ARTICLE IX, *although I despair of ever finding any other woman I could love with equal tenderness.*[13]

This is only a scrawled draft of treaty; no formal copy has been found, but we know that some treaty was signed, for Madame Brillon, years later, referred nostalgically to one. (With her usual imprecision, she then ascribed it to 1776, when Franklin had not yet come to France, and quoted articles that do not exist in the draft.) Nor is it altogether improper to speak of a "peace treaty," because a batch of mildly complaining letters reveal passing moments of tension in an otherwise harmonious relationship.

Her possessiveness and his craving seemed forever locked in a verbal tug-of-war. On a Thursday, she gave the first pull:

Do you mean that I shall see you only Saturday? And you give up so easily a Wednesday with me? Then, after that, you will say, as usual, I love you furiously, I love you too much? *I, my dear papa, love you not* furiously, *but very* tenderly; *not too much, but enough to feel sorry every time I could see you but do not. Now, which of us two loves more and better?*[14]

* Footnote: "The women can go and get drowned."

By return mail, the following day, he countered:

It is true that I have often said that I love you too much, and I have told the truth. Judge, by a comparison I am going to make, which of us two loves the most. If I say to a friend: "I need your horses to take a journey, lend them to me," and he replies: "I should be very glad to oblige you, but I fear that they will be ruined by this voyage and cannot bring myself to lend them to anyone," must I not conclude that the man loves his horses more than he loves me? And if, in the same case, I should willingly risk my horses by lending them to him, is it not clear that I love him more than my horses, and also more than he loves me? You know that I am ready to sacrifice my beautiful, big horses.[15]

But she felt more threatened than flattered because of that counterdrive toward respectability that made her, in a way, a pre-Victorian figure in a society where marriage vows were taken lightly – in the upper classes at least. So she said no, no to the horses who would run away with her good name, no to the little pagan Cupid whom Franklin had asked her to fatten. She took refuge in Greek philosophy, such as she vaguely knew it,

the gentleman, great philosopher that he is, goes by the doctrines of Anacreon and Epicure, but the lady is a Platonist. He wants a fat, chubby love, a love of flesh and bones, spoiled and pampered . . . the lady tries to blunt his little arrows, while giving him full freedom to run by hills and dales and attack anyone in sight . . . Platonism may not be the gayest sect, but it is a convenient defense for the fair sex. Hence, the lady, who finds it congenial, advises the gentleman to fatten up his favorite at other tables than hers, which will always offer too meager a diet for his greedy appetites . . . Apart from this, the lady awaits the gentleman tomorrow for tea, and forever pledges him her tender and inviolable love.[16]

A little later, Franklin hurt her feelings by leaving one of her parties too early, while she was showing the garden to some ladies:

Do you know, my good papa, that you played a mean trick on me? You order your carriage for eight o'clock, and at half-past seven you run away, to punish me for having endured the boredom of walking around with ladies, while I could have had fun, staying with you . . . I came back, I got very angry, I fumed against the ladies, against the voisin, *against you, against the whole world, against myself, against all that deprives me of the pleasure of being with you, whom I love from the depths of my heart. Another time, consider that it is a great sin to harm one's fellow creature, and stay till eight, nine, or ten o'clock.*[17]

Franklin apologized: after arising at four in the morning, working steadily, going to Paris and back, he found himself falling asleep during the conversation. And, he added pointedly:

Half an hour spent with an old man, who is not allowed to put it to its best use, is a mighty small matter, and you should not get angry over small things. Saturday evening, I shall stay with you until you long for my departure, and in spite of the usual courtesy of your spoken words, I shall know that the time to leave has arrived when you will refuse me a little kiss.[18]

Thus Franklin kept pressing his campaign, Madame Brillon kept fending him off, both playing the game in the artificial terms of conventional gallantry, yet yearning perhaps for an end to the stalemate, a breath of fresh air and simplicity. The break came, fittingly enough, in the midst of nature. In the summer of 1778, Madame Brillon went off to Anet, a small village on the western approach to Paris. Franklin joined her there, and on a fine day the friends made an excursion together to Moulin-Joli, on the banks of the Seine. Moulin-Joli was an estate belonging to Claude-Henry Watelet, a rich patron of the arts, who dabbled in painting and poetry. It was a meeting ground for professional and amateur artists, a sounding board for such discussions as the raging controversy between the partisans of Gluck's music and those of Piccinni. Musical tempers flared, but the physical surroundings, an English garden surprisingly in bloom in the middle of the Seine, were serene. Madame Vigée-Lebrun, that graceful portraitist of Marie-Antoinette and the beauties at the Court, evoked the charm of Moulin-Joli long after it had disappeared:

Imagine a large island, covered with woods, orchards, gardens, cut in two by the Seine. One crossed the river on a bridge of boats, decorated on both sides by boxes full of flowers ... Benches, here and there, invited you to enjoy the fragrance in the air, the vistas in the distance, the reflection of that bridge in the water ... the left bank was covered with huge poplars, and weeping willows made an enormous arch, under which one could rest and dream with delight.[19]

Here, even one of the sharpest wits of the century, the Prince de Ligne, waxed melancholy: "Whoever you are, if your heart is not made of stone, sit down under a willow at the Moulin-Joli ... read, contemplate and cry." Anyone sitting under that willow, the Prince went on, "would see his soul as in a mirror." [20] In the heat of the afternoon, while the other guests were chatting in the distance, Franklin sat in the shade of the willow and daydreamed. He watched the shimmering water, and, on its surface, the little insects called ephemerae, who are born, breed, and die in less than a day. He reflected that most discussions are pointless, that life is short, whether you are an ephemere or a man, that he was an old man now, that the universe itself may come to an end, and that everything is vanity. Back home, he wrote, with Madame Brillon in mind, a sad little piece called *The Ephemera*.

The theme was not new. Almost sixty years earlier, an unknown English writer had published in an English magazine a short essay, later reprinted in Franklin's *Pennsylvania Gazette*, where an incidental remark of Cicero on the strange insects "that never outlive the Day in which they are born" furnished a pretext for an exhortation to live for glory and virtue rather than for the pursuit of a "limited term of Happiness." [21] Then, in 1745, the famous French naturalist Réaumur, philosophizing on the same subject, had pronounced equally worthless the search for riches and the thirst for glory. Franklin had read Réaumur and still remembered the anonymous English essay. With far greater literary skill than the essayist, and with a lighter touch than the French scientist, he retold the story:

You may remember, my dear Friend, that when we lately spent that happy day in the delightful Garden and sweet Society of the Moulin Joli, I stopt a little in one of our Walks, and staid some time behind the Company. We had been shown numberless Skeletons of a kind of little Fly, called an Ephemere ... I happen'd to see a living Company of them on a Leaf, who appear'd to be engaged in Conversation . . . They were disputing warmly the Merit of two foreign Musicians, one a Cousin [*a variety of mosquito*], *the other a Musketo; in which Dispute they spent their time seemingly as regardless of the Shortness of Life, as if they had been Sure of living a Month.*

At this point, "an old grey-headed [ephemere], who . . . was single on another Leaf" gives vent to cosmic pessimism:

It was, says he, the Opinion of learned Philosophers of our race . . . that this vast world, the Moulin Joli, could not itself subsist more than 18 hours since by the apparent motion of the great Luminary that gives Life to all Nature, and which in my time has evidently declin'd considerably towards the Ocean at the End of our Earth, it must then finish its Course, be extinguish'd in the Waters . . . and leave the World in Cold and Darkness, necessarily producing universal Death and Destruction. I have lived seven of these Hours, a great Age, being no less than 420 minutes of Time. How very few of us continue So long . . . by the Course of Nature, tho' still in Health, I cannot expect to live above 7 or 8 minutes longer. What now avails all my Toil and Labour in amassing Honey-Dew on this Leaf, which I cannot live to enjoy! What the political Struggles I have been engag'd in for the Good of my Compatriots, Inhabitants of this Bush, or my philosophical studies for the Benefit of our Race in general! . . . My Friends would comfort me with the Idea of a Name they Say I shall leave behind me; and they tell me I have lived long enough, to Nature and to Glory; *– but what will Fame be to an Ephemere who no longer exists?*

After this unusual display of despondency, Franklin-the-Ephemere pulls himself together and concludes in a bitter-sweet vein:

*To me, after all my eager Pursuits, no solid Pleasures now
remain, but the Reflection of a long Life spent in meaning well,
the sensible Conversation of a few good Lady-Ephemeres, and
now and then a kind Smile and a Tune from the ever-amiable*
BRILLANTE.[22]

After the outing at Moulin-Joli, Madame Brillon returned
to Anet, Franklin to Passy. As always, when they were
separated, she missed him deeply and begged him to pay her
another visit:

*perhaps you will come and spend a few more moments in my
humble cottage; yes, you will come, to make us perfectly happy
. . . my papa, the weather is still lovely, won't you come back,
won't you write me a word in French – for in English I would
feel worse than Tantalus?*[23]

A few days later, on Thursday [September] 17 [1778],
faithful Le Veillard announced that Franklin would come and
stay from the 26th to the 28th. Madame Brillon, in her joy,
sent two letters of such passion that, read out of context of
the whole correspondence, they could easily lead one to see a
mistress awaiting her lover:

*to see you, to see you in my house, my dear papa, is the greatest
happiness I have ever enjoyed or that I could imagine; my soul,
made to love true and strong, has become so accustomed to seeing
you often, that it misses you dreadfully, looks for you, calls
you . . . Wednesdays and Saturdays, especially, do drag so
slowly! Now, at least, hope will sustain me; Saturday, I shall
say: one more Wednesday, Wednesday I shall say: that good
papa is coming Saturday; and that Saturday I shall say: I am
happy . . .*[24]

And again:

Wednesday you will have tea without me, Saturday you will have it with me; if that idea gives you one hundredth part of the pleasure it gives me, you must be very happy, my papa. There comes a point, they say, beyond which friendship cannot increase. I believe it, and I think my friendship for you has reached this point. And yet, it seems that I love you more with every day that passes; I think it is simply because every day I have been loving you for one more day. We shall go into this question Saturday, oh my dear papa, Saturday . . .[25]

3 Madame Brillon's Papa

For you my soul harbors
every feeling there is ❦ MADAME BRILLON

Saturday came. And Sunday and Monday. They sat on the grass and talked. And everything was changed between them.

Not that she yielded: on the contrary, she set herself apart from all other women, whom she now allowed him to woo, if he pleased. She proposed that he become, for her, instead of the pseudo papa with whom one flirts, the father whom one loves. And he accepted. He may have felt old, like the old ephemere of his story, and more in need of a dutiful daughter than of a tempestuous young mistress. The letters do not reveal exactly what was said on the grass, but suddenly the rapport between them lost frivolity, and gained depth. Soon, Madame Brillon stopped signing her letters altogether, referring to herself simply as Franklin's daughter.

Shortly after his departure, she celebrated, in her own brooding way, the new order of things:

I was too happy Saturday, Sunday and Monday; yes, my dear papa, I was too happy, my present sadness proves it! I have not gone yet to tidy up your rooms, for everything would be telling me that you are no longer there. But I have been back to our meadows; I saw everywhere the trace of our steps. The trees seemed a sadder green, the river seemed to flow more slowly . . . It is to her father that his tender and loving daughter is speaking; I had a father once, the best of men, he was my first, my closest friend. I lost him too soon! You have often asked me: Couldn't I take the place of those you regret? *And you have told me about the humane custom of certain savages who adopt their*

View of Passy, aquatint by Madame Brillon

prisoners of war and put them in the place of their own dead relatives. You have taken in my heart the place of that father whom I loved and respected so much.[1]

Franklin, in his answer, sounded pleased, fatherly, and determined to act his age:

I accept with infinite pleasure, my dear friend, the proposal you make, with such kindness, of adopting me as your father. I shall be very happy in the parentage of such a good daughter;* and as, by coming to this country, I have lost the sweet company and respectful care of my own affectionate daughter, this loss shall be amended and I shall have the satisfaction to trust that if I spend here the little remains of my days, another affectionate daughter will take care of me during my life and tenderly close my eyelids when I must take my last rest. Yes, my dear child, I love you as a father, with all my heart.

After this solemn beginning, the faun could not help showing the tip of his pointed ear: "It is true that I sometimes suspect that heart of wanting to go further, but I try to conceal it from myself." But then, resignedly: "if at my age it is not fitting to say that I am in love with a young woman, there is nothing to prevent me from confessing that I admire and love an assemblage of all female virtues and of all admirable talents."[2]

There was a flood of letters from Madame Brillon during the fall and winter of 1778. Many of them rang with the language of mysticism: idolatry, cult, devotion, fusion. She never tired of telling Franklin what he, apparently, never wearied of hearing: that her heart was pure and her soul

---

*   Here, he coined the word *enfante*, a nonexistent, but very practical, way of designating the female child in French.

fiery; that she worshiped her friends, that he was the best of them. "Oh, my friend, who will ever love you as much as I? I."[3] One day, at a loss for an adequate way of expressing the hundred shadings of her affection, she simply exclaimed: "For you, my soul harbors every feeling there is!"[4]

Remembering how diligently Franklin had worked at self-improvement as a young man, she insisted that she, too, was planning to improve, read serious books, become worthy of him: "Always, I am seeking some way of pleasing you, and I shall not be truly happy until I read in your eyes that you are proud of your daughter."[5] She kept all his letters, she said, and felt that soon there would be a whole volume of hers. Unconsciously, perhaps, she was trying to write with Franklin one of those romantic epistolary novels, of which it has been said that any woman can produce at least one – the story of the love she would have liked to live.

The love Madame Brillon would have liked to live had nothing to do with the senses:

Your daughter is not content to please you by the kind of charms you can meet any day, and to a higher degree, in many other women, but by a combination of all virtues which will make her your friend, in the true sense, were she old, were she ugly, were she a man.[6]

Whether Franklin approved or not of such a radical devaluation of her female assets, Madame Brillon proceeded to eliminate what little physical favors she had granted him at first:

You remember what I told you on the meadow, about evil tongues in this country; my dear papa, no matter how pure our intention, we are judged only on appearances; it is unfair, I agree, but people are often unfair. A wise person pities them and does not try to reform them; let us be wise, then, accept their injustice, and conform.[7]

And on another occasion, more pointedly: "Do you know, my dear papa, that people have criticized the sweet habit I have taken of sitting on your lap, and your habit of soliciting from me what I always refuse?"[8]

She never let him forget that her position as daughter was sacred and inviolable. Franklin tried, every now and then, to revert to his former irreverent ways. Having exhausted the possibilities of sins and commandments, he settled for an imaginary bishop and told the following story:

A beggar asked an Archbishop for an alm of a Louis. – A Louis for a beggar, that would be extravagant! – Just an ecu then. – Still too much. – Let us say a farthing, or your blessing. – My blessing, now, there is a sensible idea. – I don't want it any more, for if it was worth a farthing, you would not give it to me.

Such was the love the Bishop had for his neighbor. Such was his charity. If I examine yours, I find it no greater. . . . You, who are as rich as an Archbishop in all Christian and moral virtues, you could sacrifice for my sake a little portion of those virtues without the loss being sensible, but you tell me it is asking too much. Such is your charity toward an unfortunate who used to enjoy plenty and is now reduced to begging your alms.[9]

All he got for his pains was a calm reply:

My dear papa, your Bishop was a rascal, your beggar a rather funny fellow. . . . What would you say of your beggar if, after the Bishop had given him his Louis, he had protested because he had not received two of them? Yet such is your case, my dear good friend. You adopted me as a daughter, I chose you as a father. I love you as a daughter should love her father. . . . you asked for a Louis, I gave it to you; and now you grumble about the second Louis, which it is not in my power to grant.[10]

So certain was she of having tamed his baser instincts that she was able to accept the famous bathtub scene with equal serenity. Franklin and Le Veillard had become so engrossed in a game of chess, one evening, that they forgot the time and stayed quite late while Madame Brillon was soaking in the tub, under her wooden plank. Back home, at eleven, he penned a note in imitation of her handwriting, apologizing not for the strangeness of the situation, but for the "inconvenience" of detaining her so long in the water: "Tell me, my dear Friend, how you feel this morning. Never again will I consent to start a game in your bathing room.* Can you forgive me for this indiscretion?"[11] Changing the topic in the next sentence, he talked about a scholar who had translated the *Iliad* and wondered if he might bring him to tea. Madame Brillon, the following morning, replied that it would be an excellent idea to bring along Monsieur [Paul-Jérémie] Bitaubé, promised to read his Homer, joked about the imitation of her writing, and dismissed the bathtub casually: "No, my good papa, you did not do me any harm yesterday, I am so happy to see you that the good it does me more than balances the little fatigue of overstaying in the tub."[12]

The only ripples ever to ruffle the calm waters of that happy period were Franklin's occasional offers to see less of her, in

---

* This is what the draft says. The fair copy adds and underlines: "With the Grand Voisin."

order to avoid public criticism – and, perhaps, not to antagonize Monsieur Brillon:

No, my dear papa, your visits have never caused me any trouble; all those who surround me respect you and love you, and feel honored by the friendship you grant us. I told you that certain criticisms had been uttered by persons whom I meet in society concerning the kind of familiarity that reigns between us. I despise the back-biters and am at peace with myself. But that is not enough: one must submit to what is called propriety (the word varies in every century, in every land!). Though I may not sit upon your knee so often, it certainly will not be because I love you less; our hearts will be neither more nor less pure, but we shall have shut the mouths of evil speakers, and that is no small feat, even for a sage.[13]

Having thus made her peace with the outside world, the lady was free to focus once more on the only topic she deemed of interest, Franklin and herself.

Many of her letters were dated from La Thuillerie, her mother's estate where she spent about six weeks every autumn, with fresh outbursts of frustration each Wednesday and Saturday she had to spend away from her Papa. Nothing else seemed to matter, not her music which she never mentioned, not her painting, not her husband – equally absent from her letters, not even her mother and children, who only floated somewhere in postscripts, eternally sending their compliments. In postscripts, too, sending her "respectful compliments," was the girls' governess, Mademoiselle Jupin. Mademoiselle Jupin was that "plain and clumsy woman" whose presence in the Brillon household, when she was notoriously Monsieur Brillon's *amie*, had so shocked John

Adams. At the time of his visit, however, far from being worldly and cynical about the situation, as Adams had surmised, Madame Brillon had been simply unaware.

But she did find out, eventually, more than a year after Adams' remarks. And when she did, she burst out with the classic fury of the outraged wife. Mademoiselle Jupin was turned out of the house. She must have cast a strong spell upon Monsieur Brillon, for she still had him, his wife felt, in her grip. And, to make matters worse, there was talk that she might move into Franklin's household, probably as a housekeeper.

This was too much. Madame Brillon fell ill. Franklin enquired after her health. She replied, on May 3 [1779]:

I thank you, my good papa, for the interest you take in my health; it is somewhat better, but my soul is very sick. It is that soul, honest and too sensitive, that is killing me. I must absolutely have a long and detailed conversation with you. I want you to know thoroughly my heart and those who have cruelly wounded it . . . and it may be important for you to know a thing that may concern you some day. Would you, could you receive me Wednesday, the day after tomorrow, at ten in the morning, and close your door for an hour, so that my soul can open itself to yours and receive comfort and advice. Send me a word right away; it must not be known that you are writing to me or that I am going to see you. You are my father. It is the father's love that I need more than ever.[14]

Alerted by so dramatic a message, Franklin received her on May 5 and listened to a story he had known for a long time. He probably did not say much, but sat and nodded, as was his custom. He did reassure her on one point, though: he was not going to take in Mademoiselle Jupin. This was a great relief to Madame Brillon: "Passy, Saturday, May 8 [1779]. My soul is calmer, my dear papa, since it has unburdened itself into yours, since it does not fear anymore that Mlle j—— might settle down with you and be your torment, as well as that of your dear [grand]son."

Coming back in her letter to ground she had undoubtedly covered with him during their conversation, she wondered again how all this could ever have happened. Under shock, Madame Brillon reveals herself at her worst: blinded by self-adoration, whining, cut off from reality. The thought that she might have been something less than a perfect wife for Monsieur Brillon never seems to have entered her mind; indeed, she felt that far from having any shortcomings, she was being punished for the very excess of her virtues:

In the sad story I told you the other day, in the letters I showed you, you saw your daughter's soul laid bare: her extreme sensitivity, her frankness, her too easy affability, no distrustfulness to shield her from evil because she never suspects it, not being capable of evil herself; a yearning to love and be loved which has caused her to confide too promptly in such as proclaimed their own goodness and virtues – there, my friend, is the cause of all my sorrows. Shall I love less from now on? No, probably not, but I shall not love with such haste: reason and reflection will come to the aid of a heart that is too tender and too weak.

No matter how tender and weak she fancied herself, though, she could not quite let go of the enemy:

The more I examine myself, the more I see that my hope to prove useful to someone I thought unhappy and in poor circumstances has led me into a terrible trap. Mademoiselle j——, forever extolling virtues which she never practiced, a delicacy she herself knew nothing of, a frankness she does not possess, was clever enough, after being disowned by her own family, and expelled from two households, to take advantage of me to such an extent as to make all her adventures turn out to her credit; so much so that I pitied her, loved her, and always refused to listen to the repeated warnings I received to beware of her real character. I almost paid with my life the ingratitude, the falsity with which she deceived me. My husband will be perhaps for a long time under her spell; but I dare hope that my eagerness to please him, the affection of his children, the contempt which all our old and good friends have conceived for that girl, and which they are not prepared to conceal, will open his eyes some day. Meanwhile, I surrender entirely to the cleverness she will display in trying to make me appear as ridiculous as possible.

She concluded with a pledge to behave with dignity, and a new appeal to Franklin: "keep my secret within your soul, keep my heart there, too. I deposit it with you to heal it from its wounds and weaknesses. I shall expect you this evening for tea; never, never have I had a greater need of spending a few hours with you."[15]

Franklin did not try to take advantage of this moment of despair. Putting aside all thoughts of courtship, he made himself immediately into the wise, mellow father she longed for, and he even indulged in a little preaching:

You told me, my dear daughter, that your heart is too sensitive. I see, by your letters, that that is too true. A keen awareness of our own faults is good because it leads us to avoid them in the future. But to be very sensitive to, and afflicted by, the faults of

other people, – that is not good. They are the ones who should be
sensitive and afflicted by what they have done wrong. As for us,
we should preserve that tranquillity that is the just portion of
innocence and virtue. But you say that "Ingratitude is a terrible
evil." *That is true – an evil to the ungrateful – but not to the*
benefactors. . . . If they do wrong, reflect that even though they
may have been your equals beforehand, they have now placed
themselves beneath you. If you exact a vengeance . . . you restore
them to the state of equality that they had lost. But if you were
to forgive them, without any punishment, you would fix them in
the low state into which they have fallen.

If Madame Brillon derived some comfort from the thought
that her papa spent a sleepless night pondering her problems,
it is to be hoped that she never came across the *Poor Richard*
Almanack for 1749, where, exactly thirty years before her
plight, he had written: "Doing an injury puts you below
your enemy; revenging one makes you but even with him;
forgiving it sets you above him."

But if "the enemy" was singular in *Poor Richard*, it had
become "they" in this letter. What did the plural mean? Not
Mademoiselle Jupin alone, certainly not Monsieur Brillon.
Were "they" the same backbiters who had been gossiping
about Madame Brillon's relationship with the Doctor? Could
Franklin have opened his heart to her about his own American
critics? Whoever "they" may be, Franklin, groping for
words of comfort, proceeded to paint a rosy, edifying picture
in which Madame Brillon occupied the center. He hovered
benevolently on the fringes. Even the "enemies" eventually
came back in repentance:

Follow then, my very dear and always amiable daughter, the
good resolution that you have so wisely taken, to continue to

fulfill all your duties as good mother, good wife, good friend, good neighbor, good Christian, etc. (without forgetting to be a good daughter to your papa), and to neglect and forget, if you can, the wrongs you may be suffering at present.

It is interesting to note that Franklin's last editor, Albert Smyth, suppressed the words between parentheses, "without forgetting to be a good daughter to your papa," probably because he felt they were flippant and detracted from the dignity of the letter. It does go on in a dignified tone:

And be sure that, given time, the rectitude of your conduct will win over the minds of even the worst people, and still more the minds of those people whose nature is basically good, and who also are endowed with good sense, even though they may be right now somewhat led astray by the trickery of others. Then all of them will ask with compunction for the return of your friendship and they will become in the future your most ʒealous friends.[16]

So carried away was he by his new role of mentor, that in one of the many conversations they held during that month of May, Franklin kept calling his friend "Madame," thus precipitating new anguish: "don't ever call me anything but daughter, yesterday you called me madame and my heart shrank, I examined myself to see if I had done you any wrong, or if I had some failings that you would not tell me of."[17] But, on the whole, he struck the right chord, and Madame Brillon promised to do her best to follow his advice. However, she stressed, her health was so shaky that it influenced her morale. It was at a tremendous sacrifice that she kept herself under sufficient control not to destroy the happiness of those around her, "but I suffer, my friend, often, when I am alone, my eyes fill up with tears ... I shall always be a gentle, virtuous woman; try to turn me into a woman of strength, who knows, perhaps you are the one to accomplish that miracle."

Then, for the first time, she turns the spotlight on her husband. Her prime complaint was not, strangely enough, about his unfaithfulness – at Versailles, in those days, as André Maurois pointed out, "a faithful husband cut a ridiculous figure"[18] – but about his insensitivity to the fine arts or, as she calls them, "the amenities of life":

I am not unfair, I know that the man to whom fate has bound me is a worthy person; I respect him as I should and as he deserves; perhaps have I always loved him beyond the capabilities of his own heart; a disparity of twenty-four years in our ages, his austere training, my own, it may be, a trifle too much directed toward the amenities of life, have contracted his heart and uplifted mine.

Their personalities were obviously incompatible, but what parents considered such trivia when arranging a marriage contract?

In this country, my papa, marriages are made by weight of gold; on one side of the scale you put the fortune of a young man, on the other that of a girl, and when a balance is struck the matter is settled to the satisfaction of the parents. No one would dream of consulting the tastes, the souls, the temperaments of the two parties; a young girl, whose heart is filled with the burning desires of youth, finds herself married to a man who has already extinguished them.* And then, one demands from this woman perfect propriety.[19]

---

*   Here Madame Brillon had added "through libertine practices," but she crossed it out.

Actually, this picture of her husband as a tired old man does not fit at all the reality of a Monsieur Brillon caught cavorting with Mademoiselle Jupin. What comes out quite clearly, though, is that in his wife's eyes, he is of much coarser clay than her fragile self. The historian, who knows that sanguine Monsieur Brillon did not have many more years to go, while his frail wife would live to a ripe eighty, cannot repress a fleeting smile and a twinge of sympathy for a man married to such self-acknowledged perfection.

What about Monsieur Brillon? If we are to judge by his letters, the first word that springs to mind is "jolly." Even in the few business transactions he had conducted with Franklin, acting as a go-between for French merchants anxious to sell weapons to the colonies, Brillon generally managed to slip some little joke. His "you have surely just been kissing my wife, my dear Doctor, allow me to kiss you back," denoted a guilty conscience of his own, perhaps, but at least a tolerant mind. He was capable, also, of a dash of irreverence. He forwarded to Franklin Turgot's famous epigram: "Eripuit coelo fulmen sceptrumque tyrannis" ("He stole the thunder from heaven and the scepter from the tyrants"), and he added, "thank goodness, you also abandon the heavens sometimes for the shepherd's crook." [20] Over the years, Franklin grew quite fond of Monsieur Brillon. Endowed himself with a robust sense of humor, he must have enjoyed climbing down from the celestial heights of his relationship with the wife to an occasional earthy laugh with the husband. As he would write a year later:

Your good husband's visits during my illness have given me much pleasure. His conversation has relieved and amused me. I regret that instead of seeking it, when I was at your house, I lost so much time playing chess. He tells many stories, and they are always to the point.[21]

But at the time of the Jupin crisis, of course, the best that Franklin dared say about Monsieur Brillon was that he was basically good-natured, if temporarily misled. It took more than two years for Madame Brillon to reach the same conclusion. She did, eventually, when she had regained, under new skies, the poise and serenity that time alone can bring. In the months that followed the storm, the best Madame Brillon could muster was not to mention her husband at all. This is particularly striking in an "afterlife" utopia she dreamed up, borrowing a leaf from Franklin's book. She had taken her annual trip to the country in the fall, and wrote from there, in her own half-jesting, half-disenchanted way, that there was not much happiness to be expected on earth, but

In paradise, we shall be reunited, never to leave each other again! We shall live there on roasted apples only; music will be made up solely of Scottish tunes; all chess games will end in a tie, so that nobody will be sorry; the same language will be spoken by all; the English, there, will be neither unjust nor wicked; women will not be coquettish, men will be neither jealous nor too enterprising . . . There shall be no gout, no nervous upsets . . . ambition, envy, conceit, jealousy, prejudices, all will vanish at the sound of the trumpet; a lasting, sweet and peaceful friendship will animate every society. . . . In the meantime, let us get all the good we can from this earthly life.[22]

Modest, girlish wishes, on the whole; they did not elicit a prompt reaction from Franklin, so that Tuesday 9 [November

1779] Madame Brillon indulged in some gentle reproach. Her mind was cross, she said, even though her heart still found excuses for him: too much work perhaps, a touch of the gout, or, she hoped, nothing more serious than pretty ladies to take up his time.

Far from neglecting her, Franklin had been studiously preparing a long epistle. Their friendship was now evolving from the battle of love to the joys of literary alliance. Always a realist, Franklin accepted the fact that Madame Brillon would never offer him more than her particular blend of chastity and exaltation. Still, her presence stimulated his mind and his pen.

This new phase opened on November 10, with *The Story of the Whistle*. The draft, a laborious affair full of addenda and corrections, was written in two columns, with the French on the left and the English (partly transcribed below) on the right. Also extant is a manuscript of the fair copy, in French, sent to Madame Brillon for her corrections:

Instead of spending this Wednesday Evening as I have long done its Name-sakes, in your delightful Company, I sit down to spend it in thinking of you, in writing to you, and in reading over and over again your Letters.

I am charm'd with your Description of Paradise, and with your Plan of living there. And I approve much of your Conclusion, that in the meantime we should draw all the Good we can from this World. In my Opinion we might all draw more Good from it than we do, and suffer less Evil, if we would but take care not to give too much for our Whistles. For to me it seems that most of the unhappy People we meet with are become so by Neglect of that Caution.

You ask what I mean? – You love Stories, and I will excuse my telling you one of myself. When I was a Child of seven Years old, my Friends on a Holiday fill'd my little Pocket with Halfpence. I went directly to a Shop where they sold Toys for Children; and being charm'd with the Sound of a Whistle that I met by the way, in the hands of another Boy, I voluntarily offer'd and gave all my Money for it. When I came home, whistling all over the House, much pleas'd with my Whistle, but disturbing all the Family, my Brothers, Sisters and Cousins, understanding the Bargain I had made, told me I had given four times as much for it as it was worth, put me in mind what good Things I might have bought with the rest of the Money, and laught at me so much for my Folly that I cry'd with Vexation; and the Reflection gave me more Chagrin than the Whistle gave me Pleasure.

This however was afterwards of use to me, the Impression continuing on my Mind; so that often when I was tempted to buy some unnecessary thing, I said to my self, Do not give too much for the Whistle; *and I sav'd my Money.*

As I grew up, came into the World, and observed the Actions of Men, I thought I met many who gave too much for the Whistle.[23]

He went on to explain how the overambitious courtier, the man bent solely on accumulating wealth, and the inveterate spendthrift, all paid too much for their whistle "because of the false Estimates they had made of the Value of Things."

The Whistle was eventually printed on the private press Franklin had set up in Passy and reprinted many times, both in French and in English. It appeared in such sundry places as the *Daily Advertiser* for May 10, 1786, and *Le Jardin des Dames et des Modes* for April 5, 1809.

In the manuscript sent to Madame Brillon, Franklin added two little postscripts: the first told her that since their common neighbors had also left Passy, he was now reduced to singing "I have lost my Eurydice"; the second stated, "Voila une grande Exercice pour vos Corrections," the need for corrections made obvious by his putting *exercice* in the feminine. Madame Brillon may have wondered what connection there was between her letter on paradise and the tale it inspired. If one rejects the notion that Franklin was simply practicing his French – it is hard to conceive that he was not trying to make *some* point – a likely guess is that he was warning her not to squander the emotions of her impulsive, ardent nature on unworthy people or situations. At any rate, Madame Brillon, reporting that her husband laughed heartily upon reading it, chose to interpret *The Whistle* as applying to her misfortunes:

I assure you, my kind papa, that I shall be very careful not to give too much for the whistles. If they have not cost my purse very much, they have taken a big toll from my heart, and your letter proves still better than my own experience or thoughts, that I have often paid a high price for bad whistles. *I believed, for instance, that when I loved, one was bound to love me back, since I judged others by the standards of my own soul. I have seldom gotten back the worth of what I gave, which is called* paying too much for the whistle. *I believed what people said, because they said it, and I did not imagine that one could say one thing while believing another.*[24]

Her own conclusion was that no matter how much Franklin loved her, for that particular whistle he would never be paying too much.

Since *The Whistle* had obviously not raised her spirits, Franklin went back to her own fantasy about Paradise. His ideas of perfect bliss, however, were more specific than hers. First of all, the problem of Monsieur Brillon had to be met, not simply forgotten:

More than 40 years will probably elapse from the time of my arrival there until you follow me. I am somewhat fearful that in the course of such a long period you may forget me. Therefore, I have thought of proposing that you give me your word of honor not to renew there your contract with Mr. B, while I give you mine that I shall wait for you. – But that gentleman is so good, so generous towards us – he loves you so much and you love him – that I cannot think of this proposition without scruples of conscience. Yet, the idea of an eternity during which I would not be more favored than by being allowed to kiss your hands, or sometimes your cheeks, and to spend two or three hours in your sweet company on Wednesday and Saturday evenings, is horrendous. . . . But since (with all those who know you) I wish to see you happy in all things, we can agree not to speak about it any more for the·present, and to leave it to you, when we shall meet in the other world, to decide and to settle the matter as you may think best for your own happiness and for ours. Decide it in what way you want, I feel that I shall love you for all eternity.

At this point, as always when he has reached a certain lyrical intensity, Franklin injects a note of irony – his way of stepping back: "If you reject me, perhaps I shall address myself to Madame d'Hardancourt, whom it may please to take up housekeeping with me; then I shall pass my domestic hours agreeably with her, and shall be nearer at hand to see you." Madame d'Hardancourt was Madame Brillon's mother.

She must have doted on the Doctor almost as much as her daughter; Madame Brillon describes the old lady's disappointment when Franklin failed to visit her: his bed had been made up in the best room, his favorite dishes prepared, and the garden paths carefully raked for his strolls.

In his final apotheosis, Franklin did not content himself with a paradise *à deux*, as she had, but in an outburst of generosity included all their friends – and music:

I shall have enough time during those 40 years to practice on the armonica, and perhaps, I may be able to play well enough to accompany you on the piano-forte. From time to time, we shall have little concerts: good Pagin will be of the party; your neighbor and his dear family; M. de Chaumont, M. B. – . . . and other chosen friends will form our audience; and the dear good girls, accompanied by some other young angels whose portraits you have already given me, will sing the alleluias *with us; we shall eat together apples of Paradise roasted with butter and nutmeg, and we shall pity those who are not dead.*

This, again, is presented as an exercise in French, "with many mistakes, admittedly, and many follies." Since *exercice* is still in the feminine, it is obvious that Madame Brillon's pupil needed more drill. She returned his manuscripts with her corrections lightly written between the lines, and Franklin, forever eager for progress, dutifully noted them on a separate page:[25]

More than 40 Years	Plus *de* (not *que*) 40 années
To think of a thing	Penser *à* (not *de*) une chose
To be permitted	D'*avoir* Permission (not *d'être permis*)

Perhaps I shall address myself   Peut-être m'addresserai-je
                                             (not *Je m'addresserai*)

Aside from correcting his grammar, Madame Brillon tried
bravely to reply in the same vein:

*If your French is not very pure, it is at least very clear! I give
you my word of honor to become your wife in paradise, on
condition, however, that you will not ogle the virgins too much
while waiting for me; when I choose one for eternity, I want a
husband who is faithful; do you hear, my dear papa?*

*I shall tell Maman tonight about your good intentions toward
her; I fear, though, that if she plans to oppose my claims on you,
it will arouse a kind of jealousy between us. I am willing to yield
anything to my mother except you, my good papa.*

*I accept the kind of life you suggest for paradise: music,
friends, of that I will never tire, however long eternity is.*[26]

But she could not conjure up more than a weak smile.
Melancholia was closing in on her. Although she had warned
him, early in their relationship, that she suffered from
"maladie des nerfs," Franklin believed, or pretended to
believe, that her ills were purely physical. He would enquire
about her cold or her headache; invariably, she would reply:
"It is my soul that is sick."

She knew what was wrong, and she described her disease
with remarkable lucidity:

*It is a disease of which people cannot help seeing the effects, but
the causes, I believe, have not yet been discovered, since there are
no known remedies, and we are still trying out palliatives. It is
said to be due to an excessive sensitivity. Some women simulate
it in order to arouse interest. Many people make fun of this*

disease and do not believe in it. Those who are really attacked by it suffer cruelly and are terribly unhappy! Depression, deep melancholia are the sequel of such attacks; everything tires you, everything distresses you, you can hardly think.[27]

On another occasion, she mentioned that the wind upset her. The cure? "When I am ill," she said, "I need still more to be loved."

Yet Franklin kept talking about matter-of-fact remedies, even in the summer of 1780, when she showed signs of falling seriously ill. On July 10, he wrote:

Let me hear from you, my dear friend. Did the bloodletting relieve you? Do you think we may hope for the pleasure of having you here, with the dear children, next Wednesday, for tea? . . . It seems to me that when you are in good health, you do not take enough exercise to keep yourself well. I advise you to take a walk every day for an hour, in your beautiful garden if the weather is good, otherwise in your house. Or, if you don't have sufficient leisure, take a more strenuous but shorter kind of exercise, and the result will be the same. You can do that by going up and down the steps of your garden or your house for a quarter of an hour every day before dinner.[28]

Running up and down steps, however, was not the treatment Madame Brillon was looking for. She answered sadly:

My good papa, I have had a violent attack and am now exceedingly weak. I shall receive you with pleasure when you have a moment to spare, but I shall not be able to go and seek you for a long time. My machine is weak, my friend, fate has destined me to suffer. I accept its decree, which I am unable to change anyway. I have nothing to reproach myself about. I take some exercise, I live moderately, I love my friends, and especially my papa.[29]

Manuscript of the *Dialogue between Dr. Franklin and the Gout,* with Madame Brillon's corrections

This was to be a protracted illness, stretching from September 1780, to February 1781. And Franklin himself, during the fall of 1780 came down with one of his most severe attacks of the gout. Separated for several months, the friends corresponded from sickroom to sickroom, trying to cheer up and entertain one another, while Pagin and Monsieur Brillon (also a frequent sufferer from the gout) ran errands between them. On the Doctor's side, the outcome of this period of enforced immobility was a humorous little gem, his famous *Dialogue Between the Gout and Mr. Franklin.*

Not so well known, by any means, is Madame Brillon's *Le Sage et la Goutte,* a fable in the style of La Fontaine, which probably served as the inspiration for Franklin's *Dialogue.* His is dated Midnight, October 22, 1780 (the night the gout struck). Hers is dated simply, "Tuesday, from my bed." But the exchange of letters makes it clear that Franklin had received, read, and shown others her *Fable* before he responded with his *Dialogue.* Both elaborated on the same themes, she more briefly, he more fully; Madame Brillon's poem contains in a nutshell all the ideas that her friend was to develop more wittily in his prose. He was not ungrateful; a few years later, in 1784, he was to pay tribute to her role, graciously if implicitly, by including her *Fable* in the collection of his own printed *Bagatelles.*

Here is a free translation of Madame Brillon's opening verses:

An affliction that all men redoubt,
That untreatable sickness, the Gout,
At a Wise Man establish'd her room,
Thus intending to plunge him in gloom.

He did howl. Wisdom knows how to preach,
But the ears of a patient can't reach.
Reason yet at long last won the day,
After Wise Man and Gout said their say.
"Moderation, dear Doctor," said the Gout,
"Is no virtue for which you stand out.
You like food, you like ladies' sweet talk,
You play chess when you should take a walk,
You like wine. This may seem good and well,
But your fluids meanwhile rise and swell.
When I come to flush out what offends,
Why not thank me as the best of your friends?" [30]

The wise man talks back, not without indulging in some bragging: "I loved, I love, and always shall I love"; "one pretty mistress, sometimes two, three, four," and if his own wife had forgiven such transgressions, why should Gout be more intransigent? Only "dupes and fools give up their pleasures," concludes the poem. Madame Brillon displays in it that felicitous blend of flattery and mockery Franklin found so irresistible. Wine, women, and (in lieu of song) chess; it would be the unusual man of seventy-four who would not like to be told he is reckless on those three counts. That year, not long before the gout struck, Franklin had written: "Being arrived at seventy, and considering that by travelling farther in the same road I should probably be led to the grave, I stopped short, turned about, and walked back again; which having done these four years, you may now call me sixty-six." [31] A self-mocking illusion, to be sure, but it was good to find Madame Brillon a willing partner in the game of youth.

One, two, three, four pretty mistresses – no doubt, if

Madame Brillon did not feel like climbing steps to cure her nerves, neither could Franklin be inclined to chase pretty women on his sore feet. But this was no reason to brush away her hint; instead, he took it as a pretext for a sly rejoinder:

One of the characters of your fable, Madame la Goutte, seems to me to reason pretty well, except when she supposes that mistresses have had a share in producing this painful malady. I, for one, believe the exact opposite; and here is my argument. When I was a young man and enjoyed more of the favors of the sex than I do at present, I had no gout. Hence, if the ladies of Passy had shown more of that christian charity that I have so often recommended to you in vain, I should not be suffering from the gout right now. This seems to me good logic.[32]

She answered, on November 18, 1780, with some twisted logic of her own, pondering on the nature of pain, and concluding firmly: "For me, nothing remains but the faculty of loving my friends. You do not doubt, surely, that I will do my best for you, in a spirit of Christian charity – but to the exclusion of *your* brand of Christian charity."[33]

Meanwhile, she kept busy making notes on his *Dialogue.* For her *Fable* she wanted no publicity at all; indeed, she had sent Franklin a letter in mock anger because he had allowed Temple to make a fair copy of her draft. Quoting Molière's *Misanthrope,* she had stressed that a woman's lot is modesty, and that her writings were to be restricted to the closest circle of her friends. But the *Dialogue* was another matter: Franklin had written it with great care, no doubt with an eye to publication, one of his friends had revised it (Abbé de la Roche? Le Veillard?), and then he sent it to Madame Brillon for further suggestions. Could anything have been more therapeutic for her than this tender reliving of their hours together?

GOUT: *You know Monsieur Brillon's gardens and what fine walks they contain; you know the handsome flight of one hundred steps, which lead from the terrace above to the lawn below. It has been your custom to visit this amiable family twice a week, after dinner, and it is a maxim of your own, that "a man may take as much exercise in walking a mile, up and down stairs, as in ten on level ground." What an opportunity for you to have had exercise in both ways! Did you embrace it, and how often?*

FRANKLIN: *I cannot answer that question offhand.*

GOUT: *I will do it for you; not once.*

FRANKLIN: *Not once?*

GOUT: *Not once. During this glorious summer, you went there at six o'clock. You found that charming lady, with her lovely children and friends, eager to walk with you and entertain you with their agreeable conversation. And what did you do? You sat on the terrace, you praised the beautiful view, contemplated the beauty of the gardens below; but you did not take a single step toward going down and walking through them. On the contrary, you called for tea and the chessboard. And there you were, glued to your seat, until nine o'clock. All this, after you had already played some two hours at the house where you dined. Then, instead of walking home, which might bestir you a little, you step into your carriage ... You philosophers are wise men in your maxims and fools in your conduct.*

FRANKLIN: *But do you regard as one of my crimes that I return by carriage from Madame Brillon's?*

GOUT: *Yes, indeed. For you, who have been sitting all day long,*

cannot say that you are tired from the work of the day; therefore,
you cannot need the relief of the carriage.

FRANKLIN: *What then would you have me do with my carriage?*

GOUT: *Burn it, if you wish; for once, at least, you would get*
some heat out of it.[34]

Madame Brillon's notes, scribbled in the margins, reflect
the depth of her adulation. Under the title, she quipped:
"corrected and enriched with several mistakes by a learned
man and embellished with critical notes by a woman who is
not learned."[35] The gist of her comments was that whoever
amended Franklin's original text was making a blunder. His
own French, untampered with, had more pungency and
flavor. She even argued, in favor of his use of such nonexistent words as *indulger*, that it was not his fault if the French
language was poor; *indulger* should be accepted by the
Academy. She pressed her point on November 26, once more
in surprisingly modern terms, in a letter accompanying the
Dialogue:

A few purists might quibble with us, because those birds weigh
words on the scales of cold erudition; but I don't weigh, I don't
compare, I am a female guided by instinct, and since you seem
to express yourself more forcefully than a grammarian, my
judgment goes in your favor, against all learned men, past,
present and future. ... I might build long dissertations on the
basis of my instinct, yet my reasonings might not be more
unreasonable than those of your admirable, illustrious Encyclo-
pedists – economists – moralists – journalists – theologians –
atheists – materialists – and all imaginable sorts of ———ists![36]

This outburst against the isms of the eighteenth century
responded to an about-face by Franklin three days earlier,

when he had suddenly switched from treacherous logic to trustworthy instinct:

Human reason, my dear daughter, must be a very uncertain thing, since two sensible persons, like you and me, can draw diametrically opposed conclusions from the same premises. I think reason is a blind guide; true and sure instinct would be worth much more. All inferior animals, put together, do not commit as many mistakes in the course of a year, as a single man within a month, even though this man claims to be guided by reason. This is why, as long as I was fortunate enough to have a wife, I had adopted the habit of letting myself be guided by her opinion on difficult matters, for women, I believe, have a certain feel, which is more reliable than our reasonings.[37]

Was Franklin really tired of sophistry and nostalgic for the uncomplicated ways of Debbie, or was he talking of instinct merely to ease the mental tension of his sick friend? Madame Brillon, it seems, never allowed her "female instincts" to lead her in any path more adventurous than the correction of his grammar. Even though Franklin had stated modestly, "I have the impression that you are making fun of me when you say that my bad French is better before corrections than after," Madame Brillon's repeated assertions that his French was good pleased and flattered him exceedingly. He made one more valiant attempt to play coy: "If you were a journalist, I would almost decide to get some of my little French works* printed and brought to the light of day. But since this is not the case, they will sleep in the darkness, they will rest in peace, and so will I."[38] But he could not

---

* Here, he enriched the language by the word *œuvret*, a freshly minted diminutive of *œuvre*, in the wrong gender.

wait. By November 23, he had already dispatched another *œuvret*, not in his own French, this time, but translated from the English by Pierre-Georges Cabanis, a friend we shall meet later. Franklin did not mention the title of the piece in the accompanying letter to Madame Brillon, but since she alluded to good and bad legs in her answer, it can only have been *The Handsome and Deformed Leg*. Written more in the homespun, moralistic style of *Poor Richard* than in the urbane vein of the *Dialogue*, the new *Bagatelle* exhorted the reader to concentrate on the successful side of life, on the handsome rather than the deformed leg.

Perhaps because, for once, it had not been written with her in mind, the message left Madame Brillon unmoved. She commented ironically, "between the two of us, we would not make two instruments equipped with good and bad legs, for I fear that our four legs are not worth a single mediocre one."[39] In this, Franklin had to concur. In the last weeks of 1780, he had found out what was really wrong with his legs. They would not carry him to her. "This is Wednesday evening, one of the two little portions of the week that will always be dear to my heart. I have a great wish to visit you; but as I am not yet strong enough to climb up your stairs, and you are too weak to come down, we must give up that pleasure for the moment and try to be patient."[40] In the meantime, he received visits from her family and friends: "M. Pagin did me the honor of coming to see me yesterday. He must certainly be one of the best people in the world, for he was patient enough to listen to me play a tune on the armonica, and to hear me through to the end."[41] Since Pagin was one of the best violinists of his day, he must, indeed, have been patient. Monsieur Brillon also came and told stories, much to

Franklin's delight. His wife was not fully pleased. "My plump husband often goes to visit you and tell you jokes; I am worried to death that he has stolen some I have been keeping for the day of our reunion." [42] But Franklin quickly reassured her: "if he stole some of your tales, you can repeat them, for coming from your lips, they will always please me." [43]

And yet, she was right. During the long separation, Madame Brillon had become *la famille Brillon* in Franklin's mind. "Mon Dieu," he once exclaimed, "how much I love them all, from the grandmother and the father to the smallest girl!" [44] As Franklin's emotional life centered more and more on Madame Helvétius and her circle in Auteuil, the long, overdrawn tête-à-tête with Madame Brillon was giving way to a multiple relationship. The young generation began to count. "If you want to come for lunch next Monday or Tuesday," she wrote on December 7, "you will do a good deed, with the wholehearted support of our children. I answer for my daughters, and beg you to ask the opinion of your son." [45] Finally, on Sunday, December 10, Franklin was able to announce triumphantly:

I shall come to see you, my dear daughter, tomorrow morning, with great pleasure. And if it is too much trouble for you to come down, I shall be strong enough, perhaps, to climb your steps. The wish I have to see you will give me some extra strength. My son will gladly help me, for he never objects to my proposals to accompany me to Madame Brillon's. [46]

And thus the friends met again. This must have been one of the few happy moments in what was, perhaps, the most somber period of Franklin's life in France. He was, as he wrote in his diary, "much fatigued ... from tenderness of feet and weakness of knees"; he "suffered by the cold";[47] his efforts to get clothing and weapons for the American troops across the Atlantic were bogged down; his enemies endeavored to blacken his reputation at home; and Congress bombarded him with bills for which he had no funds. No wonder he took refuge in the haven of a friendly family. He had breakfast with the Brillons on December 30, received their wishes on New Year's Day, 1781, and was invited for tea and Christmas carols as often as his friend, who still suffered from fever, insomnia, and lack of appetite, felt a little better.

During a good spell, she composed in his honor a bucolic *Conte*, entitled *The Four Seasons*.[48] This time Franklin was compared to a devastating, unfaithful shepherd who changed mistress every season. Written in a precious, artificial style, à la Marie-Antoinette, à la Boucher, this poem, unlike *Le Sage et la Goutte*, elicited no Franklinian counterpart. The Doctor did rise to the bait, though, and defended his character with sly logic:

I shall bring along your pretty Conte. . . . *It has only one fault, in my opinion, and that is to take away from Mr. F. practically the only virtue left to him as a lover: his constancy. Now that is very unfair, for it is as clear as the clearest Euclidian proposition that he who is constant to many shows more constancy than he who is constant to only one.*[49]

Throughout the spring of her convalescence, he humored her, even in her possessiveness. When she wondered why he had not come on a certain evening and cried out: "The days you do not come seem to be crossed out of my life," [50] he sent, in apology, one of his tenderest messages:

I did not have the pleasure of seeing you Wednesday evening, my dear friend, because my horses were in Paris with the young man [Temple], and at the moment I have neither feet nor wings. Had I wings, I would have come to you; and I fancy that I would sometimes scratch on your bedroom window. It is a very mean trick of Nature to refuse us what she has granted so lavishly to so many little good-for-nothings, birds and flies. . . . I shall come this evening, or tomorrow evening, or maybe both evenings, for I am always happy in your sweet society. [51]

"Always happy in your sweet society." Those were not idle words. Franklin, now seventy-five, was trying to map the evening of his life. In a rare mood of depression and self-

Franklin's sketch of a garden in Passy

doubt, during that spring of 1781, he sent his resignation to the President of Congress:

I find that the long and severe fit of the gout which I had the last winter has shaken me exceedingly, and I am yet far from having recovered the bodily strength I before enjoyed. I do not know that my mental faculties are impaired; perhaps I shall be the last to discover that; but I am sensible of great diminution in my activity. . . . I purpose to remain here at least till the peace; perhaps maybe for the remainder of my life.[52]

To step out of public life, take a long trip with Temple, come back to Paris, give the balance of his days to philosophic leisure, and close his eyes in France – not alone, but surrounded by his intimates – such was now his dream.

I shall forever repeat that I spent eight years with
Dr. Franklin ❦ MADAME BRILLON

Of all the counsels of wisdom Franklin dispensed, through the *Bagatelles*, to his French admirers and friends, none seems to have struck closer to their hearts than his plea for religious toleration. The most promptly acclaimed, reprinted, and adapted of his *Bagatelles* was the short piece entitled simply *Conte*. By 1798, it had been republished by others no less than five times, with or without modifications, not to mention the original printing in French by Franklin himself. Though no more than a debonair anecdote, the *Conte* may still elicit a smile from the modern reader:

There was once an officer, a good man, called Montrésor, who was very ill; his priest, believing that he was going to die, advised him to make his peace with God, in order to be received in Paradise. "I don't have much uneasiness on that score," said Montrésor, "for last night I had a vision which entirely reassured me." "What vision did you have?" asked the good priest. "I was at the gates of Paradise," replied Montrésor, "with a crowd of people who wanted to get in. And St. Peter asked each one what was his religion. One replied: 'I am a Roman Catholic.' 'Well,' said St. Peter, 'come in and take your place there, among the Catholics.' Another said that he was of the Anglican Church. 'Well,' said St. Peter, 'come in and take your place there, among the Anglicans.' Another said that he was a Quaker. 'Come in,' said St. Peter, 'and take your place among the Quakers.' Finally, when my turn arrived, he asked me of what religion I was. 'Alas!' I replied, 'unfortunately, poor

William Temple Franklin

*Jacques Montrésor has none at all.' 'Too bad,' said the saint.
'I don't know where to place you;* but come in, anyway, you
will take a place wherever you can.'" [1]

"Wherever you can" appears in the printed version; a
manuscript version, however, states still more generously,
"wherever you wish."

Like the *Dialogue Between the Gout and Mr. Franklin*, the
Conte has a counterpart written by Madame Brillon, but in
this case we cannot tell whether she was the inspiration or the
echo, for the *Conte* is undated. Madame Brillon's letter bears
no more precise indication than "ce jeudi matin," but we may
guess at its date because in a further paragraph she alludes to
the letter of the unnamed lady who burst into tears at the
sight of Benjamin Franklin and shared her emotions with the
readers of the *Journal de Paris* on December 8, 1778. Here
is what Madame Brillon had to say about St. Peter:

*When I go to paradise, if St. Peter asks me of what religion I am,
I shall answer him: "Of the religion whereby people believe that
the Eternal Being is perfectly good and indulgent; of the religion
whereby people love all those who resemble Him. I have loved and
idolized Doctor Franklin." I am sure that St. Peter will say:
"Come in and go promptly to take place next to Mr. Franklin.
You shall find him seated next to the Eternal Being." I will go
there and enjoy everlasting happiness.* [2]

Paradise with Franklin, paradise with Madame Brillon: is
this not a perennial theme of the semiserious correspondence
between the old sage and his foster daughter? And could
Madame Brillon spell more clearly than in this letter, in the
last days of 1778, that her paradise was open to all men of good

will, whatever their religious affiliation? Franklin may have remembered it when, on April 20, 1781, he disclosed his plan for a nondenominational paradise on earth, where the kinship of spirit would be strengthened by an alliance of blood. Without any trace of playful gallantry, he penned a straightforward plea, all the more moving for its awkward French, obviously not revised by anybody but laboriously put together by his own endeavors. Franklin proposed a marriage between Madame Brillon's elder daughter Cunégonde (seventeen) and his own grandson Temple (twenty-one).

In 1777, when the friendship with the Brillons started, Cunégonde was a mere child, and Temple barely more than an adolescent. Now, four years later, he occupied a warmer place than ever in his grandfather's affection. Franklin had nevertheless consented, in 1779, to the young man's wish to serve as aide-de-camp to Lafayette in a proposed expedition against England, with John Paul Jones in joint command. The expedition, however, had not materialized, and this frustration, combined with a life of ease and pampering, had somewhat turned Temple's head. Those who wanted to approach Franklin courted "Franklinet," and Franklinet never really grew up.

To this, Franklin was blind. He never gave up trying to secure a diplomatic career for Temple. "In certain matters," observed Silas Deane, a former colleague of Franklin's in the American Commission, "the Doctor is no more of a Philosopher than the rest of the world. He has a grandson on whom he dotes, and whom he wishes to fix as Secretary in France." [3] Apart from these ambitious dreams, the aging man leaned on his grandson because he had a very real fear of dying alone and far from home. In a letter to his son-in-law, Richard

Bache, he once complained bitterly of the "malignant natures" of his enemies who would have him lose the assistance of Temple: "I am continued here in a foreign country, where, if I am sick, his filial attention comforts me, and, if I die, I have a child to close my eyes and take care of my remains."[4]

This anxiety of his was the first argument he mentioned to Madame Brillon in 1781, after having failed, during a previous conversation, to convince her husband that Temple should marry Cunégonde:

Having almost lost my own daughter because of the wide distance between us, I hoped to find another one in you, and still another in your daughter, to take care of my old age if I am to stay in France, and to close my eyes after I die.

Then, realizing that so far he had talked only about himself, he turned his attention to the young pair:

I have a very good opinion of that amiable young Lady; I have been observing her for the 4 years of our acquaintance, and I believe she will make a good wife. I also believe that my [grand] son, who has no vices, will make a good husband; otherwise I would not have wished to give him to your daughter.

About the feelings of the interested parties, he had already made such perfunctory inquiries as the custom of the time warranted:

I have noticed that they feel friendly toward one another. I have talked to him about my plans for getting him married here; he told me that he had only this objection, that his marriage in France may occasion a separation for us, should I go back to America. But when I told him that if he married Mademoiselle Brillon I would remain in France till the end of my days, he was

very pleased, saying that if I can negotiate this affair for him,
he would be most happy. – He is still young, and perhaps
paternal bias led me to form too flattering an opinion of him, but
it seems to me that he has what it takes to become, in time, a
distinguished man.

What a poor prophecy! Temple's only claim to distinction
was that he became the first editor of his grandfather's papers
– a slow and negligent editor, at that. In 1781, at the time of
the proposal, he was just another dandy, caring more for his
looks than his achievements, and Monsieur Brillon must have
sensed it, although he did not disclose any misgivings of a
personal character to Franklin. His grounds for refusing were
twofold: Temple was not a Catholic; he might take their
daughter with him to America.

To meet these objections, Franklin groped his way toward
warmth, clarity, and understanding, through a maze of corrections and deletions. In order to get Temple firmly established in France, he wrote Madame Brillon, he would remain
in the country himself and hold on to his official position until
the young man would be acceptable as his successor by the
American Government. As for the problem of different
religions, it could and should be solved by searching for the
common ground of all faiths. In pleading this cause, the
doting grandfather yields to the philosopher:

In every religion, beside the essential things, there are others,
which are only forms and fashions, as a loaf of sugar may be
wrapped in brown or white or blue paper, and tied with a string
of flax or wool, red or yellow; but the sugar is always the
essential thing. Now the essential principles of a good religion
consist, it seems to me, of the following 5 articles, viz.:

*1°   That there is one God who created the Universe, and who
     governs it by His providence.*
2°   That He ought to be worshipped and served.
3°   That the best service to God is doing good to men.
4°   That the soul of man is immortal, and
*5°   That in a future life, if not in the present one, vice will be
     punished and virtue rewarded.*
*These essential principles appear both in your religion and in
ours, the divergencies are only the paper and the string . . . .*[5]

These were perhaps the most earnest lines Franklin ever
sent to Madame Brillon, a quintessence of his innermost
belief. Shortly before his death, he was to repeat this credo,
almost word for word, in a letter to Ezra Stiles, President of
Yale College.

It was a lost cause with Madame Brillon. When her lofty
theories were put to the test, she forgot her spirit of religious
universalism, forgot her stand in favor of romantic love, and
spoke with the voice of the traditional bourgeoise she was at
heart. For once, she found herself in perfect agreement with
her husband. Conformity came first:

*Monsieur Brillon and I think precisely as you do, that there is
only one religion and one morality, common to all sages. Nevertheless, we are obliged to submit to the customs of our country.
An isolated individual may do whatever he wishes, by remaining
silent and leaving others to their prejudices. Married people,
attached to a numerous family, owe it an account of their
behavior.*

As for Temple's future, remaining in France was not
enough. The Brillons wanted a son-in-law qualified to succeed
Monsieur Brillon in his high administrative post:

We love your [grand]son and believe he has all it takes to become a distinguished person and make a woman happy; but he cannot reasonably undertake to live in this country; his property, his status, his duties bind him to his fatherland. Your very name, which he ought to uphold, creates an additional obligation for him always to do such things and reside in such places as will be useful to his fellow citizens. We, on our own side, need a son-in-law able to take over the position of my husband, who is beginning to feel the need of a rest. This position is the most important of our assets; it calls for a man who knows the laws and customs of our country, a man of our religion.

The most important of our assets! If Franklin remembered the day when Madame Brillon had complained to him that in France "marriages are made by weight of gold," he must have smiled wryly. It is true that the rebuff was coated with many flattering expressions and tempered by a promise to allay his most immediate anxiety:

Do not worry, my good papa, so long as we live you shall not be abandoned. Without being your children, we shall be your friends, and we shall give you at all times, under any circumstances, all the care that will be in our power ....[6]

What could Franklin reply? He already had been realistic enough to prepare the ground for a retreat that would save face for everybody:

I am perfectly at ease concerning this subject [of the different religions]. But since the same arguments are not equally good for all people, I do not expect that mine will be good for you, and for M. Brillon. Hence, the affair is finished, since there may be other objections he has not communicated to me, and I ought not to give him trouble. We shall nevertheless love one another, all of us. Good-bye, my dearest friend. Love me as much as you can. It will not be too much.[7]

True to his word, Franklin never brought up the matter again. Eighteen months later, Cunégonde married a Catholic Frenchman, Colonel Marie-Antoine Pâris d'Illins, who eventually became General of Brigade and was killed in action in 1809. The printed announcement of the wedding surprises the modern reader by its brevity: "MONSIEUR ET MADAME BRILLON DE JOUY ONT L'HONNEUR DE VOUS FAIRE PART DU MARIAGE DE MADEMOISELLE BRILLON, LEUR FILLE, AVEC MONSIEUR PARIS."[8]

To the copy he received, Franklin added in his own hand: "They were married Monday Oct. 20, 1783." Eleven months later, he received another announcement – one which today would seem still more peculiar since it was made by the father alone, and the name of the baby (to say nothing of weight) was not even mentioned: "MONSIEUR PARIS A L'HONNEUR DE VOUS FAIRE PART QUE MADAME SON ÉPOUSE EST ACCOUCHÉE HEUREUSEMENT D'UNE FILLE LE 26 NOVEMBRE 1784."

Without a trace of rancor, Franklin wrote Madame Brillon:

May the little girl be as good and lovable as her mother, her grandmother, her great-grandmother, etc. I remember meeting at your home, one day when your children were very young, four generations of yours, and saying, then, that I hoped to live long enough to see the fifth generation. My prophetic wish is hereby fulfilled.[9]

Three days later, he received from the raving grandmother a rapturous reply:

Your letter, my sweet papa, gave me real pleasure, but if you want to make me still happier, stay in France until you can see my sixth generation. I am only asking you for 15 or 16 years; my granddaughter will be ready for marriage early, she is beautiful, she is strong! I am now savoring a new feeling, my good papa.

Here, with her usual self-centeredness, not thinking that she might be reopening a wound, she went on to describe the wonders of her new status, going into some intimate details that previous editors felt were better omitted:

My little nursing mother is charming and fresh as the morning rose. The baby, the first few days, had some hard work getting accustomed to so firm a breast, with such a dainty, short nipple, but the patience and courage of the mother won the day. Everything is going well, and nothing is more fascinating than this sight: a pretty young woman feeding a beautiful child, a father who cannot take his eyes off them and joins his wife in taking care of the child. Often, my eyes fill with tears.[10]

In contrast to this picture of domestic happiness, Temple is usually portrayed as having found in riotous living and multiple love affairs prompt solace from whatever disappointment he may have felt at being turned down as Cunégonde's suitor. The love affairs were indeed multiple and undeniable, but historians and biographers have failed to note that, in the midst of dissipation, Franklinet cultivated a brief but sincere attachment for Cunégonde's younger sister, Aldegonde. The girl reciprocated.

The story can be reconstructed, if incompletely, from letters sent to Temple by his boon companion, Louis Le Veillard "le jeune," the son of le grand voisin, Le Veillard, Madame Brillon's neighbor and friend. Ignored by historians who have concentrated on the important figures, these letters give us a glimpse into what was going on in the hearts and minds of the younger set, a counterpoint to the more sedate themes of the older generation. Most of them were written, so to say, from exile, in 1782 and later. At the very time Temple was failing to become Cunégonde's husband, Le Veillard junior had failed to transplant himself to America as a member of the French diplomatic corps: the English had captured the ship on which he had embarked, and when they let him go home, his father sent him to Bordeaux to earn his living in trade.

Le Veillard junior never stopped pining for Paris and his former way of life. His letters to Franklinet (we do not have Temple's answers) are an amusing mixture of youthful bragging – he had hardly time enough to satisfy the Irish and local beauties craving for his love – and youthful despondency – he was too short, he was too shy, he hated his job. Whenever he was apprised of his friend's various liaisons, he heartily applauded, though he found it ridiculous that Temple should keep going with a Countess "without backbone, who can't say no," and get no other relief from that chore than "spicing the affair with some little adventures right and left." When his friend boasted of an Italian mistress, young Le Veillard congratulated him, while pointing out the dangers of associating with "women bred amidst daggers and poisons." [11] But when news came, in June 1783, that Franklinet was in love, really in love with a "demoiselle" of fifteen, and that furthermore she was Madame Brillon's second daughter, Le Veillard gave full vent to his disapproval:

A clever boy like you, who but one year ago presumed to lecture me against love, has fallen into the trap; in spite of his handsome maxims, he is sighing for a demoiselle. . . . He will waste his breath, and trouble her peace for nothing, since her father cares not a straw about the young man's sighs, and the young man is not enough of a rascal to take advantage of the said demoiselle's weakness. . . . Moreover, carried away by the said passion, you have neglected two most interesting liaisons . . . whereas it would be very easy for a skilful young man to hide a long-standing intrigue from an inexperienced fifteen-year-old demoiselle.[12]

In spite of all sarcasm, Temple remained so obdurate that the infatuation had to be taken seriously. Young Le Veillard, on August 9, tried to talk him out of it, calling on – surprisingly enough – the same arguments that the Brillon parents had used to dissuade his grandfather:

You love and you know that you are loved. . . . I see no hope of success; you cannot, you must not establish yourself in France; if you did it, you would throw away your chances. I can well understand that at the present moment you are blinded by your infatuation . . . but it is not humanly possible to remain for long in this disposition. . . . I shall add a consideration which may seem childish to you as it does to me and to three fourths of the Europeans . . . yet the difference of religion . . . has prevented countless marriages. . . . I certainly know how highly her family thinks of you . . . Nevertheless I fear they will refuse to give their daughter to you, especially as the father . . . who owes his position to his own work may be much more concerned about your getting established in France than I am.[13]

No matter how fond French society may have been of Franklin and his grandson, taking them into the family was another matter.

Ten weeks after this stern reminder of traditional ethics, Cunégonde, the older Brillon girl, married Colonel Pâris d'Illins, but "the father," if we may believe young Le Veillard, soon found out that it was not enough to be French and Catholic to make an ideal son-in-law:

I bet Monsieur B. is not at all happy with his son-in-law, who is a fool. And there is no worse fool than the nouveau riche, their pride and impertinence causing them to lose what little common-sense they had . . . they are four times more uppish, haughty, and intolerable than true noblemen.

Such lines must have been intended to salve Temple's wounded pride, but a rash of unpleasant references to Pâris – from various sources, all pointing to his arrogance – implies that he had few partisans in Passy, with the exception of Madame Brillon, who always defended him.

Less than a year after Cunégonde's wedding, a radical change in Monsieur Brillon's attitude toward Temple is revealed, once more in a letter from Le Veillard junior (September 7, 1784):

I am not surprised by what you tell me about Monsieur B., since inconsistency is typical of a great many people. . . . I have no say as to what you ought to do. . . . I agree that the new employment offered to you bears no relation to what you have been doing so far. Your present position may perhaps lead you much further up . . . but the new charge you would be given seems worth a fat dowry. It is very lucrative and, I believe, entails very little and easy work.[14]

A likely guess is that the Brillons had finally made up their mind to give Temple their second daughter and that the new employment under discussion was Monsieur Brillon's own post. But the offer came too late. Temple had become involved with Blanchette Caillot, a married woman, who bore him a child while he was still in France and sent him reams of burning letters after his return to America. In the first of these, written while her "little Excellency," as she liked to call him, was still at sea (August 1785), she related with some relief:

I saw father Br. . . . . He told me of the forthcoming wedding of his lovely daughter. I believe it may take place next October; the person in question [M. de Malachelle] is an only son, rich, only twenty-seven, and, from what I hear, very pleasant. . . . To tell you the truth, I am delighted that my charming friend will get married while you are away; I love her with all my soul, but not enough to yield her my *little Excellency.*[15]

The story of Temple and the two Brillon daughters has taken us far ahead of the spring of 1781 when Franklin, in a wave of discouragement, toyed with the idea of establishing himself in France permanently. That mood, however, did not last very long. Even before he learned (during the summer) that Congress had refused his resignation, Franklin's buoyancy was restored. Not so Madame Brillon's, whose nerves were still shaky from her protracted illness and the tension engendered by Franklin's proposal. From her mother's country house, where she had gone earlier than usual for her annual visit, she wrote:

What? not even a word . . . in twelve days since your daughter left you? This is not a reproach, but, as you know, a path leading away from reproach easily slips into indifference. I neither can nor wish to evince even the semblance of coldness toward you, hence I must complain a bit, very tenderly and gently, of your neglect.

She had heard that Franklin had been at the Opera on the night of the great fire (June 8, 1781), and, still upset by the danger, she mused:

Life hinges on very little ... life itself is very little ... only friendship, sweet friendship endears my life to me, without it I might sometimes deem it better to end it all. There are so many sorrows and so few pleasures for a sensitive being, so many fetters and privations for our sex, that without friendship — but friendship comforts me, takes the place of what may have been missing elsewhere. Do write me, then.[16]

Franklin brushed aside these somber thoughts with a brisk, impish answer:

Like you, I feel that there are many sorrows in this Life. But it also seems to me that there are many more pleasures. This is why I love life. We must not blame providence inconsiderately. Reflect how many of our duties it has ordained to be naturally pleasures; and that it has had the goodness besides, to give the name of sins to several of them, so that we might enjoy them more![17]

A longer separation was in store. By the end of September, Madame Brillon heeded the advice of her doctor, Anne-Charles Lorry, a warm-hearted, fashionable physician who had attended the late King Louis XV and believed in such simple remedies as a bland diet and a change of scenery. She undertook what was then a considerable journey to Nice, taking along her entire ménage: her husband, her daughters, and even Pagin, the violinist. Franklin, of course, remained at Passy, but she left him, as a claim, "a piece of my soul, that will flit around you." Her farewell was somber: "nothing will ever equal my pain in leaving you, except my joy in seeing you again."[18] Hardly had she left the surroundings of Paris when she wrote, from her first stop, a letter drenched in misery: "I am so tired, it looks as if my strength and I had divorced one another, I would like to be in Nice already, but my heart does not want to go any further."[19]

Then, as she proceeded south, her spirits revived almost miraculously, and the sun came back into her soul. From Lyons, she reported that she had seen great and wondrous things and eaten strawberries out of season.[20] Much as she bemoaned the lack of letters from either Franklin or Le Veillard and her depressing, Franklin-less Wednesdays and Saturdays, one can sense her excitement at the prospect of sailing down the Rhone to Avignon.[21] From Marseilles, she admitted that her nerves were better and her appetite had been increasing so much that, by the time of her return, she might conceivably work herself up to one of Franklin's favorite foods, smoked beef. Moreover, she reverted to the playful tone of their early correspondence, noting that the many pretty women she had seen in Avignon brought to her mind the Doctor, who would have been ever so pleased to kiss them.

Franklin, in turn, dotted her itinerary with some of the fondest, most gentle letters he ever wrote:

I keep thinking of the fatigues you must be enduring on such a long trip; of the poor inns, the poor beds, the poor cooking, etc.; and I fear for the delicate stuff you are made of. Such thoughts sadden me. I am cross not to be Angel Gabriel with his big wings.

For if I were, I could spare you all the trouble by carrying you in my arms, like my Chapeau-bras,* *and depositing you gently, within half an hour, in your apartment in Nice.*[22]

This image pleased her so much that her answer, for once, was a little roguish:

I could not possibly accept your proposal of carrying me in your arms, even though I am no longer very young or a virgin. That angel was a clever fellow, and your nature united to his, would become too dangerous; I would fear some miracle, and miracles between women and angels might not always bring a redeemer.[23]

He told her repeatedly how much he missed her: Passy was a desert, no Brillon hospitality, no music, no lovely girls running out to kiss him, she and the sun had left together for the duration of the winter, just when both were most needed.

I often pass in front of your house. It seems desolate. In olden days, I broke a commandment, by coveting it, together with my neighbor's wife. Today, I don't covet it anymore, so that I am less of a sinner. But as far as the wife is concerned, I still think those commandments very bothersome and I am sorry that they ever were devised. If, in your travels, you ever come across the Holy Father, ask him to rescind them, as given only to the Jews and too much trouble for good Christians.[24]

If this fond evocation of their early days was not enough to build up her strength and self-confidence, he added that merely to state that he loved her was an inadequate way of

---

* The three-cornered hat, meant to be folded and carried under the arm, which Franklin regarded as a harmless frivolity of the French.

expressing his feelings. But then, as one who was never apt to stay long on a sentimental plane, he quipped:

Long ago, when I was young, I sometimes loved powerfully at a distance of a thousand leagues. But a few years ago . . . I did not deem myself capable of loving further than a league away. Now, I discover that I was wrong, for you go every day further and further away from me, and I don't see that my feeling diminishes. That is because you are always present in my mind.[25]

He even tried his hand at a little pun in French, referring to Temple, who had been laid down with jaundice, as "le jeune et jaune homme." He said he had heard that in the provinces she was journeying through, ladies were somewhat more "libertine" than in Paris; he sincerely hoped that some of their attitude would rub off on her, that she would come back from her voyage "with more vigor and less rigor." In conclusion, "you would be perhaps less *estimable*, but much more *aimable*. The choice is up to you."[26]

She answered, of course, that upon her return she would prove, if anything, still more *estimable* than before. A lonely old age was in store for women too liberal with "their roses and their charms"; she would rather "keep her opinions, her virtue, and her friends."[27] To Franklin, however, she had already offered an indemnification for the missed carols and chess games: she commissioned him to kiss, on her behalf, all the pretty women they knew in Passy.[28] Such "bills of exchange" the Doctor readily pledged to cash, promising moreover to give back to Madame Brillon the same amount, with accrued interest, on sight after her return. To be sure, Temple was already claiming that his youth made him a more fitting collector, but "love of cash," argued the grandfather, "does not diminish with age."[29]

Away from Passy, Madame Brillon gained new perspective on the aged man who meant so much to her, and singled out the components of his charm:

I found in your letter, besides tokens of your friendship, a tinge of that gaiety and that gallantry that cause all women to love you, because you love them all.[30]

You combine with the kindest heart the soundest moral teaching, a lively imagination, and that droll roguishness which shows that the wisest of men allows his wisdom to be perpetually broken against the rocks of femininity.[31]

Nice worked out as predicted: "my health is getting stronger . . . my physician and friend was right . . . there are hardly any instances of Frenchmen who have not been markedly relieved in their nervous disturbances in the small village where I live."[32] A little town still almost unknown, Nice represented for a visitor from the northern countries the first corner of Italy, easily reached by crossing the French border into the states of the King of Sardinia. (Yet not too easily in the mind of Madame Brillon, who marveled at her own boldness in having "passed mountains, crossed rivers, skirted precipices . . . to see pounding waves."[33]) A Turkish prince, in the fifteenth century, had composed a poem in praise of Nice; an English writer, Tobias Smollett, had spent almost two years in the town (1763–65), trying to cure his lungs and keeping a most detailed record of the weather. During his second winter, there had been fifty-six days of rain in four months; in summer, he complained of flies, gnats, and other vermin. Nevertheless, he had a good deal to say in favor of Nice's balmy breezes.[34]

Madame Brillon was simply delighted at the "mild and healthy climate . . . a natural hothouse . . . protected from the northern winds by a double, and often a treble chain of mountains."[35] Her crises, her "convulsions," became less frequent. At the same time, "good Brillon's cares and attentions" made her forget the bitterness of the Mademoiselle Jupin episode and her other complaints of two years before: "my husband, it is quite clear, is my friend; when he oppressed me with coldness, it was the doing of a third party of whom we are now rid, forever."[36] In this atmosphere of détente, she opened her eyes to the world around her. She described gaily her first sea venture in the Bay of Villefranche: four miles, and a tempest in a teapot, just enough to make her and Aldegonde seasick.[37] Franklin replied that if she would only take longer and longer boat trips, she might conquer her terrors, allow him to steal her from Monsieur Brillon, and sail off to America.[38]

Brillon himself read and chuckled, happy as he was at his wife's restored health and good humor. Most of her letters to Franklin contain postscripts by the husband – he never forgot to single out Temple for special affectionate greetings, calling him "caro picolino figliolo,"[39] and Franklin began one of his own letters with a few sentences addressed to Brillon. Then he issued a playful admonition: "The rest of this letter is for Madame your good wife, and since I plan to place some gallantry in it, I am forewarning you, so that you may seize the opportunity to display your politeness and read no further."[40]

Every week, Madame Brillon wrote alternatively to

Franklin and to Le Veillard, who were to share her letters. Now and then, Madame Le Veillard sent Franklin a graceful note threatening not to show him the week's letter unless he came for dinner. As a matter of fact, before leaving for Nice, Madame Brillon had "settled" for Franklin to transfer her Wednesdays and Saturdays to Le Veillard and his wife – a safe arrangement, since Madame Le Veillard's exclusive attachment to her church and her Curé was a standing joke with her entourage. For a while, the Doctor complied with this plan; even though the good neighbors could not possibly fill the void, he said, they did their best to keep him entertained. Then he announced that his Saturdays, henceforth, would be claimed by Madame Helvétius, under the promise that she would yield the date back to Madame Brillon upon her return. The enticements of Madame Helvétius and her Auteuil group were many, and Franklin was being progressively drawn into its orbit. At this point he mentioned only one of its attractions, music, and hastened to add that, pleasant as they were, Abbé Morellet's songs were not to be compared to Pagin's violin. But to Auteuil he went.

If his chief joy there was discussing politics with competent and enlightened minds, toward Madame Brillon he kept the warm, lighthearted tone one tends to assume with convalescents. He spoke about pleasant topics, such as the birth of the Dauphin, to whom he went to offer his fond wishes before the baby was one day old, "not as a Sage from the East but as a nonsage from the West."[41] He talked about the extraordinary weather Paris was enjoying, with doors and windows open until Christmas. Most of all, he kept assuring her that she was missed, that their mutual friends comforted one another with the thought that she would come back strong and healthy, that "they all talk about you with respect, several with affection and even with admiration. It is all music to my ears."[42]

On December 12, 1781, in the midst of such homage, he casually mentioned an unspecified American victory:

As for me ... I still enjoy my good appetite, sleep well, do not suffer from the gout, in short I feel fine, our affairs are going well, and we have won a great victory. Yet I am not happy, because Madame B. is no longer in Passy. Tonight I shall go to Madame Le Veillard's and find there some other friends of yours who suffer from the same disease. . . . Only your return can cure us.[43]

But Madame Brillon had already heard about Yorktown, had understood its implications, and, one day before Franklin's letter, had burst out in happy grumbling:

Do you know, my dear papa, why I am sending you just a tiny, very tiny word? It is because I am sulking . . . yes, mister papa, sulking. What! You capture entire armies in America, you burgoinize Cornwallis, you capture guns, ships, ammunition, men, horses, etc. . . . and your friends have to learn it from the gazette. They get drunk on toasts to you, to Wasington [sic], to independence, to the King of France, to Marquis de Lafayette, Rochambault, Chatelux, [sic] etc., etc., but from you, not a peep. . . . Surely you must feel twenty years younger after this good piece of news, which ought to give us a durable peace after a glorious war. . . . As I don't wish for the sinner's death, I shall compose a triumphal march, will send it to you, will write, and will even keep on loving you with all my heart.[44]

The good-natured rebuke provoked Franklin's famous self-assessment, written on Christmas Day, 1781 (though, absent-mindedly, he dated it 1782):

You are sulking, my dear friend, because I did not send you at once the story of our great victory. I am well aware of the magnitude of our advantage and of its possible good consequences, but I do not exult over it. Knowing that war is full of changes and uncertainty, in bad fortune I hope for good, and in good I fear bad. I play this game with almost the same equanimity as when you see me playing chess. You know that I never give up a game before it is finished, always hoping to win, or at least to get a move, and when I have a good game, I guard against presumption.[45]

The contrast between French exuberance and Anglo-Saxon understatement, feminine emotion and masculine sportsmanship, could hardly be better illustrated than here. But now, the whole Brillon family was joining in humorous complaint. On Christmas Eve, they dispatched, on impressive stationery and in a perfect imitation of the handwriting and style of such documents, a *placet*, or supplication, to His Excellency – the kind of letter that had been plaguing Franklin ever since his arrival in Paris. And at first, he said, he fell into the trap. After reading the first two or three lines, "begging the Kindness of his Highness," [46] he had thrown it impatiently on his table, sighing:

Always placets! always demands of money! It is bad to have the reputation of being charitable. We expose ourselves to a thousand importunities and a good deal of expense as a punishment for our pride, nay our vanity, which lets our small benefactions be known, whereas Our Lord has given us the good and political *advice to keep our right hand from knowing what our left hand has done.*

Then, however, he had read the whole letter, seen at the

end "the dear names" of the Brillons and of Pagin, and kissed their signatures with sincere affection.* His pleasure, he admitted, had been increased by the realization that the placet begged not for money but merely for friendship; he might just as well be frank about this, without waiting for "his malicious neighbor"[47] to point it out.

Thus the year 1782, unlike 1781, opened in excellent humor. Nice might still be "an almost unknown corner of the earth,"[48] but its carnival already was very gay. Madame Brillon remarked that Temple would certainly have been happy in that corner, since there was dancing three times a week. Somewhat later, she said that her daughters regularly danced four times a week, not counting special occasions.[49] Her own musical talents opened to her the circle of English aristocrats vacationing in Nice. She soon noticed that several of them belonged to Lord Shelburne's party and held pro-American views; only the native Niçois were "English to the core," since they had fought many a war against France and derived most of their income from the British visitors.

She told of a tense moment when music and politics clashed. She had been invited to play in the home of her neighbor, Milady Rivers, the widow of the Earl of Chatham, "who at sixty is still beautiful, and reminds one of you, being both witty and good, with something of your turn of mind." Milady's sympathies were with America, and so were those of one of her guests, Lord Cholmondeley, "a tall and handsome young man, who plays the flute passably." On the other

* In fact, the placet provides us with the only instance, in the whole, voluminous correspondence, where Madame Brillon's daughters appear not simply as "mes filles," but with their first names, a clearly signed "Cunégonde" and a blurred "Aldegonde." As to the father, he italianized his name by signing: "Brillonini."

side were the Duchess of Ancaster, a close friend of the Queen of England, and her daughter, Milady Charlotte. The Governor of Nice, who was a tease, suggested that Madame Brillon play her famous "Marche des Insurgents." What could she do? She played it, hoping that the Duchess would not realize what was being performed. The malicious Governor, however, first got the Duchess to state that it was a lovely piece, then told her its title. The Duchess graciously protested that good music is above politics, but, said Madame Brillon, "she was making such a long face that I did not dare look in her direction any more." This, at any rate, did not prevent the Brillon daughters from going to a ball at the Duchess' two days later.[50]

Such colorful descriptions were interspersed with individual and collective protests about Franklin's slackness in writing. One of them, very cleverly done, took the form of a mock plea to the Goddess of Justice, written up in legalistic mumbo-jumbo and enumerating the crimes of "said Benjamin, born in Boston, formerly academician, physician, logician, presently American ambassador to France" against "said plaintiff Madame Brillon de Jouy, citizen of France, born in Paris."[51] Franklin's main line of defense was that writing in French was increasingly burdensome and frustrating for him: "When I have written a long letter, I don't like it; for upon examining it, I find that instead of uttering jokes I have uttered stupidities, and I do not know how to correct them."[52] As a matter of fact, he did commit some unspeakable crimes against grammar and gender (the lament already quoted on his perennial embarrassment with "French feminines" belongs to this period), but in almost every letter his unedited French had the redeeming flash of one perfect, graceful sentence, be it

"Je prie Dieu de vous garder et les Hirondelles de vous ramener,"[53] or, defining Christmas, "Voici arrivé le Jour de la Naissance du Dauphin du Ciel."[54]

One cannot help feeling that the language problem was a pretext. Had not Madame Brillon assured him, in the days of her deepest emotional distress and his grossest linguistic inability, that "it is always good French to say *je vous aime?*" And she had added: "My heart always goes out to meet this word, when you say it to me."[55] But now, Franklin may have felt, she did not have any longer the urgent, pathetic need of his support, a need that in turn bound him so powerfully to her. Their relationship had not soured; it gradually lost the element of anguish at its very core when her "weak machine" was shaken by her husband's infidelity, or when Franklin's "equanimity" was thrown off balance by his colleagues' unfair criticism. Then, even the shortest separation had seemed unbearable:

Since some day, my dear friend, it will be necessary for me to go away to America, without any hope of seeing you again, I have sometimes come to think that it would be a good idea to wean myself from you by degrees, seeing you only once a week at first, then every second week, once a month, etc. etc., so as to diminish gradually my inordinate desire for your enchanting society and to spare myself the great pain I would otherwise suffer upon our final separation. But trying out this experiment on a small scale, I find that absence, instead of diminishing such desire, increases it. Hence, there is no remedy for the pain I fear, and I shall come to see you tonight.[56]

But Madame Brillon's long stay in Nice made such an experiment inevitable, and Franklin became accustomed to living without her. There may have been some truth to the oft-stated complaint of many of his friends, that he tended to drop from his mind those who were out of his sight. After January 6, 1782, Madame Brillon continued to write, but Franklin spaced his answers.

Curiously, at the very moment she was slipping from her primacy in Franklin's heart, Madame Brillon unwittingly gave her one little push to the wheel of history.

One of her new English acquaintances, Lord Cholmonde-ley, had impressed her favorably, not only because of his good looks and moderate proficiency at the flute, but also because he displayed a particular interest in Franklin. He even owned a Sèvres medallion representing the Doctor. The Lord told her how much he wished Franklin's wisdom had been heeded in England and expressed the desire to meet his idol in Passy. He was accompanied by a kind of tutor, a sixty-year-old Frenchman, Monsieur De Lon, who knew many languages, had traveled all over the world, and once had carried out secret negotiations in Turkey for the King of Prussia. The cloak-and-dagger aspect of the older man, combined with the *bon enfant* appearance of handsome Cholmondeley, both fascinated and frightened Madame Brillon. She gave them letters of introduction to Franklin, but, at the same time (February 1, 1782), she wrote to the Doctor to warn him "in case they were spies." [57]

The sequel of the story is told by Franklin himself, in his journal of the negotiations for peace with Great Britain:

Great Affairs sometimes take their rise from small Circumstances. My good Friend and Neighbour, Madame Brillon, being at Nice all last winter for her Health, with her very amiable Family,

*wrote to me, that she had met with some English Gentry there,
whose acquaintance prov'd agreeable; among them she nam'd
Lord Cholmondely, who she said had promis'd to call in his
Return to England, and drink Tea with us at Passy. He left
Nice sooner than she suppos'd, and came to Paris long before
her. On the 21st of March, I receiv'd the following Note:*

*"Lord Cholmondely's compliments to Dr. Franklin; he sets
out for London to-morrow Evening, and should be glad to see
him for Five Minutes before he went. L^d C will call upon him
at any time in the morning he shall please to appoint. Thursday
ev^{ng}. Hotel de Chartres."*[58]

Franklin "had before no personal Knowledge of this
Nobleman," and previously turned a cold shoulder to English
friends who, after Yorktown, privately sounded him out as to
possible terms of peace. But as the most recent reports from
England disclosed a growing current of opinion against
continuation of the war, he welcomed the opportunity to
meet the visitor:

*We talk'd of our Friends whom he left at Nice, then of Affairs in
England, and the late Resolutions of the Commons on Mr.
Conway's Motion. He told me, that he knew Lord Shelburne had
a great Regard for me, that he was sure his Lordship would be
pleas'd to hear from me, and that if I would write a Line he
should have a Pleasure in carrying it.*[59]

Lord Shelburne, an influential member of the Opposition
soon to be swept into power by the changing tide, was an old
friend of America, of Franklin, and of Franklin's friends in
Auteuil. The letter Franklin sent him through Lord Cholmondeley adroitly mixed some cautious political comments
("I embrace the Opportunity . . . of congratulating you on

the returning good Disposition of your Country in favour of America ... I hope it will tend to produce a *General Peace*.") to some congenial gardening matters ("You have made [Madame Helvétius] very happy by your present of Gooseberry Bushes, which arriv'd in five Days."). Brought to an old friend of Madame Helvétius by a new friend of Madame Brillon, this letter was the first step on the winding path that eventually led to the longed-for peace.

What Madame Brillon was doing while the peace negotiations were getting under way is somewhat hazy. All of a sudden, the extant correspondence between her and the Doctor thins – and it is hard to tell to what extent this depends on the hazards of preservation, and how far it may bespeak a gradual lessening of intimacy, if not a cooling of hearts. We know that she lingered a while longer in Nice, suffering mild relapses whenever the weather worsened but, on the whole, feeling better and better. Then she decided that she had improved as much as she could ever expect, her nervous "frailty" being at bottom "incurable,"[60] and that the joy of seeing her old friends again would offset the inconvenience of the northern climate. So the whole family began the long journey home, by the roundabout way of the Atlantic coast.

Early in May, young Le Veillard wrote from Bordeaux to Temple that he expected to see the Brillons any day; poor Monsieur Brillon had suffered an attack of the gout in the little town of Tonneins on the Garonne, and this had held up the family for a fortnight.[61] Back in Paris, meanwhile, the old friends braced themselves for the return of Madame Brillon, taking for granted that she would immediately press her claims and restore the familiar pattern. A Madame de Baussan, who had been endeavoring for some time to arrange for a dinner party with Franklin, maliciously hinted: "It is already so hard to persuade you to come for dinner a couple of miles away, and now Madame Brillon, who is about to come back, will want you all to herself." [62]

It may have been so for a while. Once more, we watch the traditional picture of happiness in a cheerful note Madame Brillon sent Franklin when he was sick, in the fall of 1782:

I hope that by Monday you shall be strong on your legs, and that the Wednesday and Saturday teas, and the Sunday morning tea, will resume in all their glory. My fat husband will make us laugh, the grand voisin will snicker ... Père Pagin will play " Dieu d'Amour" on the violin, I will play the " Marche" on the piano, you will play " Petits Oiseaux" on the harmonica ... oh my friend, after evil days one enjoys the happy ones all the more! [63]

Yet their ways were beginning to diverge. Franklin, ever since August, was in almost constant pain from stones in his bladder, and most of his waking hours were spent at the peace negotiations. The Brillons went to live in Paris during the winter months, probably in order to introduce their daughters to society. Madame protested at first that it was almost as painful for her "to go to Paris as it had been to go to Nice," [64] but life in the capital must have offered compensations. Some months later, in a single, extraordinary instance, she actually admitted: "I am happy, my friend." [65]

She had every reason to be happy. Her older daughter had married a man who belonged to a somewhat higher social stratum (judging from the acid comments of third parties). She liked her son-in-law; she adored her granddaughter. If, because of the distance between Paris and Passy, she saw less of Franklin than before, she probably saw much more of

Temple, who was then courting her second daughter and acted as a messenger. Indeed, she became so self-sufficient that in a few instances it was she who canceled appointments with the Doctor. She did so with many apologies and regrets, to be sure; yet, such occurrences would have been unthinkable in the early days. They still met frequently: her name often recurs in Temple's appointment book for 1785, which has escaped destruction.

Franklin remained as cordial and courteous as ever. When he was looking for more spacious quarters and she suggested a house which he found "too magnificent for simple Republicans," he quickly added: "I am distressed that it cannot be suitable, since it would have brought me closer to you, my excellent Lady, whom I love, esteem, and respect from the bottom of my heart." [66] But a faint note of detachment crept into his style.

The note became more perceptible during Franklin's last winter in France, when his need for warmth and affection was happily fulfilled by the presence, in his household, of his friend from England, early-widowed Polly Hewson, with her three children. Just as Madame Brillon no longer begged and demanded, so Franklin no longer pressed – not even for gallantry's sake. Instead of asking for a kiss as payment for one of his printed "serious jokes" sent to her, on March 31, 1784, he said lightly that he would settle for a carol and an encore of the "Marche des Insurgents." Her kisses "were too precious," and she was "too stingy with them." [67] Eight days later, he sent to his "very dear daughter ... several other little things, of which some samples have been printed here in the house, solely for our friends." Together with a few more printed tracts he had given or sent her previously, they formed "a complete collection of all ... *Bagatelles* which have been printed at Passy."[68]

If, as is probable, the collection contained the same items as the unique volume now owned by Yale and possibly the very set the Doctor put together for Madame Brillon, it was inclusive indeed. Here were, of course, all the tender, witty pieces written for her in the early days of courtship as well as her own *Le Sage et la Goutte*, added to the batch as a tribute to her talent and an acknowledgment of loving bondage. "I beg your pardon," he had written in the accompanying letter of April 8, 1784, "for having put among those of my own, one of your creation, which is certainly too charming to be placed in such company."[69] The portfolio also included a few pieces written for Madame Helvétius, as well as a variety of half-whimsical, half-didactic essays meant for a wider audience, mainly masculine.*

* The Yale volume contains printed copies – in some instances, the only surviving copy – of the following pieces: *Dialogue entre la Goutte et Monsieur Franklin; Le Sage et La Goutte; The Whistle* (in French and English); Lettre à Madame B. [*Les Ephémères*]; M. F.[ranklin] à Madame H[elvétius] [*Les Champs Elysées*, two versions]; *Les Mouches à Madame He*[*lvétius*]; Franklin à Madame la Fr[et]é; *Parabole contre la Persécution, à l'imitation du language de l'Ecriture*; To the Royal Academy of —— [Brussels]; *Information to Those who would Remove to America* (in French and English); and *Remarks Concerning the Savages of North America* (in French and English). On the other hand, it does not contain two works specifically mentioned in Franklin's letter of April 8, 1784, as previously sent ("if by chance you have not lost *The Handsome and the Deformed Leg*, and *The Morals of Chess*," he says); and it is not clear whether it contains the "serious joke" mentioned in the letter of March 31. Nor is it possible to trace its history farther back than 1845, when the hitherto separate pamphlets were bound together in Paris, by the famous bookbinder Niédrée. Madame Brillon may have been the original owner, but others, such as the publisher Pierre F. Didot, a friend of Franklin, have also been mentioned.

Clearly, Franklin had aimed at letting her have the whole of his French production, all his *œuvrets*. As people will do, who know that they are about to part, Franklin and Madame Brillon hoarded mementoes, tangible proof of what had been. He asked her for some pieces of music. She sent them, with a sigh: "I have a heavy heart, the thought that you will leave is like a nightmare." She had his portrait painted, in a light blue coat and waistcoat, his gray locks falling to his shoulders, his hazel eyes sparkling with intelligence under the high, bald forehead, a half-smile on his determined lips. The painting still hangs today in the château of one of her descendants at Villers-sur-Mer, in Normandy.

Gradually Madame Brillon's pathetic need of Franklin the man, the father, had given way to a serene pride in Franklin the statesman, the genius. More than once, over the years, she had exclaimed that, easy as it would be for her to boast of their friendship, vanity counted for nothing in her tempestuous feeling for him. Now, she sensed that Franklin was her claim to fame: "Every day of my life I shall remember that a great man, a sage has wanted to be my friend. . . . I shall forever repeat that I spent eight years with Doctor Franklin!" Their last encounter took place on July 9, 1785. Although Franklin did not leave until the afternoon of July 12, she did not have the heart to see him again:

My heart was so heavy yesterday, when I left you, that I feared, for you and for myself, another such moment which would have only added to my misery without further proving the tender, unchanging love I have devoted to you forever. . . . If it ever pleases you to remember the woman who loved you the most, think of me. Farewell, my heart was not meant to be separated

*from yours, but it shall not be, you shall find it near yours, speak
to it and it shall answer you.*[70]

And Monsieur Brillon, the jolly, coarse, clumsy husband,
wrote a brief postscript: "My very dear Papa, I have nothing
to add, and even if I wanted to, my tears would not let me see."

 *5 Friends and Neighbors in Passy*

A great man's friendship is a gift from the gods ❧ VOLTAIRE

Seen at close range, the pattern of Franklin's early friendships in France was dictated more by topography than by ideological, ethical, or similar abstract considerations. The infirmities of age precluded too much traveling, even though he had a carriage. Political wisdom demanded that, for a while at least, he disappear from the public eye and operate quietly from whatever base he chose. Once it had been decided that he would live in Passy, his home became the hub of daytime activity (Ferdinand Grand, America's banker, who would become a close friend, lived almost next door); the network of his social life spread in overlapping circles, going from landlord, to neighbor, to Madame Brillon, to other congenial people in the community.

The landlord was Jacques-Donatien Leray de Chaumont. In dealing with landlords and landladies, Franklin was at the opposite pole of those standards of cool detachment we praise so highly today. He liked to be involved. His landlady for seventeen years in London, Mrs. Stevenson, remained an intimate, lifelong friend; her daughter Polly was, in a way, Franklin's spiritual child.

The same thing happened in Paris. After a few weeks, Chaumont was no longer just a landlord, but Franklin's impresario, public relations man, collaborator in business, and financial adviser. His wife Thérèse became the Doctor's witty and whimsical confidante; one of their daughters was appointed guardian of his welfare and keeper of his household accounts, earning in the process the affectionate nickname of

Madame Chaumont

"wife"; another daughter he called "my friend," another "my child." With the regrettable tendency of eighteenth-century French women never to sign their given name and parental passion for wrapping their children in anonymity, it is often difficult to tell which daughter is involved in which letter, but each little message that went back and forth is unmistakably full of warmth and good humor. The Chaumonts also had a married daughter, Madame Foucault, and a son, exactly Temple's age, who was some time later to make his mark on the New World.

It was not by chance that Franklin, two months after his arrival in Paris, decided to establish his residence in Chaumont's Hôtel de Valentinois. Passy's very location between Paris and Versailles was symbolic of his position: it was away from the capital, where his presence was provoking such an effervescent welcome that the British Ambassador was deeply disturbed; it was away – but not too far away – from a Court which had to remain officially neutral but desired to keep in touch with the American Commissioners. Passy, a conglomeration of villas and châteaux hidden among woods and vineyards, was delightful, the Hôtel de Valentinois, on a height overlooking the Seine, one of its jewels. With its spacious grounds, linden-lined avenues, multi-leveled terraces and chain of pavilions, it had once belonged to the Grimaldis, the ruling family of Monaco, and had been purchased by Chaumont only a few months before Franklin's arrival. At first, Franklin and Deane occupied one of the pavilions; John Adams, when he arrived in Paris a year later, fretted over "the Magnificence of the Place"[1] and strove in vain to discover the exorbitant rent such lodgings must cost the American public. Actually, at that time, no rent was

Franklin

charged at all; Chaumont wanted to contribute to the American cause by playing host to its representatives. In 1779, when Franklin remained alone, no longer as Commissioner but as Minister Plenipotentiary, he moved to a wing of the main building and paid rent – the figure was eventually set at 20,000 *livres* for the last five years of his residence.

Chaumont himself seemed a judicious choice as a host, a choice probably suggested by the Minister of Foreign Affairs, Comte de Vergennes. Here was a merchant prince with a deep grudge against England, extremely well-connected, but sufficiently disassociated from the government not to implicate it in his dealings. Born simply Jacques-Donatien Leray, from a middle-class family in Nantes, he had managed his East Indian trade with such acumen that by the age of thirty he had been able to acquire the fifteenth-century château of Chaumont: a former royal residence, today a high point in the classic pilgrimage of tourists to the Loire Valley.

The château had not only given him the satisfaction of adding "de Chaumont" to his name, but proved an extra source of wealth. Rather than idle away his time in parties and hunts as an aristocrat, Chaumont exploited the fisheries in the Loire, encouraged intensive cultivation of his estates (thereby gaining, on the part of the peasants, a gratitude which was to save his life during the Revolution), and took advantage of the presence of a special clay to build a ceramics factory. To insure the artistic quality of his ceramics, he had imported the well-known Giovanni-Battista Nini from Italy.

As his wealth grew, various honorary appointments came his way: Superintendent of the Hôtel des Invalides, Overseer of the King's forests, and Commissary of the French Army in charge of supplying uniforms. At this point, the need of a residence closer to Paris was felt and he had bought the Hôtel de Valentinois.

Almost every facet of this dynamic career was to be put to good use when Franklin and Chaumont joined forces. From the factory on the Loire came the series of Nini medallions, probably the most famous of all Franklin images. The artist, who may well have never seen his model, worked from a profile sent from Paris. Hearing that Franklin was accustomed to wearing a fur hat and sensing that the hat was somehow connected in popular imagination with philosophy and liberty, he used Rousseau's fur cap as a model – one more step toward an identification of two men, who were in fact very unlike one another. A vigorous, homely, intensely masculine and patriarchal representation of Franklin, the Nini medallion was soon sold throughout France and did more to popularize his features and broaden his appeal than any other work of art. For his home, Chaumont commissioned from the King's own painter, Joseph-Siffrède Duplessis, the large, majestic oil which was considered by Franklin as his official and definitive portrait and now hangs in the Metropolitan Museum of Art in New York. Dressed in a ruby coat with a fur collar, strong, solemn, purposeful, here is the public Franklin as he must have appeared on state occasions.

From Chaumont's East Indian trade ventures came his offer to procure for the colonies some bags of saltpeter, a raw material of prime importance in the manufacture of gunpowder; from his private fleet there came, for a while, packet boats plying the seas between France and America; from his experience in clothing the French Army came his complex collaboration with Franklin in the shipment of desperately needed uniforms and supplies to the continental troops; from his private wealth came the funds to equip and launch some of the ships that John Paul Jones led to victory. So eager, indeed, was the man that a scandal sheet remarked in 1777: "He would grasp, if he could, the commerce of the thirteen united colonies for himself alone."[2]

A book could (and should) be written on the projects Chaumont undertook on behalf of the insurgents. It is true that he did aim to become "le grand munitionnaire des Américains,"[3] a kind of financial counterpart to Lafayette, but he has been overshadowed in this respect by the more picturesque figure of *Figaro's* creator, Caron de Beaumarchais. Still, Beaumarchais' story and Chaumont's – and that of most French entrepreneurs who helped the young colonies shake off the yoke of England – have one element in common: a sad ending. All these early supporters wound up bankrupt and embittered, while an ungrateful and suspicious Congress turned a deaf ear to their claims.

Not even the most cautious businessman could have remained solvent under such conditions. Chaumont, moreover, was rash, tended to overextend himself, and kept tangled accounts. Finally Franklin, the soul of accuracy, balked. There followed a great deal of haggling, wrapped up in such polite formulas as "Mr. Franklin's Answer to Mr. Chaumont's Reply concerning Mr. Franklin's Memorandum written about Mr. Chaumont's Observation." Yet, even after they had to call in arbitrators to straighten out their affairs, after they challenged the original findings and turned to a new set of arbitrators, after the dossier of memos and countermemos, stretching over three years, had become enormous, Franklin and Chaumont remained the best of personal friends. And for this, much of the credit goes to the women of the family.

As she appears on another of Nini's medallions, Madame Chaumont was no beauty. Samuel Eliot Morison talks of a love affair between her and John Paul Jones, who spent some time at the Hôtel de Valentinois in 1778. Such an assumption seems scarcely warranted on the basis of his evidence.[4] It is true that Chaumont and Jones, who had been good friends, became bitter enemies – with Franklin, between them, trying to keep peace – but there were enough financial reasons (chiefly concerning the prizes taken by the ships) to explain their antagonism without our having to look for sentimental ones.

Beauty or not, Madame Chaumont "was a Wit": we can trust this judgment, since it comes from the person least suspect of being unduly partial to anything French, John Adams. It is true that these words of approval in his *Autobiography* are primarily meant to cast an unfavorable light on the irrepressible youthfulness of his older colleague: "Mr. Franklin who at the age of seventy odd, had neither lost his Love of Beauty nor his Taste for it," he says, called Mademoiselle de Passy, the beautiful young daughter of the noble lord of the village, "his favourite and his flame and his Love and his Mistress, which flattered the Family and did not displease the young Lady." When Mademoiselle, however, married the Marquis de Tonnerre, Madame de Chaumont quipped: "Alas! All the rods of Mr. Franklin could not prevent the Lightning [*Tonnerre*] from falling on Mademoiselle de Passy."[5]

This pun is unfortunately almost our only sample of Madame Chaumont's humor. There are few letters from her –

obviously she did not have to write when they were all living on the same grounds – and they are all dated from the château on the Loire, where she resided more and more because of ill health. Temple often went to visit her there, as he liked hunting and riding with her son. She never failed to tell the grandfather how much she had enjoyed the grandson's stay and how truly maternal she felt about him. She kept hoping that Franklin would come too; when at last he decided to go to Chaumont, and then had to cancel his trip at the last minute, she painted vividly the unexpected consequences of this change of plan:

I am not the only one, Sir, who felt deprived upon not seeing you. The Benedictines who run the boarding school next door spent all the time I was expecting your visit in drilling their pupils and arousing their zeal, so that they could master to perfection the exercises that you would have witnessed. Finally, the ceremonies had to take place without you. They lasted three days, and for those days nothing was applauded or admired without the refrain: what a pity that Mr. Franklin did not come!

I am sure you are not prepared for the outcome of all these celebrations. Well, here it is: I was so touched by their zeal and their veneration for you that I requested to be affiliated to their order. You don't understand this, you misbeliever, you heretic, you would never be accepted by them as an affiliate . . . but how discourteous of me to say such wicked things, for I would wager that they accepted me solely because I bragged of your friendship.[6]

The only way left for Franklin to atone for his absence, she said, was to heed the headmaster's request and help him find a new teacher of English: such was the price he would have to pay for his popularity with the Benedictine Fathers.

She did not always write in this teasing mood, however; more often, she tried to lure him with family tableaux: "The children won't stop repeating how much they would like to see you, run around you, make your tea, serve it to you, and especially kiss you on both cheeks."[7]

Of these "children," the one who played the largest part in Franklin's daily life was the eldest, who signed herself simply "Chaumont fille ainée," was nicknamed by her family "mère Bobie" – the name of one of her father's ships – and referred to by Franklin simply as *ma femme*. Her spelling is purely phonetic, and her writing has a spinsterish tightness to it, but she kept the precise kind of accounts that Franklin had tried in vain to obtain from his own wife. Thanks to her efforts, we have ample details on the way Franklin's family and entourage were fed.

By contemporary American gastronomical standards, the Doctor would have lived very well indeed; by eighteenth-century French ones, his frugality was remarkable. The Duc de Croy, who paid a visit to Franklin on March 1, 1779, in order to secure an American pledge of noninterference with Captain Cook's travels, and stayed on for dinner, marveled at the fact that "there was only one service, and then everything all at once, without soup." Fortunately, the duke was served two kinds of fish, an excellent pudding and pastry; he did not go hungry. Franklin, who was recovering from the gout, only had some thick slices of cold meat and three or four glasses of excellent wine. Such simplicity, plus the fact that the Doctor spoke very little, led de Croy to the conclusion that his American host could not possibly be anything but a Quaker.[8]

At first, Franklin and his grandson had their meals from

Chaumont's table or from Chaumont's kitchen, paying six livres apiece per meal for themselves and for any guests they wanted to bring. When Franklin gave a large dinner in his own quarters, it would be furnished by Mademoiselle Chaumont, with the Doctor paying the entire cost and providing his own wine. Over the years he built up a truly respectable wine cellar: 1,040 bottles in 1779, 1,203 bottles in 1782, with a prevalence of red and white Bordeaux, no less than five varieties of champagne, and a goodly supply of the Spanish wines (Xeres) for which he had a predilection.

After a while, the initial arrangement was modified: Mademoiselle Chaumont still kept the accounts for horses, coach, and stable expenses, but the buying of food and its preparation were entrusted to a maître d'hôtel. Those of us who think nostalgically of the happy days when so much help was available for so little money would do well to glance at the nasty pile of memoirs, bills, and recriminations built up by Jacques Finck, Franklin's majordomo. Yet the original agreement with him seemed clear enough: for 1,300 francs a month, Finck undertook to feed a household of four members (Franklin, Temple, a secretary, and a clerk) and nine servants. Breakfast, at eight o'clock on weekdays, and nine or ten on Sundays, was to consist of bread and butter, honey, coffee or chocolate; dinner, at two, was to be a joint of beef or veal or mutton, followed by fowl or game in season, with two side dishes, two vegetable courses, pastry, plus, of course, hors d'oeuvres, butter, pickles, radishes, two kinds of fruit in winter and four in summer, two fruit compotes, cheese, biscuits, bonbons, and ices twice a week in summer and once in winter.

Finck, unfortunately, never seemed to be content. On the

point of leaving France, Franklin took time in Le Havre to dissuade his friend Madame Helvétius from hiring Finck for her sister: "even if he has signed twenty times that he is fully satisfied, he will never rest, and at the end he will confront you with a memoir full of demands; he will abuse you if you don't give in, and even if you do he will complain just the same."[9] Worse was yet to come: Franklin had barely landed in Philadelphia when he learned that the shopkeepers of Passy were in an uproar. The wood merchant, the fruitseller, the butcher, the baker – none of them had been paid. They had tried to see Franklin on the eve of his departure, but Finck had tricked them once more by pretending that the Minister would give him the necessary funds in Le Havre. As if this were not enough, he went around blackening Franklin's reputation – or rather Temple's, an easier target. Informed of all this mischief, Franklin quietly commented: "He was continually saying of himself *Je suis honnête homme*. But I always suspected he was mistaken: and so it proves."[10] The last we hear about Finck is that he was happily spending his nights gambling and his days with girls of ill repute, while Chaumont was trying to get the police on his trail. His embezzlement makes one wonder once more how Franklin, surrounded by a maitre d'hôtel who was a thief, a secretary who was a spy, and a grandson who was a playboy, ever accomplished what he did.

We don't know for what reason Finck had replaced la mère Bobie. Things ran smoothly as long as she was in charge. She always tried to oblige Franklin in every possible way, from procuring him a pianoforte for a special occasion to talking her father into soliciting access to the King's special ice reserve so that the honored guest could have his drinks at the temperature he liked. In a rare reference to herself, she sighs about being thin – in her day a highly unhappy state of affairs for a woman.

She may have envied her married sister, Madame Foucault, who was in the full bloom of her beauty. "All the Family send their Love to you," wrote Temple from one of his visits to Chaumont-sur-Loire, "and the beautiful Madame Foucault accompanys hers with an *English* Kiss."[11] Whatever an English kiss may have been, Franklin replied by return mail: "My best Respects to Madame de Chaumont and my Love to the rest of the Family. Thanks to Madame Foucault for her Kindness in sending me the Kiss. It was grown cold by the way. I hope for a warm one when we meet."[12] Monsieur Brillon was to evoke Madame Foucault's charms – after the Doctor's return to Philadelphia – in a Rabelaisian vein. He dated his letter from: "Paris, across the street from Madame Foucault. By Jove, what a splendid sight to be across the street from! We saw her yesterday. She is marvelously plump once again and has just acquired new curves. Very round curves, very white, they seem to have a quality most essential in the eyes of amateurs such as you, for instance: it would be possible, I bet, to kill a flea on them. . . ."[13]

That peculiar enterprise Madame Foucault would probably not have appreciated, but during the winter of 1778 she had gone so far, in order to please Franklin, as to learn chess. The Chaumonts knew as well as Madame Brillon what a passion Franklin had for the game. Several of the anecdotes relating to this facet of the Doctor's character have been preserved by the Chaumonts' grandson, Vincent Leray, who heard them from his father. He tells of Franklin playing late into the night and sending for fresh candles only to find out that day had long since broken; of Franklin refusing to open an important dispatch from America until the game had been concluded. In turn, Thomas Jefferson relates that the Doctor, while playing with the old Duchesse de Bourbon, happened to put her king into prize and take it. "No," said the Duchess, "we do not take kings so!" "We do in America," Franklin replied.[14] Indeed, he played to win, and even though he professed to see some parallelism between his way of playing chess and his outlook on life (defiance in defeat, equanimity in victory), Franklin, at chess, was a very poor loser.

As for the young man who often watched him play and heard him philosophize, Chaumont's only son, later known as James Leray, was swept with fervor for America. Barely more than an adolescent when Franklin had arrived, at twenty-four he was considered sufficiently mature and proficient in English to go to America and plead his father's cause in Congress – as well as the cause of other French merchants who had claims against the United States Government. Fortified with letters from Franklin, Lafayette, John Jay, Rochambeau, and Vergennes, he left France early in 1785 for what was to be an absence of a few weeks, but actually stretched over five years and changed the course of his life. The news of his safe arrival in America reached Passy on the very day of Franklin's departure, bringing some cheer to the saddened family.

Franklin's preparations to leave were marked by the same peculiar admixture of warmhearted affection and hardheaded business that characterized his more than seven years with the Chaumonts. A little memo scribbled in his hand on the very last day specifies the improvements he had made in his living quarters and the value of the items he was leaving

Miniature of Louis XVI, his parting gift to Franklin

behind. He had, for instance, enlarged the kitchen window and wrought enough changes in the chimney "to cure it of its intolerable malady of smoke," this at a total cost of 172 livres. He had installed a lightning rod (150 livres), a bar for suspending pots in the kitchen (6 livres), opened two large windows in the office (20 livres), etc. What he was leaving behind included "a great deal of coal, drawers, a light for the street, a draftsboard, hammers, etc." In consideration of all this, Chaumont was to withdraw "his Demand for Reparations to Windows Furniture etc. and we agreed to strike a Ballance and that all should be considere'd as even on both sides." [15]

Now that the last financial skirmish had been fought, the last fond farewells could be said – by the women. Madame Chaumont must have expressed, privately, her desire to travel with Franklin, for in a letter he wrote her (in French, "so that she would not need a translator"), he regretfully pointed out that such a plan would not be feasible: "If you were in good health, of course, and fit to endure seasickness, the presence of such a friend as you on my trip would be a joy for me. But I have crossed the ocean seven times and having seen to what discomfort and suffering ladies are submitted on such voyages, I cannot advise you to face them." [16] He went on to say that should his trip be postponed until after the equinoxial storms, he would come to Chaumont by water and stay with her for a few weeks, if she still wanted him. But a ship was found, sailing from Le Havre, which Franklin could reach more easily than Lorient. The daughter chosen to accompany him with her father up to Nanterre was the one who spoke a little English, Sophie. But somewhere along the way, Franklin found time to send word to her elder sister, "his wife," and in a writing made still more awkward than usual by an attack of rheumatism in her hands, she cried out after him:

My dear friend, my dear husband . . . I don't know whether this will reach you before you sail . . . nobody desires your happiness more than I do, and if I could . . . I stop, but my voice and my fingers, still weak, want to join, to invite you to come back to your old room. I am sure that in my joy all trace of rheumatism would disappear, I would run up the steps four by four. . . . My husband, my friend, think of your age, your infirmities; it is such a long voyage, if the litter was comfortable make it wait and turn back . . . surrounded by our friends, you shall be free to do exactly as you please, your wishes, your least desire will be our law. . . . Even though you want to brave winds and storms to leave me, you will never find in the other hemisphere a wife who loves you more than yours.[17]

And then, she added a postscript to ask him whether he had remembered to pay a certain bill.

Franklin's trip back to the coast was a triumphal march. He carried with him the King's miniature, set with 408 diamonds, and was drawn in a royal litter, the most comfortable that could be had, while his luggage – 128 boxes of it – went down on the Seine by barge. Almost everybody in Passy, having begged him to stay, came to see him off. As young Benny Bache was to record: "A mournful silence reigned around him, broken only by a few sobs."[18] While Chaumont and his daughter went only part of the way, Le Veillard, the faithful go-between who had brought Franklin and Madame Brillon together and fostered their friendship as long as it needed an intermediary, had planned to escort his hero as far as Le Havre. But then, unable to tear himself away, he crossed the Channel and went on to Southampton. It was up to Franklin to explain this sudden change of plan to Madame Le Veillard, back in Passy. On July 22, 1785, he wrote:

You know, my dear friend, that your husband, a while ago, tried to convince me to remain in France. Now, the tables are turned, and I am trying to persuade him to come with me to America; and I have great hopes of succeeding, for I have already prevailed on him to go as far as England. Perhaps, since you are so far away, and I am so close, we will see the power of your attraction diminished and mine reinforced, so that I shall be able to drag him along.

    In such a case, I don't see any better solace for you than taking a lover, and in order to conduct this affair with more prudence and decency, I recommend Monsieur le Curé. He is a good and worthy priest whom I esteem infinitely. If you don't like this suggestion, follow us and bring along your amiable children. Thus, I shall acquire the whole family to live with me in America, which would give me infinite pleasure.[19]

Everything about this letter shows the ground Franklin had covered in eight years: its fluent, almost perfect French, marred only by a few erratic genders, its uninhibited warmth, its gay impudence in suggesting that the lady, known for her devotion to good works and charity, have an affair with the Curé. As Franklin could have predicted, she took it all in good spirit:

To tell the truth, yes, my good papa, by the time M. Le Veillard arrived here, I was terribly afraid that your attraction might have proved stronger than mine, but happily, as he will confirm,

I had not yet followed your counsel. The sorrow I felt at seeing you go and the fear of not seeing him again, must have been what kept me from taking such a step. Otherwise, impulsive as I am and coquette as you know me, I would not have tarried so long in seeking solace, since I had your approbation.

But thanks to all these circumstances, he found me just as he had left me, terribly sad about your departure, looking at your portrait every minute of the day, and daydreaming about paying you a visit. Such a daydream is sometimes expressed aloud, and my daughter wants to be part of it.[20]

The portrait that so affected Madame Le Veillard throughout the day now hangs in the New York Public Library, the gift of John Bigelow, an early Franklin scholar and United States Minister to Paris in the 1860s. Like Chaumont's, it had been painted by Duplessis – but this one was as mellow and intimate a pastel, in greys and blues, as the oil looked stately and imposing. Franklin had given it to Le Veillard in 1783. On his departure from Passy, he left instructions that a certain table of his also be sent to him. A little delay occurred, as one of Chaumont's daughters could not bear to part with this particular memento, but it was finally delivered, and Madame Le Veillard sighed: "As of yesterday, I am in possession of your table. Something keeps drawing me to it. I pass my hand over it, I look at it with a kind of sorrow that gives me pleasure."[21]

Her husband, in turn, had presented Franklin with a parting gift, not perhaps the most palatable souvenir from France, but one from his own properties that the Doctor could not fail to appreciate. Some time after reaching Philadelphia, Franklin sent word, "we are now drinking every day *les eaux épurées de Passy* with great satisfaction, as they kept well, and seem to be rendered more agreeable by the long voyage."[22]

If Franklin and Le Veillard did share a drink when they first met in 1777, they may well have filled their glasses with mineral water. Because of his stone, the Doctor had to consume quantities of it; and Le Veillard was the owner-manager of Les Nouvelles Eaux de Passy – his wife's dowry and a great source of wealth at a time when supplying 650,000 Parisians with sanitary drinking water was no small task. To be sure, a few aqueducts kept the fountains of the capital flowing, but they were inadequate. The Seine could supply unlimited amounts of water; all the sewers of its environs, however, plus many unsavory kinds of refuse, emptied into it. Great efforts were made to pump water as far from the banks and close to midstream as possible. The largest hydraulic machine was located on the eastern tip of the Ile St. Louis. The water was then "clarified," that is left to settle in huge glass containers, and distributed – at a price – by 20,000 carriers going from door to door throughout Paris. Even clarified, though, the Seine water was still somewhat murky and laxative. It was much safer, if more expensive, to buy bottled mineral water, of which there were many sources, ranging from Chatelguyon to Vichy.

In Franklin's day, royal patronage (and Rousseau's patronage) greatly enhanced the vogue of waters coming from several springs on the lovely heights of Passy. The question was: "Which is the best of the springs?" "The Nouvelles Eaux, of course," proclaimed Le Veillard, and he engaged in stiff competition with other owners. Each was armed with health experts and chemists willing to produce ever more convincing analyses. To best his rivals, Le Veillard had provided himself in 1764 with a medical degree, albeit from an unglamorous provincial university. Having thus established his scientific preeminence, he proceeded to arrange his spa with great commercial flair, embellishing it with walks, terraces, and a charming pavilion. Franklin's presence lent the final touch.

The devotion Le Veillard displayed for the Doctor knew no bounds. It often happens that powerful personalities attract lesser figures, satellites who bask in their glory, reflect their light, make themselves useful in a thousand small ways, and eventually become indispensable to the great man's welfare. Such was the case with Le Veillard: loyal, ever obliging, unsparing of his time and energy, he worked himself up gradually to a position of utmost familiarity and trust.

At first, Le Veillard, whose French was remarkably pure and elegant – if a trifle stilted – helped the newcomer with his grammar and correspondence. There are, in Franklin's files, no less than four different models of polite acknowledgment for verse dedicated to him – all four versions are in Le Veillard's hand. In each case Franklin expresses regret that his scant knowledge of French does not enable him to appreciate fully the beauty of the poem but thanks the author for such kind feelings toward America and her representative in Paris. Considering the flood of poetry provoked by his presence, the models must have been handy.

More important, Le Veillard acted as a middleman and host not only for the soirées at Madame Brillon's but also for a number of dinner parties where Franklin made new acquaintances and renewed old ones – including such well-known figures as Condorcet, Lavoisier, and Mirabeau.

Le Veillard might have seemed a most unexciting friend, compared with these brilliant men. But he had a charming family, and Franklin was responsive to the warmth of the home. There was Madame Le Veillard, who knew how to pen a graceful letter, whether it was an invitation to tea, or a reminder, countersigned by the above mentioned Curé, not to forget the poor of the parish. Back in his own Philadelphia, Franklin was to remember the comfortable, domestic side of her character: "I cannot give you a better idea of my present happiness in my family, than in telling you that my daughter has all the Virtues of a certain good lady that you allow me to love; the same tender Affections and Attentions, Ingenuity, Industry, Economy, etc. etc. etc."[23] There was their son Louis, Temple's friend and sentimental confidant, a tormented, frustrated, likable young man, who dreamed of emigrating to America, but never succeeded. And there was their daughter Geneviève.

What we know about Geneviève stems mainly from her own letters. She must have been very young, and coy, and somewhat impish. Once, she left a breathless little note at Franklin's door: "Mademoiselle Le Veillard came by to have the honor to be kissed by Monsieur Franklin."[24] No man to let a girl's kiss go to waste, Franklin surely collected his tribute. Did he tease Geneviève for not responding with enough ardor? From Normandy, where she went with her parents every year, she sent him a note that still tinkles with girlish merriment:

Do you remember, Sir, having asked the one you call your child to send you a little letter from Dreux? It is too good of you to allow her to take up your time with her person, but she feels that to be able only to write is very little; for, in conscience, she would infinitely prefer to see you, and, yes, to kiss you, even though you say she does not do it with good grace. Do you know that sometimes you are very unfair toward me?

And now, for a little lesson in French psychology:

You certainly know a great many things. You have traveled far and wide. Honors have been heaped upon you. But you have never been inside a French girl's head! Well, I shall tell you their secret. When you want to kiss one of them, and all she will say is that the idea does not pain her, it means she's glad. Now that I have revealed to you the heart of the matter, I hope you won't pick any more quarrels with me.

You told me that when you would write that you loved me a little, *it would mean* a lot. *As for me, I tell you that I love you* a lot. *I hope you shall not conclude from there that I love you* a little. *For it would be unfair, and I assure you that when I say* a lot, *that is exactly what I mean.*

Well-pleased with such chirruping, Franklin sent her a gift. She was delighted:

You sent me, my good papa, the prettiest little writing desk in the world. It gave me great pleasure, not only because it looks so nice, but much more because of him who sent it. Its one fault is that it did not contain a little letter from you, as I had hoped it would. Even two lines long, just to say that you still love me a little, *it would have caused me more pleasure than six pages from many other people.*[25]

Geneviève, being very young, loved postscripts. This one is not devoid of a little malice: "A thousand compliments for you from Papa and Maman. Five hundred for Monsieur votre fils. If the writing desk is his choice (she did not comment on the wrong gender, *sa choix* instead of *son choix*, she merely underlined it), then one may really say that he is a young man of universal good taste." [26] Temple was soon to be rewarded with an embroidered purse.

All this may sound like idle chatter, the pleasant give-and-take of country neighbors, meant to be forgotten as soon as it was uttered. Yet, Geneviève's father was destined to play a crucial role, if not directly in Franklin's life, at least in the image he was to leave for posterity; and even Geneviève participated in it.

It was in 1782 that Le Veillard stumbled upon what he was to consider, henceforth, his mission. That year, Franklin learned to his surprise that the first part of his Memoirs, written eleven years earlier and left in a trunk some miles outside Philadelphia, had not fallen into British hands, as he had presumed, but was safe and awaiting only completion. Encouraged by his friend and former publisher, Benjamin Vaughan, whom he had consulted as to the advisability of proceeding with the work, Franklin began to reconsider the idea of writing some more, but felt discouraged by the lack of relevant notes and papers.

Le Veillard, at this point, made it his life project to see that Franklin *did* bring up to date what has become known as the *Autobiography*, but was always referred to at the time as the Memoirs. It is well known that Franklin wrote a second installment at Passy, in the comparative leisure he enjoyed after the peace treaty with England was signed. It is also known that upon his departure from France he left with Le Veillard an outline of the Memoirs as he envisioned them and that a few months before his death he sent from Philadelphia one copy of the work as it then stood to Le Veillard, while another copy went to Benjamin Vaughan in London. But how much Le Veillard prodded, coaxed, and cajoled; how, over the years, he begged and nagged; how, in the hope of reaching the grandfather's ear across the Ocean, he became the grandson's errand-boy in Paris, doing anything Temple requested, from delivering love letters to a married woman to shipping him live deer; how many pages Le Veillard wrote, forever hammering away at the same theme – write your memoirs, you owe them to the world, to yourself, to me – this tremendous effort on the Frenchman's part has been largely ignored by historians.

Ironically, the spotlight focuses on Le Veillard only during the last stage of the story, when what might have been a great personal victory suddenly turned to ashes. He held it in his hands, at last, the famous manuscript. With it came a covering letter from Franklin, dated November 13, 1789:

I send you what is done of the Memoirs under this express Condition, however, that you do not suffer any Copy to be taken of them, or any Part of them, on any Account whatever, and that you will, with our excellent friend the Duke de la Rochefoucault, read them over carefully, examine them critically and send me your friendly, candid Opinion of the parts you would advise me to correct or expunge.[27]

At this point, one could expect a cry of triumph from Paris, but the next message was a blunt letter sent by Temple in May 1790, one month after his grandfather's death. Le Veillard was forbidden – absolutely forbidden – to publish the manuscript or even to communicate its content to anyone, since it was to him, Temple, that Franklin had bequeathed all his papers and manuscripts, with permission to draw any profit he could from them. The young man was planning to bring out, as soon as feasible, a complete edition of his grandfather's life and works, in France or in England, either of which seemed more propitious to him than America.

But he tarried. And the world was desperately eager for Franklin material. In January 1791, Jacques Buisson, a Paris publisher known for his unscrupulous practices, wrote to Le Veillard, proposing to buy from him any Franklin manuscript in his possession. Le Veillard, of course, turned him down, while still begging Temple, by then in London, to hurry to Paris and get the work under way. But a few weeks later, Buisson did publish a French translation of the first part of Franklin's memoirs. How he got hold of a manuscript is one of the unsolved mysteries of literary history.[28] Le Veillard promptly published a disclaimer in the *Journal de Paris*, stressing his own innocence. Temple himself, upset though he was by this turn of events, never suspected Le Veillard of double-dealing. In April, he promised Le Veillard that he would arrive in Paris within two weeks. He was still in England six months later.

All the while, with a fresh translation ready and waiting, Le Veillard fumed and fretted. His own letters have disappeared, but his frustration is reflected in Temple's answers:

Notwithstanding the Opinion you entertain, that I have neglected the Publication in question, for Business less important (which by the way you cannot possibly be a Judge of) I can assure you I have given it all the attention I could. And however I may have lost something by not publishing sooner – yet it has been amply compensated by those Pursuits you judge less

*important. A few Months will I hope satisfy your Impatience
and the Public Curiosity.*[29]

Temple's further promise "you may rely on it – the Life
shall appear *the same day* in Paris as in London" – was never
carried out. It took him another twenty years to bring out the
book, and then in English only.

By that time, Le Veillard was well beyond caring. In its
first idealistic wave, the French Revolution had swept him
into the position of Mayor of Passy; eventually it engulfed
and destroyed him. As punishment for having escorted
Louis XVI on that fateful August 10, 1792, when the King
had sought refuge in the Assembly (hadn't he been, most of
his life, the sovereign's "gentleman-servant"?), Le Veillard,
the "spoiled child of nature,"[30] as a jealous colleague once

Jacques-Donatien Leray de Chaumont

dubbed him, was sent to the scaffold, every one of his hopes unfulfilled, in the summer of 1794.

But Geneviève survived. Unmarried, she lived well into the nineteenth century. And her most treasured possession always was a morocco-bound manuscript, no longer the copy in Benny Bache's hand that Franklin had sent, but Franklin's own handwritten version, both more precious and more complete than the copy. At some point, Temple had found time to go to Paris, and for reasons known only to himself, had exchanged copies with Le Veillard. Thus, if after many decades of oblivion, Franklin's *Autobiography* was finally rediscovered in its original form, it was thanks to the neighbor's daughter who, when she was very, very young had revealed to the old Doctor what went on in a French girl's head.

6 La Comtesse d'Houdetot

Her lover gave her happiness;
her friends gave her glory ❧ CHODERLOS DE LACLOS

Comtesse d'Houdetot was the kind of woman who makes other women wonder what is it that men see in them. Friends and foes alike, as well as impartial witnesses, testify to her glaring lack of good looks: she was, we are told, thick of feature, sallow-skinned, pockmarked, and definitely cross-eyed. Yet she became one of the great romantic figures of her century: the respected wife of one man for over forty years; the cherished mistress of another for more than fifty; the passion and inspiration of a third in a brief, raging encounter; the benefactress and mentor of a fourth in a tender, motherly interlude; the beloved friend of a fifth, a much younger man who brightened her life after the others had died and held her hand on her deathbed. Those five were the most important men in her life, but she had a host of other friends besides, ranging from the powers at Court to the political avant-garde, from castaway sailors to Franklin and Jefferson.

What did Comtesse d'Houdetot have to offer? The promise of ardor, of course, what the French call *un je ne sais quoi*, something easier to feel than to explain. As Choderlos de Laclos remarked: "She knew that the great affair of life is love."[1] Coming from the author of one of the most erotic books of all times, *Les Liaisons dangereuses*, this is quite a tribute. But there was more to her personality than sex appeal. According to the numerous people who have recorded their memories of her – and none of them forgot to stress how plain she looked – she showed unfailing kindness in an

Madame d'Houdetot, 1786

age known for the malevolence of its wit, untiring zeal on behalf of those she liked, a happy tendency to see only the good in people, an utter, disarming frankness, most unusual in her day. In other words, she was blessed with that combination of esprit and sensibilité that prerevolutionary France valued higher than subsequent canons of Victorian virtue.

Life had not begun too auspiciously for Sophie de la Live de Bellegarde. Born in 1730 in Paris, near the Place Vendôme, she was married off at eighteen. Sophie met Count d'Houdetot for the first time at a luncheon organized by a friend of both families; the idea of marriage was broached between one course and the next; the terms of the contract were discussed over coffee; its draft was brought to the notary during the afternoon, signed by all interested parties just before supper, and the marriage celebrated the following Monday – a breathtaking pace even for those days.

As soon as they were left alone, less than a week after their first encounter, the young couple discovered that they had practically nothing in common. A military man of robust appetites – not unlike Monsieur Brillon – Comte d'Houdetot shared none of his wife's intellectual aspirations, although in time he grew quite fond of her. (It is said that in 1794, during the worst days of the Terror, he ran all over Paris in quest of powder for her hair, her one great asset which had remained magnificent.) At the time of his marriage, however, he had a mistress of long standing whom he never gave up. The bride shed copious tears, bore him two children, and drew some comfort from his many absences ("What a sweet, fresh soul!" wrote her sister-in-law. "She is jumping around like a puppy dog, drunk with pleasure at the thought of her husband's departure"²). In time, she recovered her spirits completely and found the man of her life, Chevalier Jean-François de Saint-Lambert.

Few reputations have been more inflated in their day than that of Saint-Lambert. An utterly mediocre poet, and arrogant as well, he was nevertheless loudly acclaimed, triumphantly received in the best salons, and raised to the honor of membership in the French Academy. As a ladies' man, too, he was no mean catch. An old story, going back to his days at the Court of King Stanislas in Lorraine, was at the source of his prestige. In 1749, when Madame du Châtelet, Voltaire's brilliant mistress, died in childbirth, Voltaire and her husband opened, with trembling fingers, a locket which she always wore. Would it contain a memento of the husband, of the lover, or both? It turned out to enclose nothing but Saint-Lambert's portrait. Voltaire recovered his wits soon enough to remark to Monsieur du Châtelet: "This story reflects no great credit on either of us."³ To a friend he complained that Saint-Lambert, that brute, was the father of the baby and the cause of her death. Now known as an irresistible man, Saint-Lambert left Lorraine for Paris and further conquests.

In Paris he met Madame d'Houdetot and embarked with her on fifty-two years of such perfect, faithful bliss, that contemporary society held up their liaison as a shining, heroic example. Monsieur d'Houdetot not only accepted it in good spirit, but once exclaimed wistfully: "How happy *we* could have been together!"⁴

Was it to keep faith with Saint-Lambert that the Countess turned down Jean-Jacques Rousseau? Did she really reject Rousseau? Or did he panic at the last minute, as he was wont to do with women of quality?

Their brief, frustrating moment came in the spring of 1757. Rousseau was forty-five, she was twenty-seven. Already famous, he was living at L'Ermitage, a quiet retreat near Paris. Sophie lived nearby, at Eaubonne, right next to Saint-Lambert's estate, from which the poet had been away for several months. One morning, she burst into Rousseau's room, in riding breeches and boots, saying that she had lost her way, laughing loudly, shaking her dark curls, childish, prankish, and – to him – madly exciting. She came back; she asked him to visit her; they saw each other every day. She described her passion for Saint-Lambert with such alluring fire that Rousseau fell in love with her more desperately than he ever had before – or after.

Soon people began to whisper about the meetings of the famous writer with the ardent lady, and someone (perhaps Madame d'Epinay, her own sister-in-law) alerted Saint-Lambert. His return brought to an abrupt ending the idyll, only three months old. But the rumors did not stop; and as they were spreading, Madame d'Houdetot stood to lose not only the trust of Saint-Lambert, but also the forbearance of her husband. Had he not expressed more than once the unwritten code of his milieu, that no matter what happened the rules of "decency" should not be broken? "Since the world now knows that you are in love with me, it would not be decent for me to see you alone";[5] with this letter Madame d'Houdetot barred any further meeting with Rousseau.

Rousseau, however, could never forget. In despair, he wove his longings and memories into the fabric of Julie, the heroine of his *Nouvelle Héloïse*, the most celebrated novel of the century. Whatever had or had not really happened at Eaubonne remained locked in the hearts of the participants;

Saint-Lambert was left sole master of the field. He had, so to speak, defeated both Voltaire and Rousseau.

Thirty-two years later, in 1788, with Rousseau dead, Madame almost sixty, and Monsieur d'Houdetot too old to worry about appearances, the posthumous publication of the second part of the *Confessions* created a sensation. In a burning passage, Rousseau told how the three months of unfulfilled desire at Eaubonne had brought his senses to a paroxysm of misery and delight. As William Short, the American chargé d'affaires, wrote from Paris to Jefferson, who had already sailed home:

The only book that has been read for some time except those relative to the revolution, is the continuation of Rousseau's confessions – as it treats of persons well known here, many of whom are still living, it is read with unexampled avidity. The secret history of Mme. d'Houdetot and St. Lambert, and Rousseau's passion for the former, is stated fully. I have not seen her since its appearance – it is difficult to say whether she will not be pleased with what is said. She is represented in such flattering colors that most people imagine few women in Paris would be displeased to be treated in that manner.[6]

The bombshell, as far as Madame d'Houdetot was concerned, was the revelation of the celebrated episode under the acacia tree. She and Rousseau had dined together, tête-à-tête, in those faraway days, taken a walk in the moonlight, sat under the tree's heavy blossoms. There, he had put his feelings for her into words of such eloquence that, after abundant tears on both sides, they were about to consummate their – or rather his – love, when Sophie suddenly remembered her pledge to Saint-Lambert (never mind Monsieur d'Houdetot), and the spell was broken. Old Madame d'Houdetot herself, in a conversation with a friend, had a different recollection: it was, she said, the curses of a wagoner whose cart was stuck in the mud that had broken the spell. Be that as it may, during the following decades of political convulsion, the "acacia by the waterfall" became the object of a pilgrimage and eventually died, its branches plucked away by Rousseau cultists.

Was it through some private symbolism, some sense of poetic symmetry, that Madame d'Houdetot chose an acacia as the tree Franklin was to plant during the *fête champêtre* given in his honor at Sannois, her husband's country estate? The year was 1781, it was spring again, and Sannois was not far from Eaubonne, in that lovely Vallée de Montmorency haunted by the memories of Jean-Jacques. Rousseau was dead, the tempestuous Sophie of twenty-seven had become "the good Countess" of fifty-one, surrounded by husband and children, and the serene old philosopher from Philadelphia, the center of the day's proceedings, was a far cry from the tormented thinker from Geneva. That day, heavy with praise, with verse, with every kind of overstatement; that day which was to be such a high point in the Countess' life that she still talked about it shortly before dying, may well have been one of discomfort and embarrassment for her guest. But, as Franklin knew well, she wielded influence, and she had decided to throw it on the American side. Wherever his thoughts may have been (on the proposal he had made to the Brillons, the day before, for a marriage between their Cunégonde and his Temple?), he was determined to do what was required of him to make the "philosophical feast" a success.

As Franklin alit from his carriage, the Countess, who had gone out on the road to greet him, recited:

Ame du héros et du sage,
O Liberté, premier bienfait des Dieux . . .[7]

Inside the house, a splendid dinner awaited the party; there was more poetry, no longer declaimed, but sung by each guest in turn as he raised his glass. Benjamin, Philadelphia, William Tell, and even the Magna Carta came in for toasts and celebration. The stanzas were, of course, dreadful, but the fact that they were sung in praise of liberty, republicanism, and revolution by French aristocrats must have made them beautiful in Franklin's ears.

Prose was used sparingly in Madame d'Houdetot's entourage. Whether her neighbor, Comte de Tressan (one of the performing guests at the party), was sending her an especially beautiful melon from his garden, or whether she was commiserating with him on the late frost that had ruined both their orchards, the notes went back and forth in verse. As a child she had been a passionate scribbler of poetry, but an aunt, bringing her up with the clear, firm ideas of a nonpermissive age, had promptly taken all paper from her, allowing only enough to keep the household accounts. For this she was to make up the rest of her life.

After the banquet, Franklin planted the famous acacia (a Virginia locust) while more verse was said – this later to be engraved on a marble plaque beside the tree. An orchestra was now in attendance at the château. The whole gathering sang a chorus in honor of the lightning rod; finally, as Franklin was climbing back into his carriage, the Countess brought the day to its climax by reciting:

Législateur d'un monde, et bienfaiteur des deux,
L'homme dans tous les temps te devra ses hommages;
  Et je m'acquitterai dans ces lieux
  De la dette de tous les âges.[8]

Whether Franklin heaved a sigh of relief on his way home and thought longingly of the uncomplicated ways of the Philadelphia gentry, we do not know.

His relationship with Madame d'Houdetot was extremely courteous, if somewhat formal. She never called him anything but "mon cher et vénérable Docteur." In another age, the Countess would undoubtedly have been president of some organization for Franco-American friendship, and it is as such that Franklin always treated her. He never failed to answer her letters promptly and to act upon her suggestions.

Shortly after the feast at Sannois, Madame d'Houdetot embarked upon the kind of project for which she was best suited: it involved America, the good of mankind, and a specific man. It had to do with a refugee from America; accompanied by his nine-year-old son, he had landed on the Normandy coast in the first days of August, 1781, penniless, forlorn, confused, having almost forgotten the language of his French forebears, vacillating even as to his own name, which he never seemed to sign twice in the same manner. He had been born in Caen, Normandy, 48 years earlier, and his original name was Michel-Guillaume de Crèvecoeur. For reasons which have remained mysterious, he had left his homeland at a very young age, emigrated to Canada and worked there as a cartographer, and then slipped into the American colonies and adopted the name of Saint John. He had done well in his new country, first traveling far and wide (to Vermont, Jamaica, Bermuda, Nantucket), then settling as a farmer in New York and marrying Mehetabel Tippet, a girl from Yonkers. After twenty-seven years in the New World, when he seemed to have cut all ties with his past, the Revolution broke out. One of his farms was burned, and, for reasons once again left rather hazy – perhaps to collect the inheritance of his mother who had died – he decided to go back to France, taking with him one of his three children.

The trip, started in April 1779, turned out to be disastrous. As soon as he arrived in New York, Saint John was separated from his son, arrested, and thrown in jail as a suspected spy. Once released, he fell seriously ill and spent more than a year in utmost poverty before being allowed to embark for England. His ship sank off the coast of Ireland. Half naked, father and son were rescued and taken to Dublin. After a while, they proceeded to London, where Saint John met a publisher and sold him for thirty guineas the manuscript of what was to become one of the best-selling books of the day: *Letters from an American Farmer*. Without waiting for publication, he made his way to Normandy, via Ostend, and reached his father's estate, still without news of his wife and two other children.

One of his first acts a few weeks after he arrived was to befriend five American officers who had escaped from an English prison and rowed across the Channel. He took them into his father's home, fed them, and invoked in their behalf the protection of an influential friend of his father, Madame d'Houdetot.

The Countess obliged immediately by writing to Franklin that she and her husband had known the Crèvecoeur family for twenty-five years, their estates in Normandy being almost adjacent, and that although she had never met the son personally, she had heard only the best about him and would be grateful if Franklin acceded to his request concerning the five American escapees. Franklin, in turn, promptly wrote to the proper authorities and took the steps he knew so well, by then, to enable the men to reach Lorient and sail home. In the process, he met Crèvecoeur by correspondence. For a while, the Doctor was understandably puzzled by the names St. Jean, Saint John, Saint John de Crèvecoeur, and Hector St. John used indifferently by his correspondent. But in his quaint, stiff, somewhat poetic, somewhat gallic English, Crèvecoeur explained that he was mixed up between the traditional St. Jean used by his family, "ever since the conquest of England by William the Bastard," and the official necessity of calling himself Crèvecoeur. Indeed, so foreign and lost did he feel in his native land that he was reluctant to leave Normandy, and he hesitated for a while before accepting Marquis Turgot's invitation to stay with him in Paris.[9]

Few prospects could have been more tempting than to live on the Ile St. Louis, in the splendid residence of Marquis Robert Turgot, brother of the recently deceased economist and Comptroller-General. Strangely enough, the reason for Turgot's interest in him and the key that opened to Crèvecoeur some of the most exclusive Parisian doors was none other than the lowly potato. Under the pseudonym of Normannus Americanus, Crèvecoeur had written a little pamphlet on the American methods of growing potatoes. It came out at a time when the more enlightened people, appalled by the hunger and suffering brought about by every crop failure, were making a vigorous effort to overcome France's massive resistance to that versatile plant.

The potato had, of course, been known to Europe since the sixteenth century, when it had been brought back, along with gold, from Peru; but, although it gained some acceptance in Germany, in Switzerland, and especially in Ireland, the French peasant stolidly maintained that it was a source of leprosy. Its champion was a humble pharmacist by the name of Antoine Parmentier who had been introduced firsthand to the potato in a prisoners' camp in Germany and devoted his life to its cause. King Louis XVI was willing to help to the extent of granting Parmentier a few acres of land and of wearing in his buttonhole a sprig of potato flowers from the first crop, in spite of some malicious smiling at the Court. Nobility soon followed suit, and, in November 1778, a grand dinner was given – with Franklin in attendance – to launch Parmentier's potato bread, "as beautiful, as fluffy, as white as the best rolls." [10] It is also reported that Franklin and his friend the chemist Lavoisier attended another banquet – this time each course consisted only of potatoes, prepared in various ways, and washed down with potato spirits. Of course the promotion of a product that was new, cheap, and useful to mankind could not fail to arouse Franklin's enthusiasm. Such was his power as a trend setter that soon potatoes were being stolen from Parmentier's experimental fields, and the battle was won. (It was also in Franklin's time that grilling beef, an English practice, was imported to France, so that the famous *steak pommes frites*, that hallmark of French cuisine, is really rather recent.)

Meanwhile, Crèvecoeur – whose name appears frequently in Parmentier's writings – was beginning to attract some attention in Paris, thanks to Turgot's patronage and to the exotic stories he had to tell. But in spite of a cordial reception by no less a celebrity than the naturalist Georges Buffon, he still felt ill at ease, very much the outsider. He could not, for instance, bring himself to meet Madame d'Houdetot.

His first encounter with her throws some light on the character of that kindly, determined woman. Seized with panic at the thought of exposing his shaky French and "foreign manners" to a lady whose refinement was so well known, Crèvecoeur pleaded illness and postponed indefinitely "the honor of presenting his respects." But his very clumsiness, far from repelling her, only whetted her curiosity, and one day, after a month of silence had made him hope that she had forgotten him, she threatened (such is the word he uses in his *Memoirs*) to fetch him at his residence. He surrendered, went to pay a call on her, and from that day started a new life:

How she received me! How soon she saw through me, reassured me! How she made a new man of me, with patience, with a thousand flattering, pleasing little attentions! What rapid progress in the knowledge of French, in the ways of the world, my desire to deserve her esteem made me accomplish! [11]

Soon he was established in her house and treated as a lifelong friend. Madame's husband, who was, as Crèvecoeur notes, much more military and businesslike than intellectual, welcomed the new guest's presence at his wife's parties and urged him to attend, so that he could slip out and have a jolly time with his own friends. The official lover, Saint-Lambert, also seems to have adopted a benevolent view of the situation. As for the Countess, she played Pygmalion in reverse with this man who was five years her junior, taking him visiting, escorting him to shows, to libraries, to concerts. As one of her acquaintances wrote, with the inevitable touch of malice,

Le Baquet de Mesmer

"Proud to possess *un sauvage Américain*, she wanted to polish him, to launch him into society."[12]

Once Crèvecoeur knew her, he met everybody who mattered in Paris. And, of course, he met Franklin. On March 13, 1782, the Countess asked the Doctor: "Could you receive me tomorrow morning at eleven, could you give me some tea, and bread and butter?" And she went on to say that she would have the honor of introducing to him the American to whom he had already shown such kindness.[13]

With Franklin's help and guidance, Crèvecoeur installed lightning rods on Madame d'Houdetot's châteaux and on the homes of her friends as well. At Franklin's suggestion and with his endorsement, he wrote to Governor Hancock of Massachusetts asking for news of his wife and children and begging for his assistance. But his letters went unanswered.

When the English version of his *Letters from an American Farmer* came out, Crèvecoeur, who had gone to Normandy to visit his son, sent a copy to Franklin. Franklin's impression was favorable enough for him to cite the book, a year later, to an English acquaintance, as the best source of information "on the manner of beginning new settlements"[14] in America. In spite of some harsh things it had to say about British rule, the book had been extraordinarily well received in England. At the urging of his ever-widening circle of friends in Paris, Crèvecoeur undertook a French translation of it. But, where the English original had been direct, earthy, and terse, the French adaptation was more idyllic, flowery, imbued with the ideas of the author's new milieu: that America offered the paradise of mature, sophisticated political institutions run in the context of an opulent and unspoiled nature by a pure-hearted, rural society. Once again, Crèvecoeur was not there to see his book appear. For 1783 had come, and with it, peace.

Suddenly, as he recalled, Madame d'Houdetot sprang into action. She made long, mysterious visits to Versailles. Her protégé, who thought that she was intriguing for her husband's advancement, was surprised to see her come back, one day, in a state of elation:

Rejoice, my friend, she said. The Minister of the Navy [Maréchal de Castries] will find good use for the knowledge you have gathered during your stay in the British colonies ... You will have to answer in writing to his questions on population, geography, industry ... Will you be able to do it? – Yes, you angel of goodness and friendship, said I, my heart swollen with joy, my eyes full of tears, kissing her tenderly ... – If such is the case, she replied, you must leave for Versailles tomorrow, and there you will occupy my husband's rooms.[15]

There followed, for Crèvecoeur, months of intense activity: he drew maps, compiled a huge report on his adopted country, and prepared a memorandum on the organization of packet boats between France and America, which he submitted to Franklin for comment.

As former Postmaster-General, and one who "had had some Share in the Management of the Paquet Boats between England and America," Franklin found the project valuable, "because not only Commerce increases Correspondence, but Facility of Correspondence increases Commerce." A fleet of five boats, rather than the suggested four, seemed indispensable to him to insure monthly departures, lest "the Regularity be broken by Accidents of Wind and Weather, and the Merchants disappointed and their Affairs deranged"; and it would be best to dispatch the boats from France on the third

Wednesdays, since boats from England left on the first. Further, Franklin suggested that the vessels' holds be divided into separate, watertight "Apartments, after the Chinese Manner," so that a leak would not provoke total catastrophe. Finally, he joined to his remarks "a Copy of a Chart of the Gulf Stream which is little known by European Navigators, and yet of Great Consequence." [16]

The upshot of Crèvecoeur's zeal, combined with much more behind-the-scenes maneuvering by his benefactress, was one of the most coveted of all new posts opening up in the diplomatic field: the first French consulship in New York. Nominated officially to this important position in June 1783, Crèvecoeur spent the summer getting ready and enjoying a new wave of popularity. Leaving his son to complete his education in France under Madame d'Houdetot's watchful guidance, he embarked, in November, on the first of the packet boats he helped to organize. He landed in the United States to learn that his farm in Orange County had been burned to the ground, his wife had died, and his children had disappeared. He eventually found them in Boston, cared for by a relative of one of the five American officers he had helped shortly after his arrival in France. He kept with him Frances-America, his thirteen-year-old daughter, sent his youngest son, aged nine, to join his other son in France, and settled down to the business of becoming an energetic and very successful consul.

His Parisian friends were not forgotten. To their complete surprise, a number of them – including, of course, the good Countess and Saint-Lambert – received the "freedom of the city" in a town they had never seen and never would: New Haven. As related in Ezra Stiles' *Journal*, Crèvecoeur himself had been granted that privilege for his part in the establishment of a botanical garden in New Haven and had asked that it be extended to the people who had helped him in his years of loneliness.[17] The news, when it reached Paris, was greeted with mixed feelings: some felt that the beneficiaries of such an honor had been ill-chosen, since the people who had really helped America were Beaumarchais and the merchants who had risked – and often lost – most of their fortunes in trade with the colonies. The philosopher Condorcet turned his new honor into a *nom de plume*, calling some of his essays *Letters from a New Haven Burgher*. As to the Countess, she was simply delighted and chose to consider the distinction as meaning that she had become an American citizen! Well aware of her "patriotism," Franklin gave her a handsomely bound edition of the French translation of the *Constitutions of the American States* as soon as it appeared, and she asserted that nothing could have pleased her more.

Madame d'Houdetot never ran short of strangers in need of assistance. Many of her letters to Franklin are appeals in behalf of stranded prisoners, the most pathetic case being that of an Irish sailor who had landed in a French jail and seemed fated to rot away in it forever, since nobody understood a word of what he said.

But life was not all charity and no fun; other letters tried to entice the Doctor with his favorite bait, an invitation to the concerts held by the Countess twice a month in her Parisian home. She also wanted him to come again to Sannois, not merely as the star of another poetico-philosophical feast, but for a longer stay:

Our valley and my garden are at the peak of their beauty, and all

*our flowers call you . . . Your coming will be one more monument
to embellish and honor my little country retreat where I keep,
carefully, all that has won my admiration or touched my heart.*[18]

Monuments are not easily moved. The Countess knew that
Franklin, now suffering from the stone, found it painful to
travel in a carriage, but she was not to be discouraged. She
arranged for him to come by boat, procured a "perfectly
comfortable yacht," and settled for a price with the boatman.
He would have only one short league to walk, she said, and
would find tea and rest midway, at a friendly home. The
invitation "for eight days at least"[19] was extended to Temple
and to Benny Bache, who had come back from Switzerland.
To no avail. Franklin wrote sadly:

*I have done nothing but think of that charming project of
spending a few days in Sannois with you . . . But the more I
think about it, the less practicable it seems; for I am still less able
to walk than the last time I had the pleasure of seeing you.
Going no further than Madame Brillon's caused me to be in pain
for several days . . . May you find everywhere the happiness that
you bring to your friends.*[20]

Even though they did not see each other as often as they
wished, Franklin consulted her on the big issue of the
moment, an issue which was agitating the minds of the
Parisians in 1784, dividing them into quarreling factions. The
problem was whether Friedrich Anton Mesmer, the man
from Vienna whose stay in Paris (1778–84) almost coincided
with Franklin's, was a genius or a quack. A genius, proclaimed
such a blue-blood as the Comte d'Artois (the King's brother
and future Charles X); a benefactor of mankind, insisted

such a hero as Lafayette; a saint, said the throngs of people who crowded his clinics or obtained initiation, at a price, into his secret societies. An impostor, maintained the respected Lavoisier; a charlatan, declared the majority of Parisian doctors; a threat to decency and public order, grumbled the more conservatively inclined. And so the battle raged.

In all fairness, we may now say that Mesmer was not an impostor; he did believe in the validity of his doctrine, even though he surrounded it with hocus-pocus and tried to make a quick fortune by it. Astrology was at its origin, but, as it evolved, it became the first link in the chain that was to lead to scientific pioneering in hypnotism, to Breuer, Charcot, and Freud.

The heavenly bodies, Mesmer felt, acted on living beings by means of a fluid they emitted, which had the power to penetrate all matter. If, for some reason, the path of the planetary fluid was obstructed, disease ensued, and the cure lay only in the application of animal magnetism, its terrestrial substitute, which only Mesmer knew how to handle. Having met with little success in Vienna and having been implicated in a scandal there, Mesmer came to Paris and associated himself with Dr. Charles Deslon, since he did not possess the medical license necessary to practice his art in France. Shortly after Mesmer's arrival, Franklin was alerted to his presence by a note in approximate English from an old friend and scientific colleague who had been the first to denounce him in Vienna:

I hear . . . the Vienna conjuror Dr. Mesmer is at Paris, that he has been presented to the Royal Academy, that he still pretends a magnetical effluvium streams from his finger and enters the body of any person without being obstructed by walls or any other obstacles, and that such stuff, too insipid for to get belief by any old woman, is believed by your friend, Mr. Le Roy.[21]

The following year, Franklin, accompanied by Madame Brillon, did pay a visit to Mesmer, but their purpose, it seems, was more musical than scientific. They were interested in the armonica Mesmer used for background music during his treatments. Franklin, it will be remembered, had an abiding interest in the instrument, partly his brainchild. That the visit was somewhat strained, with the guests trying to keep the conversation on music, and the host trying to promote his medical theories, is reflected by an exclamation of Madame Brillon in one of her several evocations of paradise – this one dated November 1, 1779 – "in heaven, M. Mesmer will content himself with playing the armonica and will not bother us with his electrical fluid!"[22]

But Mesmer did not give up hope that Franklin might come again, this time "to discover for himself the advantages of animal magnetism,"[23] and on December 1, 1779, he asked Franklin to have lunch with him on the following Wednesday, so that he could show him some arresting cases. We don't know whether Franklin went. The only scrap of evidence we have on the subject between 1779 and 1784 is that, on one occasion, Franklin lent a copy of one of Mesmer's books to his friend Jean-Baptiste Le Roy.

By 1784, Mesmer, after years of semiobscurity, had emerged as a force to be reckoned with. His séances were now so famous that they had to be dramatically organized. He invented the famous *baquet,* or trough, around which thirty or more persons could be magnetized simultaneously. The baquet, an oaken case about a foot high, was filled first with a layer of powdered glass and iron filings, then with a number of bottles, symmetrically arranged. The lid was pierced with holes through which passed jointed and movable iron branches, to be held by the patients. In subdued light, absolutely silent, they sat in concentric rows, bound to one another by a cord. Then Mesmer, wearing a coat of lilac silk, and carrying a long iron wand, walked up and down the crowd, touching the diseased parts of the patients' bodies.

Mesmer, we are told, was a tall, handsome, imposing man. Every now and then, he would place himself *en rapport* with a subject seated opposite him, foot against foot, knee against knee. This practice, often successful in provoking a trance-like state, was, of course, the germ of what would become hypnotism. But, in 1784, it aroused violent protest, especially when the subject thus treated was a woman. Suspected of putting his older women patients simply to sleep, while submitting the younger ones to *titillations délicieuses*, embroiled, further, in a bitter quarrel with his partner, Deslon, Mesmer came under fire from various directions. Tempers flared to such an extent that the King appointed two commissions to investigate the whole question independently.

The commission to which Franklin belonged was made up of members of the Faculty of Medicine and of the Royal Academy of Sciences. Tragedy, within a few years, would strike that commission. Two of its members, Lavoisier and Bailly (later the first Mayor of Paris), were to perish on the guillotine; another member, ironically, was that very Docteur Guillotin, whose name is linked to the notorious instrument, though he had not invented it, but, as a humanitarian, advocated its use as less barbarous than the hatchet. At the time of the Mesmer investigation, however, the clouds were still imperceptible and the meetings were conducted in an atmosphere of good humor – often at Passy, in deference to Franklin, the senior member, who had difficulty moving around.

Franklin's initial skepticism toward what came to be known as "mesmerism," – although officially only Deslon's practices were being investigated – is reflected in the answer he sent a sick man who had asked him whether, in his opinion, it would be worthwhile taking a trip to Paris to submit to Mesmer's cures:

There being so many disorders which cure themselves and such a disposition in mankind to deceive themselves and one another on these occasions; and living long having given me frequent opportunities of seeing certain remedies cry'd up as curing everything, and yet so soon after totally laid aside as useless, I cannot but fear that the expectation of great advantage from the new method of treating diseases will prove a delusion.

That delusion may however in some cases be of use while it lasts. There are in every great city a number of persons who are never in health, because they are fond of medications and always taking them, and hurt their constitutions. If these people can be persuaded to forbear their drugs in expectation of being cured by only the physician's finger or an iron rod pointing at them, they may possibly find good effects tho' they mistake the cause.[24]

Still, Franklin wanted to keep an open mind, and he asked the Countess d'Houdetot whether she had ever heard of a real cure obtained by the new method. On March 10, 1784, she answered that indeed she had. Magnetism had just saved from certain death her friend, whom Franklin also knew: Monsieur de Breget. That very morning, she had had a long talk with an acquaintance who had not left the patient's sickbed since the beginning of his illness and who gave her the following report: the regular doctors despaired of curing Monsieur de Breget and sent for Deslon and a disciple of his, named Bien Aimé; the patient was subjected immediately to magnetism, given barley water and lemonade the first day, broth and meat jelly the second, and solids after that; he had steadily improved, in spite of a few relapses. After nine days, he had been able to get up, dress, and come back to Paris. Once she had related the facts, the Countess gave vent to her perplexity:

It is very hard for me to believe what I cannot understand. I have no opinion on this prodigious happening, but I would be charmed to hear yours. Versailles is buzzing with this miracle, and I wish that some doctor had followed the treatment and written a report. I shall soon see Monsieur de Breget, and I will pass on to you all further information you wish. What I have sent so far comes from a levelheaded man who does not believe in magnetism any more than I do.[25]

Franklin and his fellow commissioners were bombarded with advice from all sides. Mesmer sent an extremely clever and well-worded letter, dissociating himself from Deslon and making the point that whereas Deslon had stolen some of his master's ideas – which put the commissioners in the awkward position of sanctifying a theft – he was ignorant of the true core of animal magnetism. Lafayette wrote in the same vein, calling Deslon a traitor and Mesmer an honest man.* He

---

* Mesmerism, in its heyday, had become a kind of free-masonry, with its center in Paris, and as many as twenty-four provincial branches called "Sociétés de l'Harmonie." The entrance fee was stiff, new members had to pledge clean living and abstinence from tobacco. A letter

ended with a sly allusion to the fact that Temple had been recently admitted to one of Mesmer's secret societies.[26]

Apparently unperturbed, the commission went on with its work throughout the spring of 1784. Deslon magnetized a tree in Franklin's garden, and a twelve-year-old boy fainted when he approached it. The commissioners experimented with screens, with blindfolded people. They tried their skill at impersonating Deslon and then seeing if they were capable, when wearing his clothes, of magnetizing people. They were.

On the whole, they proved to their satisfaction that the convulsions to which patients fell prey were due to imagination and nervous excitement, and that the magnetic fluid, as such, did not exist. Their report was sent to the King in August, with Franklin's signature appearing first, though he was probably not its author. Twenty thousand copies of it were printed and snapped up in no time by an eager public.

Franklin sent some copies of the report to Temple, who was in England at the time, visiting his father. He added his personal comment on this latest skirmish in the perennial battle between faith and reason:

The Mesmer Report is publish'd and makes a great deal of Talk. Everybody agrees that it is well written; but many wonder at the Force of Imagination describ'd in it, as occasioning Convulsions, etc. and some fear that Consequences may be drawn from it by Infidels to weaken our Faith in some of the Miracles of the New Testament ... Some think it will put an end to Mesmerism.

---

from Mesmer himself confirms that at some point Temple did belong to one of these societies. Whether he did it for fun, out of conviction, or because of the eternal urge of the young to spite the old is hard to tell.

But there is a wonderful deal of Credulity in the World, and
Deceptions as absurd have supported themselves for Ages.[27]

Shortly after submitting their public report, the commissioners wrote, exclusively for the King, a second one which
remained only in manuscript form for fifteen years. This
secret report dealt with the impact of animal magnetism on
matters of a sexual nature. With great emphasis, and not a
little condescension, it made the point that women, having
less stable nerves than men, a more inflammable imagination,
and a greater tendency to copy one another, were the pre-
destined victims of such a system. "Touch them in one point,
and you touch them everywhere," it said.[28] Hence, the
report concluded, the practice of magnetism should be
condemned on moral as well as medical grounds.

The first report had already dealt mesmerism a terrible
blow. An engraving of the time shows Franklin surrounded
by his colleagues and carrying the *Rapport*, whose rays cause
the baquet to overturn. A blindfolded, scantily draped woman
is about to fall from the trough, while people flee in confusion.
Mesmer and Deslon are flying away, on a broomstick and on
a winged donkey respectively. Still, Mesmer did not give up
immediately: as Franklin's secretary wrote to Temple, he
was now planning to magnetize horses in order to prove that
imagination played no part in the visible reactions he
provoked. But his fortunes kept declining, he left Paris, and
he died in obscurity in 1813. It is a pity that we do not know
Madame d'Houdetot's personal reaction to the whole problem.
If she discussed the matter at all with Franklin, it was only in
conversation.

The last of her messages to him before he left France was
pure hero worship:

My dear and respectable Doctor, in this world, where I have witnessed so much misfortune and oppression mixed with just a little happiness, my solace has been to offer my respect, my homage, the irresistible affection of a grateful heart to the great benefactors of humanity, those geniuses who have really enlightened and served it. You know what share belongs to you in these feelings of mine, and how happy and honored I am by your response.[29]

Such prose was noble and flowery enough, but Madame d'Houdetot could not restrain her poetic impulses, and she ended the letter with a little poem, in two versions – as if one were not enough. The poem was inspired by the fall of an

An American Eagle

eagle in Franklin's garden: Jupiter's bird had been sent to bring back the lightning to the gods, but Countess d'Houdetot besought Franklin, for humanity's sake, to keep the lightning in control. In the alternate version, she just assumed that the eagle, being the bird of lightning, could not help falling at Franklin's feet.

An eagle at Franklin's feet! The Doctor was certainly too courteous to tell the countess how he felt about the bird. In a letter to his daughter a few months earlier, he had expressed his disapproval of America's adopting the bald eagle, that useless, cowardly animal, as a national emblem. A much better choice, he felt, would have been that real American native, so full of good qualities – the turkey.

Cœffure
à l'Indépendance ou le
Triomphe de la liberté.

*Think how this must appear
among the Powdr'd Heads of Paris!* ❀ FRANKLIN

On the first day of spring in 1778, exactly fifteen months after
he had arrived in Paris, Franklin was received at Court. The
last few weeks had been eventful: the long hoped-for Treaty
of Commerce and Amity with France had been signed on
February 6, England had been officially informed of it on
March 13, and now, on the 20th, crowds had been gathering
since early morning in the courtyards of Versailles to see the
famous American and his fellow commissioners on their way
to the chambers of Louis XVI. This event has been most
vividly recorded for posterity by a man and by a woman.

The woman took note of what Franklin was wearing.
Being blind was no deterrent to old Madame du Deffand when
she wanted to please her friend Horace Walpole with a
graphic account of what was happening in high circles. From
the descriptions she heard, her practiced mind knew how to
sense the symbolism of clothes beyond the clothes themselves.
Franklin's striking simplicity did not escape her:

*Franklin wore a russet velvet coat, white stockings, his hair
hanging loose, his spectacles on his nose, and a white hat under
his arm. Is that white hat a symbol of liberty? One does not
know what title he will bear, but he will go to Court every
Tuesday, like all the other members of the diplomatic corps.*[1]

As for the man, the Duc de Croy was a veteran courtier
and kept his eye on the King:

*At noon ... the delegates from America were introduced. The
King, who had been in prayer, stopped and assumed a noble*

Coiffure à l'Indépendance, 1778

posture. M. de Vergennes introduced M. Franklin, M. Deane and M. Lee, and two other Americans. The King spoke first, with more care and graciousness than I have ever heard him speak. He said: "Firmly assure Congress of my friendship. I hope this will be for the good of the two nations." M. Franklin, very nobly, thanked him in the name of America, and said: "Your Majesty may count on the gratitude of Congress and its faithful observance of the pledges it now takes!" [2]

Madame du Deffand, who thought first of the social consequences of the event (and whose sympathies lay with the compatriots of her dear Walpole), went on to relate how the British Ambassador, Lord Stormont, had paid her a farewell call. The Duc de Croy, who had a political mind, indulged in bold speculation. "They" were now recognized, he mused, treated as a nation which could involve France in a war, and – you can never tell – might some day become larger than France herself and capable of subjugating Europe.

But Louis XVI, certainly not a prophet, took no special account of America's potential. According to a third witness of the reception – Arthur Lee, admittedly a perpetual grumbler – the King "had his hair undressed, hanging down on his shoulders; no appearance of preparation to receive us, nor any ceremony in doing it." Nevertheless he admitted that "the king appeared to speak with manly sincerity." Lee's brother, William, would not even concede that much: "The French say their King is as steady in adhering to his word, as our most gracious sovereign [George III]." [3]

At twenty-three, Louis XVI was already fat, sluggish, and predominantly passive. While siding instinctively with his fellow monarch George III, he had allowed himself to be pushed into a pro-American position by the anglophobia of his foreign minister, Vergennes, and by Franklin's quiet but inspired maneuvering. No wonder that the same words sounded so gracious to a French ear, so cool to an American one.

In the afternoon of that momentous day, Franklin and the other commissioners paid a call on the royal family. Marie-Antoinette bade him stand beside her, and whenever there was a lull in her gambling she spoke to him. His thoughts, in the intervals, may well have wandered back to his visit to Versailles eleven years earlier, when he had been received not by Louis XVI, but by Louis XV and his Queen, not as the representative of his beleaguered country, but in his own right as a glamorous scientist. He had been thrilled and flattered, in those days, to be invited to sit next to the Queen for no less a ceremony than *le grand couvert*, eating out of golden plates in full view of a crowd of spectators and answering the King's questions. Yet the journalist in him, ever alert, had been taking mental notes: the Queen did not apply her makeup in the same blatant way as the other women; Versailles was a mixture of magnificence and decay; the waterworks were in ill repair, many windows were broken. As for the King and Queen of France, they certainly were very kind, but "no Frenchman shall go beyond me in thinking my own king and queen the very best in the world, and the most amiable."[4]

In the course of those intervening years, Franklin's life had been racked by change. Now, in 1778, he was estranged from his king, his queen, his own son. His wife had died. His home had fallen in enemy hands. France, the very nation he had considered hostile during most of his active life, that he had branded "that intriguing Nation," was now his only hope.[5]

Those courtiers crowding around him, the rich and idle, a class he never felt comfortable with, were the people he would have to win over and please. And every Tuesday, unless countermanded by the King's secretary,[6] he would have to climb into his carriage, come to Versailles, aching or not, and submit to hours of the meaningless ritual dictated by etiquette. All this he now resolved to do.

An ambassador had to live up (or live down) to his position as a sort of inferior relative of the royal family, play the game of sharing the sorrows and joys of the Court. When a stern note from de Sequeville, "ordinary secretary of the King in charge of Messrs. the Ambassadors," instructed him that "the Court will take up grand mourning on occasion of the death of Empress Queen Maria Theresia; the Ambassadors and Foreign Ministers will dress their Personnel in black," he obliged.[7] In his diary, he recorded the gloomy ceremony as follows: "Dec. 26th (1780). Went to Versailles to assist at the ceremony of condolence on the death of the Empress Queen. All the foreign ministers in deep mourning – flopped hats and crape, long black cloaks, etc. The Nuncio pronounced the compliments to the king and afterwards to the queen in her apartments. – Much fatigued by the going twice up and down the palace stairs, from the tenderness of my feet and weakness of my knees; therefore did not go the rounds."[8]

It was much more pleasant to share the festive occasions, such as the birth of the heir to the throne, to whom Franklin duly went to pay his respects. But this, too, entailed some problems: how was he to express formally his ambassadorial joy? There is in his papers a painstakingly written unsigned note, perhaps the draft of a letter to Marie-Antoinette, which he never finished, perhaps a memo of the words he meant to read or memorize: "Je suis heureux, Madame, de cette Occasion de presenter à vôtre Majesté, les Respects et les Affections de toute [sic] les Etats de l'Amerique Septentrionale."[9]

Amid the crosscurrents of intrigue so treacherous in any court, Franklin steered a course of bland benevolence, diplomatic reserve, and, whatever his inner thoughts may have been, gratitude and respect toward the monarch. Adams thought him subservient on this point and said so, but Franklin was undeterred:

It is my intention, while I stay here, to procure what advantages I can for our country, by endeavouring to please this court; and I wish I could prevent anything being said by our countrymen here that may have a contrary effect.[10]

There is no evidence that either King or Queen ever went beyond official politeness in their dealings with him. Louis XVI may have privately enjoyed puttering in his workshop, Marie-Antoinette may have relished playing shepherdess, but the sight of a Minister Plenipotentiary who had really worked for a living and still made it a point to dress plainly was bound to be unpleasant to them. Franklin's nickname, "l'ambassadeur électrique," amused the Queen; but what could be so special about a man who, as she was informed by a courtier, had been "a printer's foreman" in his own country, and in France might have, in the best of cases, become a bookseller?[11] Engulfed as she was in class prejudice, she failed totally to sense his greatness. Her attitude is reflected in the patronizing tone adopted by two of the women who were closest to her: the court painter, Madame

Vigée-Lebrun, compared Franklin to a "stocky farmer"[12]; the lifelong lady-in-waiting, Madame Henriette de Campan, called him "un cultivateur américain."[13]

Dainty, fragile Madame Vigée-Lebrun, whose brush has immortalized the last moments of royal splendor in a series of sensitive faces haloed by masses of curls, was almost shocked by the "extreme simplicity" of Franklin's "straight, un-powdered hair, falling on his shoulders . . . in contrast with the other diplomats, all of them wearing powder, grand uniforms, and covered with gold and cordons."[14] Madame de Campan, who had access to inside information as only a lady-in-waiting would, tells us that the King grew so irritated at the mounting tide of Franklin worship that he presented Countess Diane de Polignac, one of the Doctor's most unbridled enthusiasts, with a Sèvres porcelain chamber pot displaying Franklin's portrait on its bottom.

As for Marie-Antoinette, Madame de Campan assures us that, of course, the Queen could not foresee that the American Revolution would spark a revolution in France and send her to her doom, but she felt uneasy, nevertheless, at the un-sportsmanlike means her country had adopted to hurt England by helping the rebels. Much of the same feelings were expressed by Madame du Deffand. In the sorrow provoked by the departure of her old friend, the English Ambassador, she wrote to Walpole: "I most sincerely curse that American negotiator, le Seigneur Franklin."[15]

Still, on the whole, the news of Franklin's being henceforth persona grata was greeted with enthusiasm. Even those who had not waited for the government's official sanction to welcome him into their homes felt some relief: "Now, finally, one could in all safety invite you to a concert and

Milord Stormont has yielded you his place!"[16] This happy exclamation by the Duc Louis-Alexandre de La Rochefoucauld d'Enville alludes to an incident that had taken place only a month before Franklin's reception at Court. The Duke's mother -- herself the great-granddaughter of the celebrated La Rochefoucauld, whose maxims are still quoted in France on all occasions not preempted by Voltaire – had invited Franklin to a concert at her house, and Franklin had accepted. On second thought, reflecting that these concerts were organized by subscription and that both Lord Stormont and his wife never failed to attend them, the duchess had felt it more advisable for Franklin to abstain and sent him her apologies. Franklin had answered that he "clearly saw the Impropriety of his appearing at the Concert"[17]; he could hardly wish to embarrass the hostess who, only three weeks after his arrival in Paris, had invited him for dinner. That invitation, for January 23, 1777, is the first letter from a woman among Franklin's papers of the Parisian period. The ensuing correspondence never slipped into gallantry but proceeded on the stately course that was proper with the prominent mother of a prominent son.

There was no joking, no easy give-and-take in this relationship. It was carried on in the traditional, rather lofty style that the French call *vieille France*, implying graciousness but also formality, mutual respect and admiration, but no intimacy. The duke had made Franklin's acquaintance many years earlier on a voyage to London, and he took great pride in having been the man who introduced Franklin to Turgot, almost as soon as the Doctor reached Paris. The day Turgot died, in 1781, Franklin's first thought was for the La Rochefoucaulds, as "he mingled his tears with theirs."[18]

If Madame Brillon's province was music, Chaumont's the world of business, the Le Veillard family's fun and gossip, Madame d'Houdetot's Franco–American rapprochement, the realm of the duchess de La Rochefoucauld and her son was political theory. The son knew English quite well and undertook, early in 1777, a translation of the constitutions of the thirteen states, as well as of other documents pertaining to the American Revolution, most of which appeared in the *Journal des Affaires de l'Angleterre et de l'Amérique*. At Franklin's prompting, he had been the first to translate the Declaration of Independence, a document explosive enough for the French Government to ban. It was, nevertheless, widely circulated. Franklin followed La Rochefoucauld's work closely, and a great quantity of notes went back and forth until certain subtleties of meaning had been completely elucidated. Soon, Franklin's grasp of French was good enough for him to sense that *habileté* was not an exact rendering of the English "industry" and to suggest *assiduité* in its place. [19] The duchess, who could read English although she did not speak it (a source of frustration, some years later, when Thomas Paine visited France and was her guest), took a lively interest in the proceedings, often borrowing pamphlets from Franklin and seeing to it that he met every interesting figure who came to her salon.

Widowed young, she had kept in touch with the best minds of her day and was always open to new, progressive ideas. She, too, had pioneered on her estates the cultivation of the potato; she had also attempted, though not too successfully, to improve the raising of silkworms – another of Franklin's pet projects. She corresponded with Voltaire, she befriended Adam Smith, she elicited the admiration of

Condorcet. More surprisingly, she was one of the few French women about whom John Adams did not have anything really hostile to say. He had met her at Turgot's house on his very first evening in Paris:

The Dutchess D'Anville ... and twenty others of the Great People of France were there. I thought it odd that the first Lady I should dine with in France should happen to be the Widow of our great Enemy who commanded a kind of Armada against Us,* within my Memory: But I was not the less pleased with her Conversation for that. She appeared to be venerable for her Years, and several of her Observations at Table, full as I thought of bold, masculine and original Sense were translated to me.[20]

Invited to the La Rochefoucauld mansion ten days later, and by then feeling somewhat worldly wise, Adams marveled at the power such people wielded. He could not repress one little barb, but it was directed more against the country in general than against his hosts:

Dined with the Dutchess D'Anville ... with a large Company of Dukes, Abbes and Men of Science and Learning among whom was Mr. Condorcet ... The Dutchess and her Son were said to have great influence with the Royal Academy of Science, to make members at pleasure, and the Secretary perpetual Mr. D'Alembert was said to have been of their Creation as was Mr. Condorcet afterwards ... This Family was beloved in France, and had a Reputation for Patriotism, that is of such Kind of Patriotism as was allowed to exist and be esteemed in that Kingdom.[21]

---

* The expedition of Acadia (Halifax) in 1746. Her husband was at the head of this campaign which was to win him his marshal's baton. But most of his squadron was captured, and he died shortly thereafter—of a broken heart, it is said.

Whether or not they really "made" members of the Academy, the duke and his mother leaned over backwards to avoid even the appearance of patronizing the self-made man from America. Franklin himself had become an academician long before La Rochefoucauld, who, after his own election, was gracious enough to write: "Permit me to take advantage of my membership in the Academy, which gives me the honor of being your *confrère*, to eliminate all formality from the veneration and the tender and sincere devotion I have pledged you for all my life."[22]

Franklin was not insensitive to this devotion. It was to La Rochefoucauld, as we have seen, that he entrusted the first copy of his Memoirs, the other one going to Le Veillard. The request for advice he had appended to the manuscript arrived too late to be answered. But the Memoirs supplied La Rochefoucauld with information and inspiration when, after Franklin's death, he pronounced one of the first of the many eulogies the French devoted to a foreigner so intimately connected, they felt, with their nation.[23] Unlike the others, this eulogy, remarkable for its sobriety and crisp detachment, was written very much in Franklin's own, unemotional style. (In the United States, on the contrary, only one eulogy was pronounced – a cool one delivered by William Smith, Franklin's antagonist during his lifetime.)

Underlying La Rochefoucauld's composure was a selfless idealism which led him to advocate almost passionately the abolition of the very privileges to which he and his mother owed their prestige and fortune. He took an active part in the *Assemblée des Notables* in 1787 and applauded the decree of 1788 granting a limited emancipation to non-Catholics; but he complained to Franklin that it did not go as far as the law of Virginia. Happily, the Etats Généraux were expected to meet soon, with broader powers and plans for reform: "if the meeting does take place, it will usher in a great age, for under the present condition of enlightenment, it must by the force of nature produce good results." [24] The good duke saw Liberty as a goddess, wearing the Phrygian cap as a philosophical halo, and treading the straight path to universal happiness.

But the Phrygian cap could also harbor wild, sanguinary instincts. In the Etats Généraux of 1789, the duke and other moderate idealists were overwhelmed by the radicals. Franklin, who from Philadelphia had followed with interest La Rochefoucauld's first steps away from the realm of theory and into the world of active politics, was spared the end of the story, how the gentle old duchess, about whom he never failed to enquire and who always sent her "tender regards," was to see her son stoned to death under her very eyes, in September 1792, by a frenzied revolutionary mob.

Franklin himself brought back to America a French-made Phrygian cap of Liberty, but it was a harmless golden pommel, which he was to bequeathe to the steady hand of George Washington with the following words:

My fine crab-tree walking stick, with a gold head curiously wrought in the form of a cap of liberty, I give to my friend, and the friend of mankind, General Washington. If it were a sceptre, he has merited it and would become it. [25]

Franklin had received it from one of his most fervent female admirers in France, along with the inevitable poem crammed with classical references – ranging, on this occasion, from Marathon to William Tell, and winding up with Trenton,

which in French rhymes so conveniently with Washington.
Franklin liked the poem well enough to have it printed and
the stick well enough not to lose it, as he had the one the lady
had given him previously. But she did not mind his losing it.
She liked giving him presents. How else could she keep
herself fresh in his mind when they were parted? "Forgive me
those little tricks," she wrote in a note accompanying the
gift of a pair of scissors. "They are prompted by my heart's
best interest; they are the only tricks I am capable of; now,
you see, whether you are changing your shirt, taking a walk,
or writing, you are forced to think of me."[26]

Franklin, in his answer, listed more good reasons to think
of her:

*It is true that I can now neither walk abroad nor write at home
without having something that may remind me of your Goodness
towards me; you might have added, that I can neither play at
Chess nor drink Tea without the same Sensation: but these had
slipt your Memory. There are People who forget the Benefits they
receive, Madame de Forbach only those she bestows.*[27]

Feeling, at this point, that he may have waxed too lyrical,
he crossed out the sentence that followed: "That Impression
will remain as long as the Heart on which it is stamped." On
the whole, the draft of his heavily corrected and rewritten
thank-you note, though, being in English, it offered no
grammatical problem, shows Franklin working hard to
convey a precise blend of affection and respect.

The lady in question always signed herself "M: Comtesse
de Forbach, Duchesse Douairière du Duc de Deux-Ponts."
Since the small principality of Deux-Ponts, or Zweibrücken,
in what would now be the region of the Saar, on the Franco–

German border, was a sovereign state, this would have made the dowager duchess the highest ranking of Franklin's titled friends, had it not been for one unfortunate flaw: old Duke Christian de Deux-Ponts Birkenfeld had never contracted with her more than a morganatic alliance – no doubt because she was not of noble blood and, in her young days, had been a dancer by the name of Marianne Camasse. Consequently, their two sons were barred from dynastic succession, and it passed to a cousin of theirs, brother of King Maximilian of Bavaria.

This state of affairs is never even alluded to in Franklin's correspondence. (After all, his own marriage had never been more than a common law one, without religious or civil ceremony. To avoid possible charges of bigamy, since her widowhood was not an absolute certainty, Deborah had simply come to live with Franklin and adopted his name.) He was grateful to the countess for her early and genuine support of the American Revolution – she called herself "one of your friends, more American than all the Americans in the world" [28] – especially as her connections with Germany might spread good will beyond the French frontiers. Indeed, it was under her roof that the first points of a commercial agreement between the United States and Bavaria were discussed.

When her nephew, Fontevieux, a boy of eighteen, decided to cross the seas, she not only gave him moral support (against his own parents) but financed his trip and sent him money during his first months as a volunteer in the New World. Although stoic about the possibility of the young man's dying for liberty, she worried about his welfare in the meantime, and enrolled Lafayette's cooperation in helping

him handle his money, as well as Franklin's in getting messages and packages over to him. Fontevieux, incidentally,
did not die in the American Revolution, where he fought
bravely, but perished on the scaffold in his own country,
accused of counterrevolutionary activities.

In 1780, it was the turn of Madame de Forbach's own two
sons, Christian and William, to go and fight for America
with their regiment of Deux-Ponts. They both distinguished
themselves at Yorktown where William, who later published
an interesting *Journal* of his campaigns, was wounded. He
appears in the picture of the surrender of Cornwallis, painted
by Trumbull, that now hangs in the Capitol Rotunda.

To escape the ennui of what she called "her hut" (her
seignorial mansion in the provincial town of Forbach), the
countess spent a few months in Paris each year. Whenever
she came to the capital, she plunged into a whirlwind of
activity, referred to cryptically as "mes affaires," bustled
around Versailles, attended the Opera, gave some intimate
soirées and a number of dinner parties – at a typical one,
Franklin was promised the company of the ambassadors from
Sweden and Spain. Once, she lured the Doctor to a quiet
celebration of Easter with a few chosen friends and relatives.
There would be tea, she said, for the older generation,
something stronger for the young, and would Franklin keep
in mind that playing chess with her would be the best
Christian deed for such a holy day?

Madame de Forbach was assisted in her various activities
by a Chevalier Agathon de Keralio who had been her
children's tutor and now functioned as her "private secretary,"
a title vague enough to cover a multitude of occupations.
Keralio's devotion to the countess can be gauged by the

adjectives he uses to refer to her: "celestial" was one of the more sedate. Of course, he soon became one of Franklin's most assiduous propagandists.

Keralio turned out to be a useful man to have on one's side, for apart from serving the countess, he was an inspector of the military schools of the kingdom, which he toured once a year. From every coastal town he visited, he would send Franklin detailed information on ship movements, prizes, captures, and the English blockade. Since Franklin, among his many tasks, functioned as unofficial head of American naval operations in Europe, these scraps of news, carefully preserved in his files under the headings of Intelligence from Brest, Toulon, Bordeaux, etc., must have given him a clear picture of a maritime situation he could not possibly have inspected himself. Furthermore, wherever he was, Keralio would spread the word that the colonies were winning the war, that it was good policy to trade with them, and that the English reports were nothing but lies. With his reputation of being close to the source of American news, and Franklin did keep him informed of every development, Keralio had no difficulty in inserting the right items in the few but influential newspapers of the day. Whereas Keralio referred jokingly to his intelligence work as "sending news, whether true or false,"[29] the propaganda he called "preaching the faith" and took very seriously.[30] As a reward, when Franklin had medals struck to celebrate the end of hostilities in 1783, Keralio was given a number of them for distribution, thereby gaining prestige in the eyes of friends and colleagues.

After a number of parties in honor of the two young Deux-Ponts who had come back from the United States, "their brow darkened with laurels," and were being feasted by "les Américains Français,"[31] Keralio embarked on what was to be his last tour of inspection. His duties took him to a school in Brienne (Champagne), where he noticed a fourteen-year-old boy, small for his age, but gifted for mathematics, if somewhat slow in Latin. Feeling that the lad would make a good sailor, Keralio recommended him for immediate schooling in Paris, in spite of the teachers' opinions, and even placed his name at the head of the honor list. His name? A tongue twister: Napoleon Buonaparte. And good Keralio, who prided himself on his knowledge of men, summed up his protégé's best features in a striking formula: a docile character.

Comtesse de Forbach was not Franklin's only contact with Germany. When he needed some letters translated from the German, he turned to a Baroness de Bourdic. The eager lady undertook the task in a rash moment; when confronted with the actual text, she remembered that she had left Germany at the age of four and that her German was rusty. But she struggled, as she confessed, for three weeks over an assignment that should have taken three hours, produced a translation, and immediately claimed her fee: another visit with Franklin.

Born Marie-Anne Henriette Payan de l'Etang, the baroness, married at that time to the second of her three husbands, was a *femme de lettres* of some repute. Although she professed to write only for her friends, most of the poems she turned out with remarkable facility found their way into the *Almanachs des Muses*. Best known of all and best liked by Chateaubriand, was her "Ode to Silence," which may well have pleased Franklin, himself a man of few words. Over the years, she solicited various favors from him for various friends, but, most of all, she wanted to be included in his circle.

She succeeded, and a poem published by an anonymous admirer of hers in the *Journal de Paris* explains how. Who, asked the author, could imagine that a pretty woman, the toast of Paris, would spend her time at the altar of philosophy, drink tea with a white-haired Doctor, nay a "Quakre," while the ball, the opera, the theater were kept waiting? Thank heavens for the many decades between the Nestor from Philadelphia and his lovely disciple! Had he been her age, Franklin would have been too electrified by her charms to tame lightning, too enslaved by her beauty to become "l'apôtre de la liberté." [32]

Less adept as an intellectual partner, but much more proficient in German was the former Wilhelmina von Mosheim, a beautiful girl from Göttingen who had married the Russian Count Alexander Golowkin and shared with him a sumptuous house in Paris. The daughter of a theologian, she chose Rousseau as her spiritual guide. On Rousseau's advice, her children were fed on milk and vegetables, and in the morning had to run straight from their bed and jump into a bath of cold water. Such a régime, we are told, made them strong and beautiful. [33]

Toward herself, the Countess was less spartan. Like a good many women who had read *La Nouvelle Héloïse* too hastily, she lived up to her conception of the novel by devoting respectful affection to her husband, but much warmer feelings to a host of other men. The man who filled her thoughts during Franklin's stay in Passy was the Chevalier de Chastellux, one of those versatile people that the eighteenth century produced in such abundance: philosopher, economist, poet, and major-general in Rochambeau's Expeditionary Corps in America. In her distress at the Chevalier's departure, Countess Golowkin turned unashamedly to Franklin. She was "trembling for the life of her *ami*" with whom she was "*intimement liée.*" Would Franklin, who had a "sensitive soul," condescend to give her news from Chastellux and convey her own tender messages to him?[34]

She was young, pretty, kittenish: "mon cher Papa," "mon bon Papa," "mon bon et cher Papa," "je vous embrasse tendrement," "je vous souhaite un petit bonjour," "je vous embrasse mille fois . . .". Franklin could not resist her pleas, however indiscreet. Whenever alarming rumors about the French Corps threw her into a panic, he reassured her. He placed in the American diplomatic pouch the letters she entrusted to his care and took the initiative in forwarding any information that reached him: "I have just received a News paper from Philadelphia, dated Decemr. 5. wherein there is a Paragraph that I know must give you Pleasure, as it shows that our Friend was then well."[35]

Soon, she fell into the habit of asking him for other favors: the loan of a French–English dictionary, the loan of his carriage (without horses), the loan of the *Philosophical Transactions* of the London Academy, or of Rousseau's *Romances*. She paid him back by singing one of his favorite arias, "Dieu d'Amour," by acting as his "faithful interpreter," by coquetting with him, by sending him a sprightly description of the fascinating man she had just met: Rousseau's Persian cousin, no less. Rousseau's father had a brother who had established himself in Persia as clockmaker of the seraglio and had married a local girl. Their son, remarkably gifted for languages, had become consul of the French King at Bassora and created a sensation when he visited Paris in early 1782:

He is only 41 years old and it is amazing to hear how much he has traveled. Upon seeing him, I was reminded of the Chinese mode of dressing. I counted four petticoats on him: a pink one, a brown one, a yellow one, and a flame-colored one, and surely there must have been more below those. His headdress is no less extraordinary; and then, there is his mustache, not to be forgotten.[36]

It was all very lighthearted and carefree, between Franklin and Countess Golowkin. Stepping out of his role of Cupid, the Doctor once wrote to Chastellux: "Dare I confess to you that I am your rival with Madame G——? I need not tell you that I am not a dangerous one."[37] Chastellux, it seems, would not have minded too much. Although Madame Golowkin had become a widow during his absence, he did not marry her; he married instead, some years later, a penniless Irish girl. His *Voyage en Amérique septentrionale* is one of the best books on America before Tocqueville's.

Eventually, the countess, too, found a second husband, but under tragic circumstances. The man she married in exile in Geneva, the duc d'Ayen, formerly one of the most powerful noblemen of the realm, had lost his wife and one of his daughters on the scaffold, in 1794. Another daughter, Adrienne, barely escaped the guillotine, but was saved, probably through the intervention of the American Ambassador to Paris during the Revolution, Gouverneur Morris. For if, on her father's side she had a prestigious name, and on her mother's side was a Noailles, in American eyes her married name of Marquise Gilbert de Lafayette outshone all others.

It was an irony of fate that Wilhelmina Golowkin should become Adrienne de Lafayette's stepmother. They were at opposite ends of the spectrum. Madame Golowkin was a demanding woman, flighty and volatile in temperament, and she led, by worldly standards, a successful life. Madame de Lafayette was all self-denial, abnegation, loyalty, and her life was tragic.

At the time of her first letters to Franklin, Madame de Lafayette was seventeen. She had been married three years to the provincial, gawky, red-headed boy her father had chosen, and she was madly in love with him. She had already had a miscarriage, born him a daughter, and was pregnant with another child. Lafayette, at nineteen, was, through various inheritances, one of the richest men in France. He was already unfaithful to his pious young wife, hardly ever stayed at home, had left for America without taking leave from her, but never failed to write tenderly and call her "mon cher coeur." Whereas he was bent on proving himself, on making his mark, she, like her mother, lived in the pure Christian tradition of austerity and self-effacement.

Madame de Lafayette's personality, so poignantly recreated by André Maurois in his *Adrienne*, shines through the few humble, apologetic notes she sent to Franklin. Written in a cramped, childish hand, couched in the words of a very young girl addressing herself shyly to a celebrity, they deal exclusively with her husband's welfare, his mail, and his needs. The wife who would put up with his mistresses, his debts, his vacillating political ideas; who would bask briefly in his glory, then join him in jail; strive to save part of the fortune he squandered, and wait until her deathbed to confess, at the age of forty-eight, the depth of her passion for him: that future wife is in germ here, in those hesitant little letters.

Franklin, with his marvelous knack of adjusting his style to that of his correspondent, answered her gently, respectfully. Only once did he risk a little joke, and then it was in a letter to her husband. On September 17, 1782, Lafayette sent a hurried note to Franklin, telling him of the birth of a new daughter, two months premature, but healthy, adding: "Every Child of Mine that Comes to light is a Small Addition to the Number of American Citizens," [38] and stating that the baby would be christened Virginia, in honor both of the saint and of the American state bearing that name. Good Anglo-Saxon Protestant that he was, Franklin did not pay much attention to the Catholic requirement of saintly patronymics, but had the following suggestion:

In naming your Children I think you do well to begin with the most antient State. And as we cannot have too many of so good a Race I hope you and Mme de la Fayette will go thro the Thirteen. But as that may be in the common Way too severe a Task for her delicate Frame, and Children of Seven Months may become as Strong as those of Nine, I consent to the Abridgement of Two Months for each; and I wish her to spend the Twenty-six Months so gained, in perfect Ease, Health and Pleasure.

While you are proceeding, I hope our States will some of them new-name themselves. Miss Virginia, Miss Carolina, and Miss Georgiana will sound prettily enough for the Girls; but Massachusetts and Connecticut are too harsh even for the Boys, unless they were to be Savages. [39]

Such a prospect might discourage anyone. The Lafayettes had no more children after Virginia. But when, on Christmas Eve 1779, their only son was born and Adrienne had found the appearance of that living image of Lafayette reason enough for "America to celebrate with an illumination,"[40] the first thought of the father had been to inform Franklin, in the middle of the night, that the son was to be christened George Washington. Even this name was a tongue-twister for the French, as witnessed by the great variety of ways they spelled it, but Lafayette "and his Lady," according to John Adams, were the only two people in Paris who knew how to pronounce it.[41]

In 1779, the marquis had the idea of highlighting the Fourth of July celebration at Franklin's Passy headquarters by the display of Washington's portrait; the general was represented as holding the Franco–American treaty in his hand and trampling upon King George's tyrannical decrees. But Lafayette, as usual, was unable to attend, and Adrienne – serious, tense, a little unbending – represented him. The small American colony paid tribute to her, and someone wrote bad verse in her honor.

She was much more at ease in the privacy of her home, which soon became the rallying point of the friends of America in Paris. There are among Franklin's papers several invitations to dine with the Lafayettes, one of them printed in English. The family's children, contrary to custom, mingled with the guests, and the Iroquois boy, Kayenlaha, brought back from America by Lafayette, performed the songs and dances of his tribe. After the cessation of hostilities in 1783, the young hero took mischievous delight in gathering, at a dinner party, a number of Englishmen headed by the

Marquis de la Fayette's
Compliments Wait upon
His Excellency M. Franklin and
Begs the Honour of His
Company at Dinner on
Monday —————————— next

Paris the 26. April 1785.

The favour of an Answer is Requested

Invitation to dinner from Marquis de Lafayette

younger Pitt, and a number of rebels headed by his dear "docteur."

With such avant-garde aristocrats Franklin communicated in an atmosphere so pleasant and relaxed that the difference in social background did not matter much, and the contrast between their elaborate elegance and his own deliberate simplicity merely amused him. To an English woman friend, he wrote:

I know you wish you could see me; but as you can't, I will describe myself to you. Figure me in your mind as jolly as formerly, and as strong and hearty, only a few years older; being very plainly dress'd, wearing my thin gray strait hair, that peeps out from under my only coiffure, *a fine Fur Cap, which comes down to my Forehead almost to my spectacles. Think how this must appear among the Powder'd Heads of Paris! I wish every gentleman and lady in France would only be so obliging as to follow my Fashion, comb their own Heads as I do mine, dismiss their* Friseurs, *and pay me half the Money they paid to them. You see, the gentry might well afford this, and I could then enlist those* Friseurs, *who are at least 100,000, and with the Money I would maintain them, make a Visit with them to England, and dress the Heads of your Ministers and Privy Councillors; which I conceive to be at present* un peu dérangées.[42]

He was joking, of course, but the waste of flour on French coiffures at a time when bread was scarce aggravated him. Condorcet recalls him as having remarked sarcastically to Turgot:

You have, in France, an excellent way of waging war without spending any money. All you have to do is to agree not to get

your hair curled and not to use powder as long as it will last.
Your hairdressers will make up the army; their pay will come
from your savings, and their food from the grain you usually
devote to the making of hair powder.[43]

As a matter of fact, all but the lower classes at that time
powdered their hair very heavily – even men in the military.
Ladies wore extravagantly high headdresses and kept them
in good order with a lavish spraying of starch; at night, the
whole architecture was wrapped in white muslin. Truly
great occasions demanded an extra touch. In July 1782, when
the Baroness d'Oberkirch was invited to Court, she concealed
in her powdered hair small vials of water for the fresh
flowers sprouting from it. The desired effect: "Springtime
in the midst of snow." [44]

Franklin noted with satisfaction that fashions in the
aristocratic circles at Court were a trifle less exaggerated than
they were outside Paris. At the first ball to greet his arrival,
"at Nantes there were no heads less than five, and a few were
seven, lengths of the face above the top of the forehead."
But, he added, "yesterday we dined at the Duke de Rochefoucault's, where there were three duchesses and a countess,
and no head higher than a face and a half." [45]

Altogether, what annoyed Franklin was not what he
dismissed as "harmless Frivolities," but the idleness that
often went with them.[46] Toward the loafer he was harsh.
During the months of greatest activity of his Passy press in
early 1784, he composed and printed, both in English and in
French, a little didactic piece entitled *Information to Those who*
would Remove to America. Intended to warn the French
would-be immigrants that the new country offered good

A royal banquet, January 23, 1782, drawn by J. M. Moreau the younger

opportunities only to those already possessed of skills and willing to work hard, the *Information* was mostly serious, but derived some comic relief from the following taunt at a certain class of the nobility:

[*The Americans*] *are pleas'd with the Observation of a Negro ... that* Boccarorra (*meaning the Whiteman*) *make de Blackman workee, make de Horse workee, make de Ox workee, make ebery ting workee; only de Hog. He, de Hog, no workee; he eat, he drink, he walk about, he go to sleep when he please,* he libb like a Gentleman.

The original manuscript added another stinging sentence: "He no good for noting until he dead; den he bery good – *to cut up*." But Franklin omitted the sentence in the printed edition, perhaps because he thought it might be interpreted as expressing contempt for the gentlemen who gave their lives for America.

In another passage of the same pamphlet, where Franklin was speaking in his earnest American voice, he said:

Much less is it advisable for a Person to go thither who has no other Quality to recommend him but his Birth. In Europe it has indeed its Value, but it is a Commodity that cannot be carried to a worse Market than to that of America, where People do not enquire concerning a Stranger, What is he? *but* What can he do? [47]

There is in woman a light-hearted gaiety that dissipates the sadness of man ✠ BERNARDIN DE SAINT PIERRE

What can he do? Among Franklin's fellow members at the Paris Academy of Sciences, there were plenty of people who were "doing," indeed who were reshaping the physical and spiritual world of man. The long-lasting attachments he formed with some of his younger colleagues followed the usual pattern: scientific dialogue with the husband; social relaxation with the couple; affectionate jesting with the wife.

Such was the case with the Lavoisiers. Antoine-Laurent Lavoisier, the creator of modern chemistry, was in his mid-thirties when Franklin arrived in Paris, and already famous. His wife, Marie-Pierrette, who like Madame de Lafayette had been married at fourteen, was at twenty an accomplished hostess and her husband's assistant in the laboratory. Franklin and Lavoisier promptly came together through their common passion for chemistry. Separately, they had investigated many of the same topics: weather, thunder, aurora borealis, the nature of air and gases. Jointly, they now moved on to a subject still chemical, but heavy with political implications: the manufacture of gunpowder and of its prime constituent, saltpeter. Lavoisier, who, like Franklin, preferred combining pure research with business and public life, acted both as Farmer-General and Superintendent of Explosives (*régisseur des poudres*). The *Fermiers-Généraux* were the members of a company of financiers who bought from the Government the right to collect and keep certain taxes and customs duties. Jacques Paulze, Marie-Pierrette's father, was also a

Ascension of Montgolfier balloon, September 19, 1783

Farmer-General and had known Lavoisier as a younger colleague before choosing him as a son-in-law.

Franklin was interested not only in securing ammunition, and especially saltpeter which was in scarce supply in America – hence his courtship of Lavoisier the *régisseur des poudres* – but also in finding the means of exporting the precious stuff, regulated by the stringent rules applying to royal monopolies – hence his courtship of Lavoisier the Farmer-General. In return, he helped Lavoisier draw up plans for making the powder magazine of the Arsenal (where the Lavoisiers both lived and worked) as safe as possible and conferred upon the up-and-coming young scientist the immense prestige of his intimacy and admiration.

As time went by, the bonds grew tighter. There was the joint investigation on mesmerism. There was a consultation, on Franklin's part, about the humble but important problem of a safe way to have his cooking pots tin-plated. Far from asking for his wife's opinion on this domestic problem, Lavoisier turned to his colleagues at the Academy, and came up with the answer that only pure tin would really do. This was scholarly, but also discouraging, since most boilermakers in Paris mixed tin with a large amount of lead, "thus covering one poison with another equally dangerous poison."[1] The only hope was to find an honest man and not to haggle with him over the price.

The Lavoisiers gave a number of lively dinner parties, with the company made up mostly of physicists and chemists – such as the Portuguese monk-scientist Joachim de Magalhaens, or Magellan (a descendant of the explorer), who often came in from London with the latest news from across the Channel. After dinner, Lavoisier would entertain his guests by performing some tricky experiment, or there would be music, or Madame, who had studied painting with the famous Jacques-Louis David, sat and sketched.

One sample of her work can still be seen in a private house in Princeton, New Jersey. It is an oil portrait of Franklin – much in the manner of the classic Duplessis – which she painted and sent the Doctor after his return to Philadelphia, keeping a duplicate for herself. On October 23, 1788, he wrote to thank her. He was eighty-two by then, but could still pepper his nostalgia with humor:

I have a long time been disabled from writing to my dear Friend, by a severe Fit of the Gout, or I should sooner have return'd my Thanks for her very kind Present of the Portrait, which she has herself done me the honour to make of me. It is allow'd by those who have seen it to have great Merit as a Picture in every

Lavoisier and his wife in their laboratory

*Respect; but what particularly endears it to me, is the Hand
that drew it. Our English Enemies when they were in Possession
of this City and of my House, made a Prisoner of my Portrait
and carried it off with them; leaving that of its Companion, my
Wife, by itself, a kind of Widow: You have replaced the
Husband; and the Lady seems to smile, as well pleased.*

He went on to say that he liked much "young M. Dupont,"
meaning Victor du Pont de Nemours, who had recently
emigrated to America, and whose younger brother, Eleuthère
Irénée, would soon import to Delaware the gunpowder
manufacturing techniques learned from Lavoisier, his
"adoptive father." Franklin also told Madame Lavoisier how,
in spite of the warmth and affection he had found in the midst
of his family, Paris still glowed in his mind:

*Yet all do not make me forget Paris and the nine Years Happi-
ness I enjoy'd there, in the sweet Society of a People, whose
Conversation is instructive, whose Manners are highly pleasing,
and who above all the Nations of the World, have in the greatest
Perfection the Art of making themselves belov'd by Strangers.*[2]

After thanking her husband for the books he had sent,
Franklin extended wishes for their joint happiness: "and I
think I cannot wish you and him greater Happiness than a
long Continuance of the Connexion."

The "Connexion" was to be brutally interrupted a few
years later, in 1794. The story of Lavoisier's downfall, one
of the most tragic blunders of the French Revolution,
displays the classic mixture of famous quotations and counter-
quotations ("The Republic has no need of scientists" –
"Only a moment to cut off that head, and a hundred years
may not give us another one like it"[3]), of human cowardice

(his colleagues did not lift a finger on his behalf), and of melodrama: his attractive young wife, it was rumored, might have saved him, had she shown the proper submissiveness toward his accuser, Antoine Dupin, but she chose what is commonly known as the path of honor. Her father and her husband were sent to the scaffold together, along with the other Farmers-General, who had all become odious symbols of the ancien régime, regardless of their personal honesty and competence.

Within the next few weeks she lost all her fortune, her furniture, his books, his equipment, and was herself thrown in jail. But the Terror had spent itself by then and Madame Lavoisier eventually recovered her liberty and most of her possessions. Several men wanted to marry her, Pierre Samuel du Pont de Nemours (father of Victor and Eleuthère Irénée), among others. She chose a well-known if somewhat enigmatic scientist, Massachusetts-born Benjamin Thompson, who had sided with the British during the American Revolution and had been created Count von Rumford by the Elector of Bavaria. They separated after four unhappy years.

The Lavoisier ménage, a happy one, came to a tragic end. Another of Franklin's closest scientific friends and collaborators, Jean-Baptiste Le Roy, survived the French Revolution, but did not get along very well with his wife – though Franklin managed to keep on excellent terms with both. The wife, who must have been diminutive – Franklin called her his little pocket wife, *ma petite femme de poche* – was one of the tea-serving ladies John Adams accused of contributing to the old Doctor's "discipation." As for the husband, he belonged to one of those marvelously gifted families (gifted in the

Franklinian sense, with an inventive, practical turn of mind) that seem to have sprung up in such abundance during the last decades of the eighteenth century.

His own father, Julien, had been the first Frenchman to equal and surpass the English in the burgeoning art of clockmaking; in recognition of his talents, he had been appointed clockmaker to the King and lived at the Louvre. The oldest son, Pierre, followed in the father's footsteps and perfected a marine timekeeper of extraordinary accuracy which fascinated Franklin. Another son, Charles, made a name for himself in medicine, and, on Franklin's recommendation, was elected to the Royal Academy in London. Still another, Julien-David, an architect, won a prize for his work on Greek and Roman building. Also inspired by antiquity was his project for a new kind of boat – the *naupotame* – designed to navigate both on seas and rivers, "from Paris to Philadelphia." [4] Though Franklin greeted the idea with enthusiasm and secured its author's election to the American Philosophical Society, the naupotame, for lack of funds, sank in a sea of indifference.

And finally, there was Jean-Baptiste, who devoted his life to electricity. Electricity brought him in touch with Franklin as far back as 1753, long before they met. Le Roy, together with some other scientists, undertook to defend Franklin's first electrical theories in the face of the violent attack of the Abbé Nollet in Paris. The friendship that blossomed between them as a consequence of this alliance was to last for almost forty years, sustained and nourished by an enormous number of letters – enough to fill a book.

After a formal beginning, their correspondence soon settled into the comfortable, relaxed manner of two old cronies, with notes hurriedly scribbled in French, English, or a mixture of both. Its range was vast, covering such diverse topics as the nature of water, free trade, comets, hospitals, expeditions to the North Pole, how to install a lightning rod on the cathedral of Strasbourg, optical glass, and so on. They exchanged innumerable books, periodicals, remedies, addresses, and electrical machines. Most important of all, it was through Le Roy, in charge of the King's laboratory at the Château de la Muette, that Franklin met the scientific world of Paris, both the proper Academicians and the dilettantes, such as Jean-Paul Marat.*

And Madame Le Roy, what was she doing in the midst of all this intellectual effervescence? Madame Le Roy, though herself a close relative of the Comte de Milly, a member of the Academy of Sciences, took no interest at all in the work carried out by the men around her. In the bevy of sophisticated, musical, philosophical or simply adoring women who surrounded Franklin, she strikes a different, almost refreshing note: she is a grumbler. She feels neglected, slighted, ignored, and her loud protest – that her husband does not devote enough time to her – gives her a strikingly modern appeal.

On one occasion, she was literally left out in the cold – or, rather, in the rain – and then not even for the sake of the advancement of physics, but because her husband and Franklin were having such a good time playing chess late into the night. Under stress, Madame Le Roy's spelling,

---

* Marat in the 1770s was a far cry from the sanguinary pamphleteer he was to become. As an amateur physicist, he kept pressing Franklin to witness his experiments on the nature of fire and give them the stamp of his approval, for he felt persecuted. But Franklin was lukewarm toward the whole project and never invoked the gout as often as during those weeks in 1779.

shaky at best, disintegrates completely and becomes so in-
coherent and phonetic that it may have looked to Franklin
like a French version of his own Deborah's English:

*I could not be more offended, my dear papa, by the trick you
played on us by keeping Mr. Le Roy late last night and in
closing the door so cruelly on me. I shall not expose myself
anymore to a kind of joke you would not inflict on any other
woman of your entourage, especially in that weather. You must
not doubt my desire to do anything that is agreable to you, and if
you had told me that you wanted still another game, I would
have consented with pleasure, even though it was already eleven
o'clock, and dining at that hour is bad for women whose health is
frail.*

At this point, identifying with all frail, put-upon women,
she shifts to the plural, while her style, spelling, and syntax
become more chaotic than ever:

*But since they are not selfish, they will lend themselves to any-
thing that can be pleasurable to the company, disregarding their
own wellbeing and happiness. As I don't often enjoy the privilege
of seeing Mr. Le Roy, it is only natural that I should want to
have supper with him; It is the only time that he gives me and it
happens too seldom for me not to be afflicted when I am cheated
of his presence. Thank you for the umbrella. I am sending it
back.*[5]

What a pity that Franklin's answer to this unique scolding
has not been preserved!

Even on her best days, Madame Le Roy sounds edgy and
defensive. She may raise her bids for affection to the incestu-
ously mixed formula: "the little pocket wife begs her papa
to accept a good and tender kiss," but in the same breath she

pointedly asks to be introduced to a certain couple "so that she can be a member of the party."[6] When Franklin invites the Le Roys for dinner but fails to send a reminder and provide for transportation, she asks whether it "would be an indiscretion to come; if we have made no mistake could you let us know and help us come without getting wet or covered with mud as the weather is awful."[7] To uplift this depressed creature, nothing short of air transportation will do. Such transportation was in fact forthcoming, and it is worth spending some time recalling the steps through which the air age came for Franklin and the Le Roy ménage.

In our own dawn of the space age, the saga of the first balloons comes very much alive. Here is a preview of our excitement, our frustrations, our doubts, the physical euphoria of floating, the second sunset within a day, the spiritual ecstasy of success. Here, on a touchingly small scale, are our problems: is man capable of living and functioning at such altitudes? Will the new discovery be put to peaceful or to warlike uses? Is humanity ready for it?

The pace of the first ascensions is truly breathtaking. On June 5, 1783, the Montgolfier brothers, Joseph and Etienne, paper manufacturers, sent up from Annonay, near Lyons, a balloon made of paper-lined linen. It rose to a height of almost 6,000 feet and covered a horizontal distance of 7,200 feet. What kind of lifting force they used was not divulged.

Paris, of course, started clamoring for an encore right in the capital. The Montgolfier brothers began making preparations, but before they were ready, another balloon, based on a different principle and launched by a different person, had already left the ground. The date was August 27, the place was the Champ de Mars, the balloon was made of oiled silk, the "inflammable air" (hydrogen) that carried it up was produced by pouring oil of vitriol over iron filings, the inventor was the physicist Jacques Charles, and the success was spectacular. In spite of a downpour, stoically endured by the crowd, the balloon, made still more beautiful by its being wet and shiny, as Franklin observed, stayed aloft for forty-five minutes. It fell ten miles away, in the village of Gonesse, whose terror-stricken inhabitants promptly destroyed it with pitchforks.

Not to be outdone, the Montgolfier brothers worked feverishly on their second balloon, which was being assembled by one of the most eager teams in history in the gardens of M. Réveillon, faubourg St. Antoine. One night a violent storm destroyed it. A new one was put together in four days, and, in the presence of the royal family, a sheep, a duck, and a rooster, left the earth. They came down unharmed, except for a scratch on the rooster's wing, after an eight-minute flight. This marked the end of the trial period. Soon it would be the turn of men . . . and of women.

Of course, no scientific breakthrough would be complete without both intramural and international rivalry, respectively hampering and stimulating its pace. In the case of early aeronautics, the international rivalry was between France and England. With just a trace of malice, Franklin kept Sir Joseph Banks, President of the Royal Society in London, pitilessly informed of every step the French were making. Finally, Sir Joseph, in an answer bristling with polite exasperation, acknowledged that "your friends across the water" might well be ahead in actual practice, but that England kept an undeniable theoretical lead.[8] The intramural conflict – and a vicious one it was – pitted the partisans of the Montgolfier brothers (who, it was now announced, used rarefied air, produced by burning straw and wool) against those of Charles (who filled his balloons with more expensive and more powerful hydrogen). In his usual mood of conciliation, Franklin tried to make peace by suggesting that the balloon was a baby, of which Montgolfier was the father and Charles the wet nurse.[9]

There was an eighteenth-century flavor to this race, a sense of fun, an elegant mixture of formality and nonchalance, an emphasis on the individual, all unthinkable in the modern age of the scientific team. As much time was spent on decorating the balloons – with gilded eagles and garlands, with fleurs-de-lys, with the signs of the zodiac and the King's monogram – as on building them.

The next one to go up, on October 17 (a montgolfière), was a splendid affair, the largest yet. Meant to remain captive, it boasted a novelty – a wicker basket hanging below and a

Observing the Ephemera by Night

separate place for the straw-burning apparatus. For the first time, a man soared above the earth and looked down upon Paris. His first thought, he tells us, was: "What a wondrous sight!" His second: "How priceless this would be during a battle." [10]

The real turning-point occurred on November 20, 1783. While a record crowd cheered and a record number of women fainted, the first two aeronauts – Pilâtre de Rozier and the Marquis d'Arlandes – wearing frock coats and duly furnished with champagne, were launched from the Château de la Muette on man's first free trip through the air. A delightful touch of bravado and amateurishness pervaded the venture. The Marquis d'Arlandes candidly recalled that he was so busy waving his handkerchief to the people of Paris that his companion had to remind him a little sternly: "Eh bien, mon cher ami, du feu!" whereupon the Marquis quickly threw some straw on the fire and the balloon lurched upward. As they hovered above the Seine, they noticed that the water gave off an echo and regretted not having brought along their flutes. And finally, when after twenty minutes they stopped feeding the fire and came down, Pilâtre de Rozier, whose frock coat had been ripped during the landing maneuvers, absolutely refused to parade through Paris in such an unbecoming state; he let his companion ride alone to the acclaim awaiting at the Muette. The following evening, the Marquis and Montgolfier called on Franklin. Along with Le Roy and several other scientists, Franklin signed the official *compte-rendu* of the ascension.

The grand climax came on December 1, and this time it was the turn of Charles. Riding the most scientifically sophisticated balloon yet devised – financed by private subscription, with Franklin among the subscribers – Charles and a companion took off from the Tuileries and proved that henceforth the aeronaut would be capable of regulating his flight. His instruments brought back the first data from what looked to the eighteenth century like outer space. He landed in a field late in the afternoon and in the flush of victory took off once more, by himself, thus witnessing his second sunset of the day. Alone, in the silent and icy regions above the clouds, Charles experienced a spell of such intense, mystical happiness that his narrative, after two centuries, still rings with ecstasy:

No living being, I reflected, has yet penetrated these solitudes; man's voice has never been heard here, and I struck the air with a few sounds as if to stir that tremendous silence all around me. The calm, the gathering darkness, that immensity in the midst of which I was floating, all this gripped my soul in the deepest way.[11]

On that day, December 1, 1783, the balloon came of age.

France went wild throughout that fall and winter. Hairdos, snuffboxes, tableware, fans, gloves, hats, clocks, jewels, walking sticks, swords, bird cages, wallpaper, all were under the sign of the balloon. A new liqueur (*crême aérostatique*) and a new dance (*contredanse de Gonesse*) were named after it. Plays were written to its glory. Within weeks, little hydrogen-filled contraptions were for sale, in the shape of nymphs, animals, and mythological beasts, and no party was complete without its private launching. "Come for tea and balloons," wrote Le Roy to Franklin.[12]

And Franklin was as thrilled as his fellow Parisians. He had been on hand for the first experiment in August. His famous mot: "What is the use of a new-born baby?" in answer to somebody's wondering why all the fuss about this new toy, made the rounds of the capital. But he did speculate, of course, about its practical applications. Had not his own electricity, at first, been considered a "mere Matter of Amusement?" [13] Anything that increased "the Power of Man over Matter" was, he felt, worth investigating. Writing to Sir Joseph Banks two days after the event, he first related all the information available on the machine and then recounted the musings he had heard about its potential. A footman or a horse might be slung from the balloon and, thus buoyed up, be enabled to proceed cross country, over hedges and ditches, with the speed of the wind; or an enterprising soul might rent out a captive balloon to sightseers at a guinea an ascent; or yet, the French being French, it might prove a convenient way to keep game fresh and to procure ice at any time. [14]

Franklin became acquainted with both the older Montgolfier and with Charles. In September, and again in October, he went at Montgolfier's personal invitation with a selected group of guests, including Le Roy, to watch some experiments. As for Charles, there is no doubt that he considered himself one of Franklin's disciples. In his eulogy of Charles, many years later, Baron Fourier underlined that if the young man, who had started as a financier, decided to devote his life to what was then called "natural philosophy," it was because of Franklin's immense prestige. Fourier also recalled that both Franklin and Volta had attended Charles' famous lectures and that Franklin, struck by the man's dexterity, had once exclaimed: "Nature cannot say no to him!" [15]

The balloons, it seems, rejuvenated Franklin, sprinkling his style with fresh, sprightly images: "A few Months since [ago] the Idea of Witches riding thro' the Air upon a Broomstick, and that of Philosophers upon a Bag of Smoke would have appear'd equally impossible and ridiculous." This was addressed to the staid Sir Joseph Banks the day after Pilâtre de Rozier and the Marquis d'Arlandes had taken their first flight. Carried away by enthusiasm, Franklin was not only rooting for the French but totally identifying with them. Here he is, in the same letter, chiding England in true Gallic tradition:

I am sorry this Experiment is totally neglected in England where mechanic Genius is so strong. . . . Your Philosophy seems to be too bashful. In this Country we [notice the we!] are not so much afraid of being laught at. If we do a foolish Thing, we are the first to laugh at it ourselves and are almost as much pleased with a Bon Mot *or a good* Chanson, *that ridicules well the Disappointment of a Project, as we might have been with its Success.*[16]

Still in this impish mood, he reverted to one of his favorite devices, the hoax. At some unknown date, he penned an anonymous letter to the press, pretending that he was a woman subscriber who had a suggestion to offer. Had he not started his literary career that way when, as a boy of sixteen, he had slipped under the door of his brother's printing press a letter supposedly written by Mrs. Silence Dogood, a middle-aged widow? Franklin consistently loved this kind of joke. During the second half of his life, he addressed no less than 149 letters to the American, English, and French press, many of them under assumed names. Some are probably still undetected.

This particular letter was never printed and has remained virtually unknown. It shows Franklin not only having fun with one of his favorite topics – hot air – but also spoofing himself and his famous sense of thrift. The "lady correspond-ent" starts out in fake naïve manner:

Our chemists, it is said, are sparing no effort to discover a kind of air both lighter and less expensive than inflammable air, in order to fill our aerostatic machines (the name given to balloons by our learned Academy). But it is really singular that men as enlightened as those of our century should be forever searching in art for what nature offers everywhere and to everybody, and that an ignorant woman such as me should be the first to think of the solution. Therefore, I am not going to keep my invention a secret, nor shall I solicit any recompense from the government, or any exclusive privilege.

Then she strikes:

If you want to fill your balloons with an element ten times lighter than inflammable air, you can find a great quantity of it, and ready made, in the promises of lovers and of courtiers and in the sighs of our widowers; in the good resolutions taken during a storm at sea, or on land, during an illness; and especially in the praise to be found in letters of recommendation.[17]

The manuscript is certainly in Franklin's hand; and even if it were not, its authorship would be given away by the reference to letters of recommendation, a burden of French social life that he abhorred. There are faded corrections to his French, very few in number and hardly legible, in Le Roy's hand. His principal contribution was to tone down "the sighs of our widowers" to "the sighs of those who become widowers" – no widower, after all, being expected to keep sighing after the first shock.

Madame Le Roy contributed much more than corrections,

jokes, and speculations: she herself boarded a balloon. Franklin, who had already gone back to America, was informed of the event by her husband: "Last fall [in 1785] Madame Le Roy and the Montalembert ladies traveled by free balloon (*à Ballon perdu*) from Javelle to Issy, soaring to a height of almost 400 feet. The weather was calm; they returned and descended without any trouble."[18]

Was she elated? One must assume that she was, but the enclosure she sent to Franklin with her husband's letter sounds disgruntled as ever: the little pocket wife has not forgotten her erstwhile friend, though he obviously has. That is the way men are, "new friendships make them forget older and truer ones, they cannot distinguish between those who love from the heart and those who only pretend," and yet she had been his very first "daughter" who loved him long before he adopted those other ones, and so on.[19]

The fickle friend (now eighty) apologized for his long silence, blamed it on work, and switched to a topic meant to make her feel proud: "How courageous of you to go up so high in the air! And how kind of you, once you were so close to Heaven, not to want to leave us all and stay with the Angels! I kiss you tenderly."[20] If Franklin thought that this was enough to raise her spirits, he was mistaken. Her next— and last—letter to him is one long cry of misery: blurred by tears, almost unintelligible, going back in cycles over the same points for five chaotic pages, it is one of the most poignant Franklin ever received. Women, obviously, turned to him not only for glamour and amusement but for guidance and comfort as well.

Had she been able to remain aloft longer, Madame Le Roy said, she would have crossed over to him and never gone back to Europe. Her life was one of black despair. She had separated from her husband six months earlier. She could not bear any longer his constant attentions to another woman – an unworthy woman at that – right in her country house, the one Franklin visited so often. Like Madame Brillon during the Jupin crisis, Madame Le Roy had no doubts about her own good conscience ("my behavior has been above reproach . . . my only fault was to cherish and love him too much") and was sure that their common friends would side with her ("he avoids our circle, only looks up those who don't like honest women"). But she sounds both more shrill than Madame Brillon ("I am the person with whom he has lived the least . . . I was always without him, from morning to night") and more desperate ("he is trying to kill me bit by bit . . . he is deaf to my pleas"). She does not forget to point out that only her dowry "enabled her husband to become independent."[21]

Her bitterness was only too warranted. Madame Brillon had thrown out her rival, but Madame Le Roy lost the battle and abandoned the field. What happened later? Though Le Roy himself survived Franklin and the Revolution, we hear no more about Madame. As far as the modern reader is concerned, the curtain goes down on the little pocket wife "sobbing day and night."

The ranks of the bourgeoisie were not filled only with wives of interesting husbands. Some of the women whom Franklin knew and liked made a name for themselves, generally in the one field traditionally open to their sex, the arts.

The eighteenth century witnessed the blossoming of a new type of artistic or quasi-artistic creation at which women excelled. It was an ultrarealistic type of sculpture in wax adorned with real hair, glass eyes, and genuine costumes. One can measure the popularity of philosophers by the fact that at the 1784 fair of St. Germain "the wax likenesses of the King, Queen, and Dauphin were joined by those of Voltaire, Rousseau, and Franklin." [22] No less than three artists in wax from different countries and traditions crossed Franklin's path at one time or another. From America came the ebullient, loud, and hearty Patience Wright who resided for a while in Paris and whose life-size likeness of Franklin, dressed in a suit of his own silk clothes, enabled its owner, Elkanah Watson, to stage many a practical joke, both in France and in England. From Switzerland came shrewd, pretty Marie Grosholtz, for whom he may have sat while she was still very young, and who was to become famous once she moved to London and opened an exhibit on Baker Street, under her married name of Madame Tussaud. Whether it was executed by Madame Tussaud herself or by her uncle Curtius who ran an exhibit in Paris before and during the Revolution, or reconstructed from fragments of a lost model, there has always been, and there still is, a Franklin at Madame Tussaud's; and Franklin himself, we are told, obtained from Curtius and his niece "models of many other notable characters of the day." [23]

From France came the spinsterish, pathetic figure of Mademoiselle Biheron, whose aspirations were scientific rather than artistic and whose life was one of frustration. Her passion, ever since her youth had been anatomy. But how could a girl too poor to buy books study anatomy? She managed, somehow, to witness a number of autopsies. Later, her biographers say, she bribed people to steal soldiers' corpses, so that she could dissect them in the privacy of her room. In spite of the great knowledge she acquired, and of the extraordinary collection of wax anatomical reproductions that she built, the Paris Faculty of Medicine remained staunchly antagonistic. She had to support herself precariously by opening her study to the public once a week, for a fee of three pounds. Toward the end of her life, she managed to sell the whole of her collection to Catherine II of Russia – it had become so enormous and expensive that only a sovereign could afford it.

Mademoiselle Biheron met Franklin during his first trip to France, in 1767; they were introduced by the philosopher Jacques Barbeu-Dubourg, who at the time was busy translating Franklin's work into French and spreading his fame throughout the country. Three years later, she decided to try her luck in London, and it was Franklin's turn to introduce her to the prominent medical people he knew there, Sir John Pringle and Jan Ingenhousz among others. What else he may have done on her behalf is not quite clear, but he must have been helpful, for, back in France, she referred frequently to the Doctor's "bontés" toward her and to the kindness shown by Franklin's landlady, Mrs. Stevenson.[24]

Ironically, this unmarried, single-minded career woman was always being entrusted with the most domestic kind of errand: we see her pondering over what quality of thread to send Mrs. Stevenson from France, which ribbons to buy for Mrs. Stevenson's daughter Polly, how to pack the peppermint ("peper menth")[25] water her French friends desired from London. Left to her own devices, she promptly gives in to her longing to be a doctor and endeavors to do by long distance in London what she is forbidden to do in Paris: treat somebody's disease. She begs Franklin to forward to a "poor unfortunate" some powder she is sending over to cure his eyes. Although she was one of the very first to greet him upon his return to Paris as American commissioner, there is no record that Franklin ever asked her for a kiss.[26]

Women, of course, did not confine themselves to waxwork. Many wielded a brush, some with considerable talent. If one happened, furthermore, to be young and pretty, she could even overcome Franklin's general unwillingness to pose. Such was the case of Rosalie Filleul.

The daughter of Blaise Bocquet, merchant of "curiosities," Rosalie was a true child of Paris, quick, pert, and lively. Enrolled at an early age in art school, she became the inseparable friend of two other girls, both aspiring painters like herself. One was Elisabeth Vigée, the future Madame Vigée-Lebrun, the other Emilie Vernet, daughter of the painter Claude-Joseph Vernet who worked on the decoration of Versailles. In 1777 (the wedding announcement is still among Franklin's papers) Rosalie married Louis Filleul, "garçon de chambre du Roi." How she came into Franklin's life is not quite clear. It may have been through Madame Brillon, who took the Doctor on several occasions to visit Vernet at his home or attend one of his shows. Or it may have been through Jean-Baptiste Le Roy, who worked at the Château de la Muette, of which Madame Filleul, right after her marriage, was appointed concierge.

A concierge who earned 15,000 livres a year was obviously not the kind who opens the door, sweeps the stairs, and distributes the mail. Madame Filleul, who also was one of the official portraitists of the royal family (though she was never paid for this particular function), seems to have been in charge of organizing some of the lively parties Marie-Antoinette was so fond of, even though the King frowned on them. Frivolous and extravagant as such parties were, they could not compare with what la Muette had seen in the days of Louis XV, when queens, both legitimate and illegitimate, princesses of the blood, and high-flown women of pleasure had given the castle an unsavory reputation. But even in the relatively tame days of Louis XVI, that section of court hierarchy devoted to "les menus plaisirs du Roi,"[27] that strange, parasitic, half-artistic, half-erotic world must have been fascinating to Franklin.

Madame Filleul was on terms of pleasant familiarity with him: she told him of the birth of her first son; she lent him books; she asked him to pick her up in his carriage so that they could ride together to a ball at the Brillons, since she had a lot of shopping to do in Paris that morning, and her horses would be tired – if the dear papa was so kind, she would "look forward to kissing" him.[28] When he left, she planned to buy his piano.

Unfortunately, as Le Veillard reported to Franklin soon after his departure, the cold wind of reform and economy began to blow: la Muette was about to be closed, and Madame Filleul was quite uncertain about her future. The future turned out to be grim. She was given a house in Passy, in compensation for the loss of her position, but she hardly enjoyed it. Her husband died; her resources dwindled. When the Revolution broke out, she did not follow her friend Vigée-Lebrun, who left the country and painted more queens and princesses in their unperturbed curls, but stayed in Paris and shared her home with her other friend Emilie Vernet, who had separated from her husband. It was a disastrous error. Together they were arrested (it was rumored that Jacques-

Louis David, the famous painter, an unsuccessful suitor of Emilie, had a hand in their fate); they were accused of having stolen state property from la Muette and having indulged in a scandalous friendship with Marie-Antoinette. Sentenced to death after a mock trial, they went together to the scaffold three days before the end of the Terror.

An attractive, poignant figure, Rosalie Filleul was not a great artist. If her name is still known, it is mainly because of her portrait of Franklin, a Franklin done in a vigorous manner, looking years younger, with an open shirt and an expression more intellectual than benign. The portrait was immediately made into an engraving and put on sale in her father's bric-a-brac shop.[29]

Everybody wanted a likeness of the Doctor while he was in France. Owning one, whether in oil or pastel, life-size or miniature, sculpted in the round or etched in metal, became for the Parisians more than a tribute or a token of devotion: it became a status symbol. What makes a status symbol, of course, is that you have it and your friend or neighbor does not. The emotions that agitated Madame Fournier, "la belle Madame Fournier," as Le Veillard called her, are a case in point.[30]

Her husband, Simon-Pierre Fournier le Jeune, was one of a dynasty of Fourniers, all typefounders, all remarkable craftsmen. Franklin got in touch with them as early as 1777, to buy some type for the press he meant to set up in Passy, and during the following years he ordered large quantities of printing equipment. Fournier type was used to print not only all the *Bagatelles*, but also blank orders against American bank balances in France, blank promissory notes, and passports.[31]

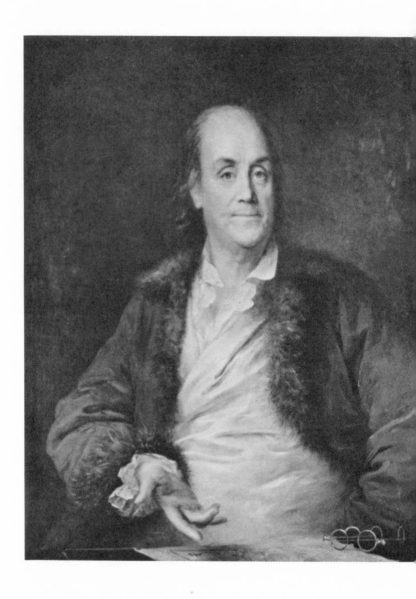

Portrait of Franklin, by Rosalie Filleul

Rosalie Filleul's Self-Portrait

Behind the technical-sounding business letters of Fournier le Jeune, however, looms the pleasant face of Madame, who never forgot to acknowledge Franklin's compliments or send her own. In the spring of 1780, when Fournier asked Franklin to do him the immense favor of posing for an unspecified artist, he was careful to stress that this would "give him great credit" with his father-in-law, and especially with his wife.[32]

As usual when confronted with such requests, Franklin had mixed feelings. To the French he always professed mild exasperation with their national mania for portraits, even protesting on one occasion that he had suffered a stiff neck twenty times within a week from the long hours of posing. But when writing back home to his daughter, he betrayed his deep satisfaction with such mass adulation:

The clay medallion of me you say you gave to Mr. Hopkinson was the first of the kind made in France. A variety of others have been made since of different sizes; some to be set in the lids of snuffboxes, and some so small as to be worn in rings; and the numbers sold are incredible. These, with the pictures, busts and prints (of which copies upon copies are spread everywhere), have made your father's face as well known as that of the moon, so that he durst not do anything that would oblige him to run away, as his phiz would discover him wherever he should venture to show it. It is said by learned etymologists, that the name doll, *for the images children play with, is derived from the word* IDOL. *From the number of dolls now made of him, he may truly be said,* in that sense, *to be* i-doll-ized *in this country.*[33]

Lest we think that Franklin was indulging in a little bragging, the contemporary writer Félix Nogaret notes that "he now appears on all mantelpieces, revered no more no less than a Penate god."[34]

When presented with Fournier's request, Franklin balked somewhat and resorted to a suggestion he had made in several other cases: why not copy the splendid, the definitive portrait that Chaumont had commissioned from Duplessis and that hung, for all to see, in the Hôtel de Valentinois? Furthermore, Franklin had understood that he was supposed to bear the cost of this project himself, and here he really drew the line: "I shall tell you that I am neither rich enough nor vain enough to get portraits made at 8 or 10 Louis a piece, in order to give them away as presents."[35] Fournier hastened to reassure him on this count. Never had such a thought entered his head, he said. All he wanted was two or three sittings. The painter's fee had already been settled, and were it to amount to as much as 20 Louis, he, Fournier, would spend them with pleasure, since this portrait was to be the glory of his life and of his posterity.[36]

Could Franklin turn down a colleague, a man of his own craft? Could he disappoint the attractive woman who was obviously behind all this insistence? He sat. The artist, an obscure Alexis Judlin, made a miniature that sent the Fournier ménage into raptures of delight. As a further favor, Fournier begged Franklin to come and visit his foundry, which he did. Thirty years later, when another generation of Fourniers had taken over, their workmen still practiced their craft under the benign half-smile of the printer from Philadelphia, whose bust was displayed with pride to an American visiting Paris. To show his gratitude, Fournier devoted the greatest care to designing type for Franklin. When Benny Bache came back from Switzerland, and his grandfather decided to have him learn the printing trade, he boarded with the Le Roy family and procured from Fournier the type he was to bring back to America.

Was Madame Fournier pleased with her miniature, really pleased? She was. That is, until a year later when a Monsieur Pierre, whose job it was to print proofs of the type meant for Franklin, stated his desire to become, too, the possessor of a portrait, in view of the work he was doing. The Fourniers were shocked by such impudence. The husband wrote:

My wife, who is wise and prudent, told him, as I did, that you do not give away your portrait to unknown people and that to obtain it, it is imperative for one to have special worth in your eyes. He retorted that he was planning to write to you. I tried to make him feel the rashness of such a move. In case he makes it, anyway, I shall be glad to have warned you, while begging you not to compromise me and not to let him know that I said anything ... I shall be curious to hear what you have answered.[37]

Since there is no trace of any correspondence between Franklin and a Monsieur Pierre, we may safely assume that the Fourniers' prestige was unimpaired and that, in the hierarchy of the printing world, they remained on whatever rung of the ladder Franklin's miniature had enabled them to ascend.

If a portrait was unobtainable, status could still be gained by having the great man to dinner. Hundreds of invitations clutter Franklin's files – generally undated, often cryptic, altogether an unwieldy mass of tokens of good will and social climbing, so closely intertwined that they defy posthumous disentangling.

Occasionally the problems of the would-be hostess stand out in ominous relief. One Madame de Baussan prevailed on Joseph Caillot (the actor whose wife was Temple's mistress) to forward a dinner invitation to Franklin and his grandson for a Sunday 19. She did not know that Franklin reserved his Sundays for "le diné amériquain," a semi-official party he gave for the most distinguished members of the American colony. The Doctor (or Temple; the reply is not on file) suggested the preceding Friday 17, but this threw Madame in the greatest confusion: "my house is full of workmen who need time until Sunday to let me have a dining room fit to receive you *convenablement*." [38] Could the date be changed to Friday 24? Temple said it could, and Madame went ahead with determination. She saw to it that the decorators did not slacken on the job, hired two Italians who would perform "their tricks, their mimicry, and their music," sent out, as an extra enticement, an invitation to Madame Brillon, her family, and, no doubt, a number of minor stars.

The party fell flat. Madame Brillon was out of town. Much worse, Temple had forgotten that his grandfather had to go to Court in Versailles on that Friday, instead of Tuesday as usual. Madame de Baussan was so upset that she could hardly express her disappointment *convenablement*:

That journey to Versailles has really grieved us, very dear papa. We had made our plans, and we felt sure we would have the pleasure of having you with your grandson, who certainly deserves some reproaches for his forgetfulness. We had engaged two Italians for after dinner. They would have amused you.

That cursed trip to Versailles has harmed us; it is already so hard to persuade you to come for dinner a couple of miles away, and now Madame Brillon, who is about to come back, will want you all to herself. Well, I beseech you, very good papa, to remember that you have promised to make up for this another day. If I may, I shall come one of these mornings at tea time and ask for it.[39]

One wonders what part of the elaborate preparations made for that ill-fated Friday were permanent embellishments, and to what extent Madame de Baussan had filled her house with workmen in vain. One of the most conspicuous features of formal dinners in the late eighteenth century was the ephemeral beauty of the centerpiece: unusual figurines, tiny sugar carvings, imitations of Oriental rugs combining powdered marble, colored sand, crushed glass, and tinted breadcrumbs. Love for Arcadia expressed itself in winter landscapes made of artificial frost which would melt during the meal, turn into flowing rivulets, gradually revealing miniature trees and flowers, and bursting into spring just as the desert – more often than not a *bombe glacée*, another novelty – was brought in.[40]

All this, of course, went with the finest porcelain, and the vogue was for Sèvres, rather than China or Saxe. The most lavish care was spent on the food itself. Indeed, the reign of Louis XVI marked one of the peaks of French gastronomy – a cuisine less extreme in its spicing, less baroque in its flavoring than that of Louis XV, but relying for effect on chopping, mincing, and puréeing until the stupendous result bore no resemblance whatsoever to the original product. Several interesting new specialties were introduced at the time of Franklin's stay: pâté de foie gras was invented in 1782, and camembert had made its appearance only a few years earlier.

From abroad came not only beefsteak but caviar and such exotic spices as curry and soya.[41] The wines that enhanced such feasts were early harbingers of the *grands crus* of France.

A great amateur of wine, Franklin must have appreciated the choice bottles of Burgundy sent to him by the Chevalier O'Gorman, brother-in-law of the much talked-about Chevalier d'Eon. Though not quite fitting into any category, this enigmatic figure who spent part of its life as a man and part as a woman cannot be bypassed in a cross section of the "women" of Paris whom Franklin met.

Born in Tonnerre (Burgundy) in 1728, as Charles-Geneviève-Louise-Auguste d'Eon (ominously two masculine names and two feminine ones), the Chevalier embarked on a brilliant military and diplomatic career. While serving as a special envoy to the Court of Russia, he suddenly switched to women's clothes and became Empress Elizabeth's favorite "reader" – whatever this term may have meant to a sovereign whose sex life was notoriously tempestuous. Back in the role of a man, he passed himself off as the reader's brother (as in a Shakespearean comedy), returned to France, took up his post as officer of the dragoons, distinguished himself in several battles, and wound up with the post of Minister Plenipotentiary in London. At this point, the plots and counterplots in his career, along with changes in sex, undercover activities, innuendos, accusations, and refutations, become too thick to follow. He fell in disgrace – though still paid a pension by Louis XV – and was denied permission to go back to France unless he accepted a woman's name and clothes. He refused, and lived in England for a number of years, while bets about his true nature were raging. One more scandal: in order to pay off his debts, he pawned some state papers in his possession, and the playwright Beau-marchais, no dilettante himself in intrigue, was sent to London to retrieve them.

The year Franklin arrived in France, 1777, was also the year the chevalier finally returned to his native country – under strict orders to stick to a woman's identity. D'Eon's one extant letter to Franklin, dated January 24, 1778, is duly signed *la chevalière* and consistently uses the feminine gender. It is not in itself an extraordinary letter: the writer says that she had gone to pay the Doctor a visit and upon discovering that he was not home she had drunk to America's freedom with the amiable Chaumont family.

But one of the few slanderous writings circulated about Franklin makes more of his rapport with la chevalière.[42] The purported narrator of the story, published simultaneously (and anonymously) in French and English in 1779, is none other than a louse, born on the head of a woman of pleasure. Entitled *Story of a French Louse, or the Spy of a New Species*, it follows the protagonist's adventures from head to head (from countess, to queen, to soldier, to laundress), until the louse settles on Mademoiselle d'Eon, who is invited to dinner at Franklin's. There follows one of the cruelest descriptions of the old man: one third of his face concealed by glasses, warts in such and such a place, a heavy jaw, teeth like a row of cloves. Yet such a man appeals to Mademoiselle d'Eon. They drink thirteen toasts to the thirteen colonies, she reads him some of her work, they kiss, and make a further appointment. This much for Franklin's lechery; in another episode, the louse shows him to be Beaumarchais' dupe as well as a profiteer and impostor.[43]

One can scarcely believe that such a gross tale could have

harmed Franklin's reputation. That of d'Eon, however, was not so easily vindicated: in 1784, persecuted, disheartened, he went back to London, made a living as a fencing teacher, wrote extensively – on grain trade, among other subjects dear to Franklin – and only after his death was he pronounced, by the doctor who examined his body, to have been a man.

Since the fictional louse is the only undignified character we have been able so far to observe at close range, one is led to wonder whether Franklin, the self-made man and preacher of equality, ever met any Frenchman of the lower classes apart from his butler and servants. And though it is logical to assume that such contacts, if they existed, would not have left any trace in his correspondence, one cannot help feeling that the American philosopher, like his idealistic French friends, could not or did not care to pierce the wall separating the privileged, moneyed classes from the mass of the people. He may have smiled at the throngs watching him come out of his carriage – modestly dressed and unescorted, as the tearful lady who wrote to the *Journal de Paris* observed – but apparently he spoke to nobody, and nobody in the crowd was bold enough to speak to him.

"Nobody," perhaps, is too strong. Next to invitations for dinner, the largest number of undatable and unclassifiable items in Franklin's files are the placets, begging letters penned in a peculiar style, with great flourishes every time the hoped-for benefactor is mentioned. Like most other letters preserved by Franklin, they usually bear a brief endorsement mentioning the name of the sender and the subject, such as: "Placet d'Ester Brickland femme d'Ignace Adolphe Dumay implorant l'assistance de Mr. Franklin." There is no trace of any of them ever being answered.[44]

No doubt the most insistent beggar is not the neediest. Few of the petitions come from the destitute, unkempt, angry people who would storm the Bastille, overrun Versailles, and watch the guillotine at work a few short years later. On the contrary, the supplications tell over and again the same hard luck story: a sudden turn of fortune, an undeserved fall from the top to the bottom of the ladder. Here is an example:

Sir: Be not surprised at my action. It can only mean praise for your kind heart, since it is prompted by your reputation. Be willing to read me before passing judgment.

Were it not for an illness which has kept me in bed for the last six months, I would have come personally to beseech the grace I am asking of your beneficent heart. I know I am addressing my prayers to a most respectable Man, who is the glory of his Country and the pride of ours, and who will be forever famous and immortal.

Shall you be willing, Sir, to listen to the most unhappy woman who is in tears – a woman whom you may have seen when she was sufficiently well off to be an object of envy. For the love of God do not add to my sorrows the mistrust one ought to feel for the crowd of impostors who are besieging the Doors of the Rich.

This very woman is now imploring you to buy a most valuable ring for four Louis. It became a part of my collection in happier times; now, it would enable me to rise from the bed where I am suffering. If you ever have felt that charity filled your heart with joy, here I am offering you a good opportunity to do so.[45]

Franklin endorsed the letter but did not take the opportunity. Nor did he answer the placet of a certain Gérard, who "through enthusiasm for the universal good of mankind had embraced the profession of literature," but had been driven by poverty to "relinquish the pen, that interpreter of his lonely thought." [46] It is true that Gérard took up his pen again to write the placet and gave the placet to his wife, who put it in Franklin's hands. To no avail; the following day, Gérard wrote again, deploring the "blunt, humiliating refusal" he had endured, protesting that "his soul was too proud to beg," and pouring his bitterness half-way into the final sentence, but not so far as to forget the standard formula for concluding a letter: "To yield to the violent drive of a noble despair rather than to debase myself, these are the feelings which make me resolve to die, while still remaining, Sir, respectfully your most humble servant." [47]

A faker? A deranged mind? A talented but unhappy man? Franklin did not find the time to ask the wife, and we shall never know.

In your company we are not only pleased with you, but better pleased with one another and with ourselves. ❧ FRANKLIN

She was the queen of them all, the only one to whom he wrote more often than she answered, who did not call him papa, but, as an equal, *mon cher ami*, the one woman with whom he did not want to have merely a flirtation, a passing adventure: he wanted her for a wife.

What was the fascination of that woman, a widow in her late fifties, only thirteen years Franklin's junior? Though she had been beautiful, her enemies compared her now to the ruins of Palmyra,[1] and it took more than ordinary devotion for one of her protégés, Pierre-Georges Cabanis, to forecast that she, alone, would remain forever young:

... Et vous paraîtrez à cent ans
Sortir des mains de la Nature.
Ce destin qui vous est promis
Sans doute a bien quelque avantage,
Mais vous y perdrez vos amis,
Car vieillir est notre partage,
Et bientôt, je vous le prédis,
Nous ne serons plus de votre âge.[*2]

[*2] *When you're a hundred, you'll look as though*
From Nature's bosom you just sprang out.
The special fate that will treat you so
Has some advantage for you, no doubt,
But you'll forfeit your friends at last;
For growing old is our destination,
And all of us, I predict, will fast
Become too old for your generation.

Portrait of Madame Helvétius, by Louis-Michel Vanloo

Without going quite so far, Franklin broadcast his admiration for her grace, dignity, and charm. Madame Brillon called her "my charming rival,"[3] and as time went by, "my charming and redoubtable rival."[4] Those two centers of Franklin's social life, Madame Brillon and Madame Helvétius, knew one another but slightly. They moved in different circles, one in Passy, the other in Auteuil. Their personalities were, indeed, poles apart: Madame Brillon was tender, moody, self-absorbed, and bourgeoise to the core; Madame Helvétius was brisk, outgoing, exuberant, with that touch of the earthy and the bohemian that only a born noblewoman can afford.

She belonged to one of the four great families of Lorraine, "the four horses" as they were called, related to the imperial dynasty of Austria and hence to Marie-Antoinette. But Anne-Catherine de Ligniville d'Autricourt, the tenth of twenty children, had no dowry, and in the high society of her day, this generally gave a girl no alternative but the cloistered life. To a convent she went, with her sister, when she was fifteen – the age of marriage for girls with a dowry – and remained there until, at thirty, she was told that the pension granted her by Cardinal de Rohan had expired with the Cardinal himself, and she had to leave. What would she find at home? "Fifteen children, a pregnant mother, and six hundred pounds of income,"[5] that is, decent starvation.

The catastrophe was a blessing in disguise. An aunt, Madame de Graffigny, who had grown fond of "Pussycat" (Minette) when she was a child, felt sorry for her, brought her home to Paris, and introduced her to the brilliant men who frequented her salon. Madame de Graffigny, separated from a brutal husband, supported herself by writing. Of the several novels she wrote, the most successful one – indeed, "the most successful French novel between 1740 and 1760"[6] – was *Les Lettres d'une Péruvienne,* in which she extolled directness and simplicity, two outstanding qualities of her niece's personality. The aunt wrote in the polished, epistolary mode so in vogue since Montesquieu's *Lettres persanes* and Richardson's *Pamela;* the niece was throughout life a wretched letter writer, with a scrawl almost as atrocious as her spelling. No matter. She had a lively presence, was pretty, and soon found herself surrounded by a number of suitors, including a former seminarist, Anne-Robert Turgot, who would become one day Comptroller-General, Minister of the Navy, and one of the great economists of all times.

At the time of the courtship, however, Turgot, who was eight years younger than Minette and almost as penniless as she, appeared as a poor choice. He was passed over in favor of an older, more established man: Claude-Adrien Helvétius, a dashing talker, dancer, ladies' man, and, to boot, one of those powerful Farmers-General who, in the words of Voltaire, "leased the kingdom . . . and paid the monarch a small rent for it." They were married in 1751; she was thirty-two, her husband four years older.

Marriages between an indigent aristocrat and a rich financier were not infrequent in the society of the time. At the beginning of the eighteenth century, it would still have been regarded as a misalliance, but when the wedding took place, the social prestige of the chief tax collectors was catching up with their power. Moreover, Helvétius, though not a nobleman, had a distinguished ancestry. He was descended from a long line of eminent physicians, whose original name was Schweitzer; they had moved from Germany to Holland, then to France, and became in the process doctors to the Court. Claude-Adrien was the first who abandoned the family profession in order to build a fortune. Then, once married, he promptly gave up his lucrative position to devote himself entirely to family and philosophy.

For the next twenty years, the Helvétius ménage settled into the leisurely pattern of eight months in the country (alternating between their two châteaux) and four months at their Paris mansion, rue Sainte Anne. Here every Tuesday gathered some of the most brilliant spokesmen of the Enlightenment, those bold thinkers who were so wittily – and unwittingly – preparing the downfall of their way of life: Diderot, the novelist and philosopher, whose *Encyclopédie*, thirty years in the making, would be the mainspring of the French Revolution, and the mathematician d'Alembert, his collaborator; Baron d'Holbach expressed his doubts on the existence of God, Condorcet proclaimed his faith in the "progrès de l'esprit humain." Turgot, Raynal, Morellet debated problems of economics and colonization, Abbé Galiani and David Hume brought, from time to time, a whiff of Italian or British thought. A sumptuous dinner was served at two o'clock, and the discussions that followed often lasted far into the night.

Such guests were difficult to please. To some, the hostess appeared frivolous. "Because of her beauty, unusual wit, and stimulating temperament, Madame Helvétius disturbed philosophical discussions considerably,"[7] Abbé Morellet, one of her closest friends, grumbled many years later. But most philosophers took such disturbances in their stride. The famous "Oh, to be seventy again!" is already attributed, in its long line of attributions, to the almost centenarian writer, Fontenelle, catching Madame Helvétius in one of her more casual and generous *déshabillées*.[8]

Helvétius himself, however, came in for more severe criticism. Many attacked his unsophisticated brand of hedonism which reduced all men's faculties to physical sensations, made love of pleasure the origin of all human activities, and put more stock in the power of education than in the might of God. There were those who insinuated that the guests' ideas invariably turned up in his books. Yet when his long-expected major work, *De l'Esprit*, came out and because of its blunt godlessness incurred the Sorbonne's wrath, Helvétius was promptly disavowed by most of his entourage. His wife never wavered.

He died in 1771, still rather in disgrace, in spite of an elaborate apology. The widow, far from retiring to a convent or devoting her life to her children, showed that independence of spirit Diderot had praised in her years before, when he noted that, unlike most women, "she was not a slave."[9] Within a few months, she had married off her daughters (significantly, to men of their own choice), given each daughter one of the châteaux, sold the Paris residence, and bought from the Court painter Quentin de la Tour a charming little estate in Auteuil, next to Passy, on the fringe of the Bois de Boulogne.

Soon, the shady corners of her park were ablaze with rhododendrons, and there appeared everywhere a profusion of flowers in the artful English disarray, far from the prevailing French formality and symmetry. Wherever they traveled, friends brought back specimens of local flora to be, somehow, crowded into the gardens; Lord Shelburne, it may be remembered, had sent gooseberry bushes from England even before the opening of peace negotiations. The grounds were not large, as a young officer on the make tactlessly remarked to Madame Helvétius a few years later. "General," she replied to Napoleon Bonaparte, "you cannot imagine how much happiness can be squeezed into three acres of land!"[10]

Along with the plants came the animals, for whom Madame Helvétius had a fondness verging on mania. Deer throughout the park, ducks, pigeons, hundreds of chickens, a great variety of birds housed in huge aviaries, an ever increasing number of cats and dogs roaming at will – all these she fed and loved. This facet of her personality became so well known that the librettist of Beethoven's "Fidelio," Jean-Nicolas Bouilly, was prompted to write a fanciful tale entitled *Les Oiseaux de Madame Helvétius*.

Finally, people: much as she liked nature, she hated solitude. She was not alone for long. A former Benedictine monk, Abbé Martin Lefebvre de la Roche, who had been secularized by a brief from Rome obtained through Helvétius, rushed to the widow's side from his post as librarian in Holland. His purpose was to put in order his late benefactor's papers and prepare his manuscripts for publication. He was set to work in a pavilion on the grounds. Thirty years later he was still there, surrounded by his beloved classics, rare editions, fine bindings, and etchings. Another old friend, the Abbé Morellet, who used to ride in the Bois with Madame Helvétius, also gravitated toward Auteuil, was given temporary lodgings, and found the arrangement so warm and satisfactory that he took the habit of spending several days a week away from his Paris home.

The two abbés were different in both appearance and

temperament: de la Roche, in his late thirties when he settled in Auteuil, was tall, fair, blue-eyed, handsome, and placid; Morellet, who had been a fellow student of Turgot's at the Sorbonne, was forty-seven when he moved in. He had the reputation of being a grump. Voltaire, who esteemed him, called him "l'abbé Mords-les" (bite them).[11] Madame Necker, wife of Turgot's archenemy, branded him as "un ours mal léché," an ill-licked bear symbolizing to the French the combination of a lone wolf and a crank. But Madame Necker, whose tongue was as sharp as that of her famous daughter, Madame de Staël, may have been somewhat unfair. Toward Franklin, at least, about whom he wrote abundantly in his *Memoirs*, Morellet always showed himself perfectly friendly and congenial.

Morellet's niece, a very young girl, had just married the mature writer and academician, Marmontel. Marmontel initiated the habit of visiting Auteuil; others followed, and soon there were enough men of note flocking to Madame Helvétius' new home to form what was jokingly referred to as "l'Académie d'Auteuil." This gathering of scientists and men of letters almost duplicated the Lodge of the Nine Sisters (the nine Muses), a high-caliber masonic group that had been Helvétius' dream. He did not live to see it, but his widow helped bring it into being. Eventually, Voltaire (who inherited Helvétius' apron) became its most illustrious member, Franklin its *Vénérable*, or grand master.

At the core of Madame Helvétius' Académie was Turgot, the faithful admirer of her youth, who had never married and now proposed once more. His reputation as an economist and his position in government were high and still soaring in the early 1770s, but Madame turned him down once again, on the grounds that she intended to remain faithful to her husband's memory. One wonders if she was not prompted, rather, by a desire to enjoy her new freedom. Turgot, at any rate, accepted this second rebuff with good grace. He maintained an intense devotion toward his old friend, and she, in turn, provided warmth and support when his liberal views on taxation, commerce, and religious toleration brought his political downfall in 1776. A wealthy man, Turgot entertained lavishly in his own home and also made frequent trips to Auteuil, bringing new and interesting friends.

One of his protégés was a dark, brooding young man with the high forehead, long face, and thin features of the intellectual: Pierre-Georges Cabanis. At twenty-two, Cabanis, a medical student, already had an eventful life behind him, including a time in Poland as a tutor. Taken by Madame Helvétius into her house almost as a waif because he needed good food and fresh air, Cabanis soon became the pet, the favorite, the son she had lost in infancy. Still at the threshold of his career when Franklin came to Paris, he later grew in fame as a medical theorist (a philosopher of medicine as it were). But he always remained at the side of his foster mother, even after his marriage, and he nursed her through her final illness. It was to him that she willed her estate. Thus, the house at Auteuil, which had known the ferment of prerevolutionary days and was a haven to bewildered liberals caught in the whirlwind of the Terror, became, during the Empire, the seat of the bright-eyed, ineffectually discontented group of the *Idéologues* who were, in turn, to have so profound an influence on the Italian Risorgimento. From the eighteenth century deep into the nineteenth, the highest human aspirations were nurtured under that roof.

Turgot did not bring Cabanis only. He also brought Franklin, whom he had known and liked for years, both as a human being, a brother sufferer of the gout, and as a fellow economist engaged in the battle for more freedom in the exchange of goods.

Franklin was conquered at once. He does not seem to have seen anything incongruous in the ménage of an elderly widow surrounded by three younger men. Rather, he was puzzled by the appeal she held for such a variety of men and tried to analyze its elements in a letter addressed almost as much to himself as to her:

I have in my way been trying to form some hypothesis to account for your having so many friends and of such various kinds. I see that statesmen, philosophers, historians, poets, and men of learning attach themselves to you as straws to a fine piece of amber.

It is not that you make pretension to any of their sciences, and, if you did, similarity of studies does not always make people love one another. It is not that you take pains to engage them: artless simplicity is a striking part of your character. I would not attempt to explain it by the story of the ancient, who, being asked why philosophers sought the acquaintance of kings, and kings not that of philosophers, replied that philosophers knew what they wanted, which was not always the case with kings.

Yet, thus far the comparison may go that we find in your sweet society that charming benevolence, that amiable attention to oblige, that disposition to please and be pleased, which we do not always find in the society of one another. It springs from you; it has its influence on us all; and in your company we are not only pleased with you, but better pleased with one another and with ourselves.[12]

Franklin wanted very much to become part of the charmed circle. He promptly embarked on a multi-faceted campaign of seduction, from the lady of the house (rechristened by him "Notre Dame d'Auteuil"), to her daughters ("the stars," as he called them), to the two abbots ("les bons abbés"), to serious-minded young Cabanis. He won quick acceptance in that vibrant, somewhat chaotic household and soon became so much a member of it that his place at table was always set. The tone of the house, a kind of bantering, of loving impudence, was one he came by easily. He soon learned the inside jokes: Abbé Morellet had an inordinate fondness for cream and for specious reasoning; Madame was hopelessly disorganized; Abbé de la Roche did not really care about anything but his books.

The delicious flavor of intimacy could hardly be conveyed better than Franklin did it in his letter to Madame de la Freté, later to be published among the *Bagatelles*. Addressing himself to a mutual friend who had tried to warn him that a projected breakfast was not going to take place, but whose message had not been forwarded by absent-minded Madame Helvétius, he describes his disappointment in a choppy French admirably suited to the subject matter:

As the invitation was for eleven o'clock . . . I expected to find a breakfast in the manner of a dinner; that there would be many guests; that we should have not only tea, but also coffee, chocolate, perhaps a ham and several other good things. I resolved to go there on foot. My shoes were a little too tight. I arrived nearly crippled.

On entering the court, I was a little surprised to find it so empty of carriages, and to see that we [Franklin and Temple] were the first to arrive. We climb the stairs. No noise. We enter the dining room. No one but M. l'Abbé and M. C. The breakfast ended, eaten! Nothing on the table but some morsels of bread and a little butter. They exclaim. They run to tell Madame H. that we had come for breakfast. She quits her dressing table, she comes with her hair half-combed. They are surprised that I have come. . . .

Finally, a new breakfast is ordered. One person runs for fresh water, another for charcoal. A watched pot never boils, *as Poor Richard says. Madame departs for Paris, leaving us. We begin to eat. The butter is soon finished. M. l'Abbé asks if we want some more? Yes, certainly. He rings. No one comes. We chat. He forgets the butter. I was scraping the plate; then he seizes it and runs to the kitchen, looking for some. After a while, he returns slowly, saying sadly: there is none in the house. In order to entertain me, M. l'Abbé proposes a walk. My feet will not allow it. Consequently, we leave breakfast there and go up to his room in order to find something with which to finish our repast – his good books.*[13]

After the pomposity of Versailles, the tautness of negotiation, it must have been good to unwind in a house that was not too well run, to laugh at and with one's friends, to belong once more to a group, just as in Philadelphia, just as in London.

Disarming and wholesome as the Auteuil household appears through Franklin's eyes, it takes on darker and more morbid overtones when viewed by a critical John Adams. In April 1778, five days after he had been shocked by the ambiguous presence of Mademoiselle Jupin in the Brillon household, Adams was shocked all over again. He had been

invited to dine at Madame Helvétius', together with Franklin
and his grandson. He granted that the dinner was "elegant"
and marveled at the fresh grapes he was offered, so utterly
out of season. Told that they had been preserved in a vacuum,
"sans air," he made note in his diary of the technique em-
ployed.[14] In those days, America borrowed money from
France, while France taught America how to preserve.

Adams remarked further that Madame Helvétius was "a
Lady of established Reputation, the Widow of the famous
Helvétius, who, as Count Sarsefield once said to me, if he had
made a few millions of Livres the more as one of the Farmers
General, and written a few Books the less as a Philosopher, it
might have been better for France and the World."[15] He
paid tribute to the lady's devotion to the memory of her
husband by recording that she had erected a monument to
him and kept a model of it in her house, a statue of herself
weeping over his tomb. Adams even went to the trouble of
transcribing the inscription on the monument's replica.* Then
he lashed out:

*That She might not be, however, entirely without the Society of
Gentlemen, there were three or four handsome Abby's who daily
visited the House and one at least resided there. These Ecclesi-
asticks, one or more of whom reside in allmost every Family of*

---

*   *Toi dont l'âme sublime et tendre*
     A fait ma gloire, et mon bonheur
     Je t'ai perdu: près de ta cendre
     Je viens jouer de ma douleur.

     You, whose sublime and tender soul
     Was all my glory all my joy
     I have lost you: near your urn
     I come to savor my despair.

Distinction, I suppose have as much power to Pardon a Sin as they have to commit one, or to assist in committing one. Oh Mores! said I to myself. What Absurdities, Inconsistencies, Distractions and Horrors would these Manners introduce into our Republican Governments in America; No Kind of Republican Government can ever exist with such national manners as these. Cavete Americani." [16]

Without matching the pitch of Adams' sanctimonious indignation, other people probably saw mischief in a household where a still attractive widow lived with and (partly or totally) supported two abbots and a bachelor, respectively ten, twenty, and thirty years younger than herself.

The participants in these "Absurdities" and "Horrors" seem to have taken a placid view of their life. Abbé Morellet recalled in his *Memoirs* the tranquil years he and his two companions spent "together under the same roof without having the slightest altercation" and attributed this happy state to the fairness of their common friend, "who did not exhibit for any one of the three a preference which would have displeased the other two." [17] As for Abbé de la Roche, the nostalgic memory of the hours spent in such joyous company prompted him to write, years later, when the ocean lay between him and Franklin:

We were so happy, were we not, when sitting all together around a good table; when we discussed ethics, politics, philosophy; when Notre Dame d'Auteuil led you on to flirt, and the Abbé Morellet, while fighting for the cream, set his arguments in magnificent sequence, so as to convince us of what we did not believe. In those days, we would gladly have renounced that other

Paradise to keep the one we had, and live, just as we were, for all eternity.[18]

Coming from the pen of one professionally committed to the afterlife, this is a strong statement; it is true, however, that de la Roche was not too deeply committed. When accused by the Jacobins of counterrevolutionary feelings, he was able to assert that during the twenty-two years he had spent so far at Auteuil, nobody had ever seen him exercise the functions of a Catholic priest. Furthermore, the idea of postponing paradise in favor of immediate enjoyment was one Franklin himself had propounded, tongue in cheek of course, in a note sent to the abbé toward the beginning of their acquaintance.

M. Franklin never forgets any Party at which Madame Helvétius is to appear. He even believes that if he were to go to Paradise that morning, he would beg to be allowed to remain on earth until half past one, to receive the embrace she was kind enough to promise him at their last meeting in M. Turgot's house.[19]

It is rather curious that Franklin should have addressed this and a number of other flirtatious little messages not to the lady herself but to one or another of her three satellites. Such courtship by proxy is one of the dominant features of Franklin's relationship with Madame Helvétius. She wrote little: short, hurried notes inviting him to dinner or begging him to disentangle her from some mixup. No self-analysis like Madame Brillon, no poetic flights like Madame d'Houdetot, no coquettish teasing like Madame de Forbach, no firm data or dates on which to build anything but a most tentative sequence of events. Her personality was all in her presence, and she must be re-created through the impression she made on others.

Such an impression was not always favorable. When Abigail Adams first met Madame Helvétius, she etched a portrait in which the physical decay of the aging French-woman seems to symbolize the moral decadence of France. What else could the descendant of many Puritan generations expect to find in the widow of a freethinker? Here is Boston judging Paris:

She entered the room with a careless, jaunty air; upon seeing the ladies who were strangers to her, she bawled out, "Ah! mon Dieu, where is Franklin? Why did you not tell me there were ladies here?" You must suppose her speaking all this in French. "How I look!" said she, taking hold of a chemise of tiffany, which she had on over a blue lutestring, and which looked as much upon the decay as her beauty, for she was once a handsome woman.

Her hair was frizzled; over it she had a small straw hat, with a dirty gauze half-handkerchief behind. She had a black gauze scarf thrown over her shoulders.

She ran out of the room; when she returned, the Doctor entered at one door, she at the other; upon which she ran forward to him, caught him by the hand, "Helas, Franklin!" then gave him a double kiss, one upon each cheek, and another upon his forehead. When we went into the room to dine, she was placed between the Doctor and Mr. Adams. She carried on the chief of the conversation at dinner, frequently locking her hand into the Doctor's, and sometimes spreading her arms upon the backs of both the gentlemen's chairs, then throwing her arm carelessly upon the Doctor's neck.

I should have been greatly astonished at this conduct, if the good Doctor had not told me that in this lady I should see a genuine Frenchwoman, wholly free from affectation or stiffness of behavior, and one of the best women in the world. I own I was highly disgusted, and never wish for an acquaintance with ladies of this cast.

After dinner, she threw herself on a settee, where she showed more than her feet. She had a little lap-dog, who was, next to the Doctor, her favorite. This she kissed, and when he wet the floor she wiped it up with her chemise. This is one of the Doctor's most intimate friends, with whom he dines once every week, and she with him.[20]

A straitlaced woman would not, of course, imagine the charm such rollicking abandon in dress and deportment could hold for a man, himself full of joie de vivre. Here was relief from the stiffness of diplomatic circles, from the affectation of blue-stockings and blue-bloods, be they as attractive as Madame Brillon or as influential as the Countess d'Houdetot. With Madame Helvétius, Franklin yielded to his wholesome appetite for the simple, robust pleasures of life. There was no need for sophistication, but only an unself-conscious exchange of notes, such as this undated message from her: "Do you want, my dear friend, to have dinner with me on Wednesday; I have the greatest desire to see you and embrace you – and a little bit your son, too."[21] To which he replied: "Of course I shall not fail to come next Wednesday. I get too much pleasure from seeing you, hearing you, too much happiness from holding you in my arms, to forget such a precious invitation." [22] With her, he could joke and speak boldly, without fear of being misunderstood. Through Cabanis, he sent an impudent remark:

If Notre Dame is pleased to spend her days with Franklin, he would be just as pleased to spend his nights with her; and since he has already given her so many of his days, although he has so few left to give, she seems very ungrateful in never giving him one of her nights, which keep passing as a pure loss, without making anyone happy except Poupon [the cat]. Nevertheless, he hugs her very tightly,* for he loves her infinitely in spite of her many shortcomings. [23]

It may have been such a letter which gave rise to the anecdote that when a French lady did tell Franklin she would yield to his entreaties and let him spend the night with her, the Doctor, taken aback, begged to be allowed to postpone this joy "until the nights were longer." [24] Such *bons mots*, of course, were the currency of polite conversation in the eighteenth century, but under the sparkling veneer he had so easily acquired, Franklin's restlessness began to show.

To Cabanis – once more – went the following Valentine, referring mysteriously to four Mesdames Helvétius:

Mr. Franklin, being up, scrubbed, shaved, combed, beautified as best he can, fully dressed and on the point of going out, his head full of the four Helvétius Ladies, and of the sweet kisses he intends to steal from them, is very mortified to find the possibility of this happiness put off to next Sunday. He will bear it as patiently as he can, hoping to see one of those Ladies at M. de Chaumont's on Wednesday. He will be there early, to watch

---

* To say "tightly," Franklin coined the rather useful adverb *serrement*, from *serrer*, to squeeze.

her enter, with that grace and dignity which have charmed him. . . . He even plans to capture her there and keep her to himself for life. The three others, remaining at Auteuil, ought to suffice for the canaries and the Abbés.[25]

"To capture her there and keep her to himself for life" – Madame Helvétius, for once, answered herself, not through the good offices of one of her friends. And her answer, unsigned, undated, hardly legible, never yet published or even assigned to her, made a point of keeping to a tone of carefree camaraderie – and nothing more:

The sweet letter you wrote me, my dear friend, made me feel all the more keenly my loss in not dining with you Wednesday. I hoped that after putting such pretty things on paper, you would come and tell me some; and now, I am vexed for having hoped too much. For I confess that I love pretty things, especially those that come from you.

I shall receive your news today, and I trust that I will hear nothing but good tidings about the pain in your shoulder. By the way, what did you do to that shoulder? Would it be, by any chance, a rheumatism caught under the windows of one of my rivals? Surely, you are young enough to go and spend all clear, fair nights playing the guitar, while blowing on your fingers!

Mind you, I am not going to feel sorry for you. At any rate, it will be a good lesson, and I see better every day how much a flighty, irresponsible youth needs to learn. What reassures me is that your son watches over your behavior; and I recommend that you follow his advice.[26]

She had decided, evidently, to take his advances very lightly. She once told Comtesse de Forbach, who repeated it to Keralio, who repeated it to Franklin, that Franklin "loved

An eighteenth-century salon

people only as long as he saw them." [27] But he did see her very frequently and, being basically a family man, wanted deeply to fit into a niche. "A bachelor," he used to say, "resembles the odd half of a pair of scissors." [28]

A man alone is helpless, and what can be more appealing to a woman than a man's domestic helplessness? In a "billet à Notre Dame d'Auteuil," sent to Madame Helvétius through Abbé de la Roche, Franklin slyly incorporated his bid in a petition ascribed to the flies buzzing in his home. If she did not take care of destroying the spiders, how could they survive? (And how could he, without her?)

The Flies of the Apartments of M. F. request Permission to present their Respects to Madame H., and to express in their best language their Gratitude for the Protection she has been kind enough to give them,

Bizz, izzz ouizz a ouizzz izzzzzzzz, etc.

We have long lived under the hospitable Roof of the said bon-homme F. He has given us free Lodgings; we have also eaten and drunk the whole Year at his Expense without its having cost us anything. Often, when his Friends and himself have used up a Bowl of Punch, he has left a sufficient Quantity to intoxicate a hundred of us Flies.

We have drunk freely from it, and after that we have made our Sallies, our Circles and our Cotillions very prettily in the Air of his Bedroom, and have gaily consummated our little Loves under his Nose.

Finally, we would have been the happiest People in the World, if he had not permitted to remain over the top of his Wainscoting a Number of our declared Enemies, who stretched their Nets to capture us, and who tore us pitilessly to pieces. People of a Disposition both subtle and fierce, abominable Combination!

You, very excellent Lady, had the goodness to order that all these Assassins with their Habitations and their Snares be swept; and your Orders, as they always ought to be, were carried out immediately. Since that Time we have lived happily, and have enjoyed the Beneficence of the said bonhomme F. without fear.

There only remains one Thing for us to wish in order to assure the Stability of our Fortune; permit us to say it,

Bizz izzz ouizz a ouizzzz izzzzzzzz etc.,
It is to see both of you forming at last but one Ménage.[29]

But one ménage! Franklin was ignoring the three long-entrenched lodgers. Abbé Morellet, during one of his absences from Auteuil for work in a library, hinted humorously at a compromise:

For three deadly months, I have been deprived of the pleasure of seeing Monsieur Franklin. . . . He will easily believe that it is none of my fault when I tell him that I have not seen Notre Dame d'Auteuil either. If I were the master of my life, if I were not bound to my desk by a chain, I should always want to be between her and him. This, perhaps, would not suit Mr. Franklin who loves to be very close *to the lady. Well, I should consent to place her between him and me. I think this arrangement is fit for two philosophers who believe in the principle of freedom of trade and who do not like exclusive privileges.*[30]

Nothing but innocent joking, it would seem, but soon another believer in commercial freedom, the very man who had introduced Franklin to Madame Helvétius – Turgot –

was in for a great surprise. The "bonhomme Franklin," whose "pretty little stories" had enchanted him only a few months before, had now contrived a plot that did not amuse him at all; he had formally proposed to Madame Helvétius. What was worse, Madame had not turned down Franklin as promptly as she had Turgot, but had taken the proposal seriously enough to write her old friend for advice.[31]

Actually, the whole episode of Franklin's proposal is both revealed and concealed in later innuendos.[32] Neither Madame Helvétius' letter nor Turgot's reply have survived, but Turgot must have been irritated enough to tell Madame rather bluntly that both she and Franklin had passed the age for romance. That much can be surmised from a somewhat cryptic reference in a letter Turgot wrote on December 18, 1779, to his intimate friend Pierre Samuel du Pont de Nemours: "My answer to Madame Helvétius has been delivered the day after you left. No matter what you say, it is a great dupery to show oneself too chivalrous, and had I been so, I am quite certain that I would not have elicited more gratitude."[33] Turgot had forgotten that he was dealing with a man not easily discouraged. Franklin, now that he had started, pursued his campaign with a characteristic mixture of positive vigor and negative irony: vigor might ultimately carry him to success; irony would provide a convenient and graceful means of exit in case of failure.

It is this very mixture that makes his famous *Bagatelle* on the Elysian Fields so elusive. If he were truly in love, why did he broadcast, in an almost sacrilegious vein, what must have been a deep disappointment? If he were not in love, why insist upon and publicize a game which Madame Helvétius would not play and Turgot found ludicrous? The great nineteenth-century French critic, Sainte-Beuve, was puzzled, too, by this ambivalence; turning upon Franklin, the rationalist, the searchlight of his own romantic era, he commented that the American had never allowed himself to be carried away by feeling, whether in his youth or in his old age, whether in love or in religion.[34]

The theme of the *Elysian Fields* is, in a way, the elaboration of an idea Franklin had once broached to Abbé de la Roche, a rather touching identification between himself and the late Helvétius: "I have often noticed, when reading the works of M. Helvétius, that even though we were born and brought up in opposite parts of the world, we have often met one another in the same thoughts; and it is very flattering for me to reflect that we have loved the same studies, the same friends, and the same woman." An asterisk beside the word "friends" sends us to the bottom of the page, where Franklin enumerates them: "Messieurs Voltaire, Hume, Turgot, Marmontel, Le Roy, Abbes Morellet, De la Roche, etc., etc."[35]

In this case, Franklin was, as we know, rather wide of the mark; his personality had little in common with that of Helvétius. But the notion appealed to him so much that he now carried it further and pointed out the basic similarity between his robust Debbie and the uncomplicated Madame Helvétius. Here, in a new, unabridged translation from the French, is Franklin's famous piece, whose youthful, somewhat cynical whimsy defies summary:

Saddened by your barbarous resolution, stated so positively last night, to remain single the rest of your life, in honor of your dear husband, I went home, fell on my bed, believing myself dead, and found myself in the Elysian Fields.

*I was asked if I had a wish to see some Important Persons –
Take me to the Philosophers. – There are two who reside quite
near here, in this Garden: they are very good neighbors and very
good friends of each other. – Who are they? – Socrates and H. –
I have prodigious esteem for both of them; but let me see H. first,
for I understand some French and not a word of Greek.*

*He received me with great courtesy, having known me by
reputation, he said, for some time. He asked me a thousand
questions on war, and on the present state of religion, of liberty,
and of the government in France. – But you are not enquiring at
all about your dear friend Madame H.; yet, she is excessively in
love with you, and I was with her but an hour ago.*

*– Ah! said he, you are bringing back to my mind my former
felicity. But one must forget, in order to be happy in this place.
For several of the first years, I thought of nobody but her. Well,
now I am consoled. I have taken another wife. One as similar to
her as I could find. She is not, to be sure, quite as beautiful, but
she has just as much common sense, a little more wisdom, and
she loves me infinitely. Her continuous endeavor is to please me;
and she has gone out right now to search for the best nectar and
ambrosia to regale me with tonight; stay with me and you shall
see her.*

*– I notice, said I, that your former friend is more faithful
than you: for several matches have been offered her, and she has
turned them all down. I confess that I, for one, loved her madly;
but she was harsh towards me and rejected me absolutely for the
love of you.*

*– I pity you, said he, for your misfortune; for she is truly a
good and lovely woman, and most amiable. But Abbé de la R.
and Abbé M., aren't they anymore in her home, every now and
then?*

– *Yes, of course; for she has not lost a single one of your friends.*

– *Now, if you had won over Abbé M. (with coffee and cream) and got him to plead your cause, you might have met with success; for he is as subtle a debater as Duns Scotus or St. Thomas; he puts his arguments in such good order that they become almost irresistible. Or, better still, if you had convinced Abbé de la R. (by the gift of some fine edition of an old classic) to argue against you: for I have always observed that when he advises something she has a strong tendency to do the exact opposite.*

As he was saying this, the new Madame H. came in with the nectar. I recognized her instantly as Madame F., my former American friend. I claimed her. But she said coldly, I have been a good wife to you for forty-nine years and four months, almost half a century; be content with that. I have formed a new connection here, that will last for eternity.

Grieved by this rebuke from my Euridyce, I resolved there and then to abandon those ungrateful shadows, and to come back to this good world, to see the sun again, and you. Here I am! Revenge! [36]

Madame Helvétius received the *Bagatelle* "one morning, after spending the previous day in uttering with Franklin a great deal of follies," says Morellet in his *Memoirs*. [37] It can be dated almost exactly, thanks to a circumstance that only one of Franklin's biographers, so far, has noticed: Debbie states that she has been married to Benjamin for the last forty-nine years and four months. Since their wedding took place on September 1, 1731, the encounter in the Elysian Fields must fall shortly after New Year, 1780, a few weeks after Turgot's letter to du Pont.

In the *Elysian Fields*, Sainte-Beuve concluded, "one can sense a deep emotion underlying the playful surface."[38] True: yet, at the very moment when Franklin was painting for Madame Helvétius an attractive pagan paradise, fully equipped with Greek philosophers – a fitting afterlife for the widow of a philosopher and freethinker – he was also redecorating an alternative paradise, complete with Christian angels and chamber music, for Madame Brillon. "Since you have assured me that we shall meet one another in paradise," he wrote her, "I have kept thinking of how we shall arrange our affairs in that Country; for I trust your assurances, and implicity believe all that you believe." And, as if one spare wife were not enough, he added: "If you turn me down, perhaps I shall address myself to Madame d'Hardancourt."[39] No wonder Madame Helvétius, recalling the *Bagatelle* long after Franklin's return to America, agreed that they would meet again after death, she with a husband, he with a wife, but added: "I believe you have been a rascal and will find more than one wife up there!"[40]

A mere joke, "a great deal of follies,"[41] one might be tempted to say with Morellet. Didn't Franklin convert the *Elysian Fields* into a pleasantry for public consumption by printing the piece almost at once, so early that Grimm could reprint it in the April, 1780, issue of *Correspondance littéraire*?

Yes and no. After a cooling-off period, Franklin returned to the attack. Far from being chastened, he trespassed over and again, and in a letter to Cabanis, who had gone away for the summer, he bragged of it:

We often talk of you at Auteuil, where everybody loves you. I now and then offend our good lady who cannot long retain her

Portrait of Turgot, from the portrait in pastels by J. N. Ducreux

displeasure, but, sitting in state on her sofa, extends graciously her long, handsome arm, and says: "là; baisez ma main; je vous pardonne," *with all the dignity of a sultaness. She is as busy as ever, endeavoring to make every creature about her happy, from the Abbés down thro' all ranks of the family to the birds and Poupon. I long for your return.*[42]

This was written on June 30, 1780. By this time, however, Madame Helvétius was ready to bring all insistence to an end by fleeing the battlefield. On Saturday, June 24, six days before Franklin wrote Cabanis, Turgot had written du Pont:

I have seen one of our friends whom I have found in pretty poor shape. Her tranquility has been again troubled, and always by the same vagaries. I shall tell you all when I see you. She has decided to go and spend the summer in Tours, at the home of a relative; she brings her older daughter along. She will settle in the country and busy herself only with her health and that of her daughter, that she may forget, if possible, all the turmoil that has tormented her. I think this decision is very reasonable and most appropriate, not only for her own tranquility, but also to reestablish it in that other head that has agitated so ill-advisedly. I shall try to visit both of them the day after tomorrow. She has arranged her departure for Monday.[43]

She was to leave on "Monday," but "the day after tomorrow" already was a Monday. We know that on Monday, June 26, Turgot actually invited Franklin for dinner, alone, and "did not talk to him either about Charlestown [Charleston, just lost by the Americans to the British] or about the bankruptcy of [American] paper money": these sardonic words, in another letter to du Pont,[44] may indicate by innuendo that Turgot tried to talk Franklin out of pressing Madame Helvétius.

One can only guess. At any rate, the storm at Auteuil, if it can be called such, subsided at last. Franklin settled graciously for what he was being graciously offered, a choice seat in the inner circle. As he wrote to Madame Helvétius: "Here is a problem a mathematician would be hard put to solve. Usually, when we share things, each person gets only one part; but when I share my *pleasure* with you, my part is doubled. *The part is more than the whole.*"[45]

Keep the chain bright and shiny ❦ FRANKLIN

They shared pleasures; they shared ideas. In the absence of contemporary records of those leisurely talks around the table or under the huge acacia, we must be content with the memoirs left, years later, by the participants. A little blurred, suffused in the golden haze of happy memories recorded in unhappy times, they nevertheless provide a framework for what took place at Auteuil.

Never mind if, at times, the spotlight falls less on Madame Helvétius than on her three companions; whoever was speaking, she was the soul of the group, its catalyst and raison d'être. Its sovereign, too: "you know well that one does not resist her will," Morellet wrote Franklin.[1] A benevolent despot, though: "Even if you totally mistake the way to spell *bonheur*, still, from the eminence of your ignorance, you shed it," the same Morellet told her.[2] The pursuit of happiness was her province, her personal contribution; it was for the others, who knew so much more, to investigate the rational and scientific means of prolonging life and promoting liberty. How Cabanis, de la Roche, and Morellet viewed Franklin, how he responded to them, what problems they debated, what stories they traded – all this recaptures something of the climate Madame could so well generate.

The first time Franklin met Cabanis, the young man was talking animatedly in a corner of the Auteuil salon. "At your age," remarked the old philosopher, "a man's soul is still at the window, looking outside."[3] It was, indeed, a soul thirsty for communication, and communication soon established itself on various levels. First and foremost, medicine,

Portrait of Franklin, by Philippe-Amédée Vanloo

but in the eighteenth-century vein, an extension of philosophy rather than a scientific specialization. Cabanis had started his studies relatively late, on the advice of a famous doctor who regarded the practice of medicine as a healthier way of life than the youth's first vocation, writing poetry. He had abandoned poetry reluctantly, taking time from his studies to translate parts of Homer, composing in verse his rendition of the Hippocratic Oath to be delivered on his graduation in 1783. From then on, he devoted himself entirely to the new discipline. Throughout his career, which was a brilliant one, Cabanis always remained a theoretician. He investigated the reciprocal influence of mind and body, fell briefly for Mesmer, composed an important work on method (*Du Degré de certitude de la médecine*), and propagated the ideas of the new or "sensualist" school of medicine: the physician should rely only on what he can see and touch.

With one notable exception, he limited his practice to a few needy cases around Auteuil. The notable exception, who almost cost him his own life, was none other than the early leader of the Revolution, Mirabeau. Mirabeau, whose star was already waning, died while under the care of his friend Cabanis, and this gave rise to the suspicion that Cabanis had poisoned him. He defended himself in his *Journal de la maladie de Mirabeau*, was absolved, but never abandoned again the safe paths of theory which eventually led him to a chair on the Paris Faculty and a Senator's seat under Napoleon.

A very different outlook, it would seem, from the eminently practical one of Franklin, yet their minds may have met on at least one concrete point. The very first of Cabanis' works, his *Observations on Hospitals*, published in 1789, was close to Franklin's heart. Franklin had written extensively on the subject of ventilation, particularly the ventilation of hospitals, first in London in collaboration with Alexander Small, then in Paris, with his friend, Jean-Baptiste Le Roy. The destruction by fire, in 1778, of the Hôtel-Dieu, the largest hospital in Paris, gave him scope for grandiose plans of reform of the kind he liked best, applying a new scientific principle to everyday human needs. An ardent believer in the virtues of fresh air, Franklin would urge his French friends to emulate his own practice of taking an air bath in the nude upon arising in the morning. The few who followed his advice promptly caught cold and closed their windows, since, as Cabanis explained, it took a man of the Doctor's constitution to withstand such shock treatment.[4]

The relationship between the two went far beyond the realm of medicine. Cabanis was that dream of the elderly: the eager young listener, avid for stories of the olden days, in quest of a pattern for his own life and thought. Franklin, who at various times of his life had taken delight in molding the minds of a number of young women, had gone completely unheeded by his own son and grandson. Now, in his seventies, he found a willing, attentive disciple. To this sophisticated Frenchman from the Corrèze he poured out the simple joys of his childhood in Boston: the romping on the snow and ice, the endless summer swimming, his mother's love and understanding, her amused view of his early bout with vegetarianism. He reminisced with delight, telling many anecdotes, among them the famous story of the whistle, which he had written out for Madame Brillon. Cabanis drank in every word.

With such a listener, how could Franklin have helped indulging in a little moralizing? He stressed his dogged efforts toward self-education: Plutarch, Xenophon, Socrates – who was to remain his model for life – Locke, Shaftesbury, *The Spectator*. What about France? asks Cabanis. No French author, no French thought? Yes, of course, he had read Pascal's *Provinciales*. The translation was rather poor, but he had loved the book, read it several times over, and it was still one of his favorite French works.

From the young Franklin's studies they moved on to his flight from Boston, to his arrival in Philadelphia, penniless, facing the world all alone, "without any other guide for conduct than his good luck, or rather his good sense."[5] When, at this point Franklin compared his situation to that of Adam or Tom Jones, Cabanis could fully identify with him, for he, too, had been expelled from school because of a rebellious spirit, sent by his father to Paris, and abandoned to fend for himself. The reference to Tom Jones is not devoid of a certain piquancy: the actor who created his part on the Parisian stage happened to be Joseph Caillot, husband of that very Blanchette who was having a tempestuous affair with Temple. But such mundane considerations would never enter Cabanis' recollections. His "Notice sur Benjamin Franklin," published, as he says, because Franklin's own family was so deplorably slow in bringing out the great man's biography, maintains a highly moralistic tone.[6]

Passing from his protagonist's mind to his soul, Cabanis deals at some length with the spiritual crisis which had led the restless young American to "doubt the existence of God."[7] The crisis comes to its triumphant conclusion in the proclamation by the now serene and vaguely deistic old American of a pragmatic morality according to which it pays to be virtuous: "One day that he had dwelt at length on that topic, he wound up by telling us in his French, all the more graceful and forceful for its awkwardness: 'If the rascals only knew all the advantages of virtue, they would become honest through sheer rascality!'"[8]

The ethical side of Franklin's personality appealed most to Cabanis. Although a scientist himself, he paid rather scant attention to Franklin's scientific achievements but dwelt on his hero's early striving toward self-improvement and his mature achievement of inner harmony. There is a note of ecstasy in the page where he tells how Franklin, in his Philadelphia beginnings, kept an agenda of his weekly and monthly progress in the various virtues he had decided to cultivate. "We touched this precious booklet," exclaims Cabanis, "we held it in our hands. Here was, in a way, the chronological story of Franklin's soul!"[9]

It was a rosy picture, on the whole, that the Doctor drew for his young friend: Debbie, bustling happily in the shop, filling with her intuition the gaps in her husband's more reasoned views, helping him on the road to prosperity; Poor Richard, brought back to life by his creator, uttering once more his homespun aphorisms against the elegant background of the Auteuil salon; Benjamin himself, dressed as a workman, toiling among his workmen, "not in the manner of European speculators who direct their business from the depths of an office,"[10] but right in the midst of manual labor; around him, his friends, the Philadelphia merchants, bristling with energy and good will, forming a club, organizing a public library, raising money for schools, setting up an insurance system for the sick and the old, founding the Philosophical Society.

And beyond the friends loomed those famous "savages"

about whom French curiosity and idealism knew no bounds, the noble savages, extolled from afar by a whole school of thought, but whom Franklin had actually seen, talked to, listened to, and dealt with. His *Remarks on the Politeness of Savages* were read avidly by his Parisian entourage, though Cabanis had some private reservations about the idea that uncivilized nations are happier than civilized ones. Between the two trends of his day, the one pointing back toward naïve primitivism and the other striving toward full exploitation of the human mind, Cabanis sympathized with the latter. But he took pleasure in the Indian legends Franklin told and noted some of their more felicitous, poetic expressions, such as the famous "Keep the chain of friendship bright and shiny" that the Doctor was particularly fond of quoting.

So much for the young Franklin re-created by the old Franklin for the benefit of the Auteuil society. While reminiscing, the Doctor may have indulged too much in his moralistic, self-righteous vein; at that time, he was writing the second part of his autobiography – the very pages Mark Twain would brand as "a thing which has brought affliction to millions of boys since, whose fathers had read Franklin's pernicious biography." [11] But the Franklin whom Cabanis was in a position to observe almost from day to day for eight years did not only preach the unsmiling virtues of a Puritan background; he told Cabanis that bad humor was a vice, an "uncleanliness of the soul." [12] Of this man Cabanis drew a full-length portrait, whose essential and familiar features are those which have struck less resentful modern biographers than Mark Twain: Franklin's composure, his cunning reserve ("faith saves us in the next world, loses us in this one" [13]), his passionate longing for clarity in communication, his talent for simplifying complex problems, his overwhelming interest in the useful and the applicable, his rich and selective memory, the freshness of his style and mind: "his art of living at peace with himself and with others." [14]

When Franklin told Cabanis stories of his youth, he was convinced that his own memoirs, written long before and left in America, had been destroyed along with his other papers by the British. Thus, it may indeed have been with an eye to posterity that the old philosopher, knowing the eighteenth-century French passion for memoirs of all kinds, spoke of himself at such length; thus he wished to be remembered – be it through his autobiography, if it ever were completed and printed, or through the testimony of his Auteuil friends, if they would put it in writing. Of the less successful part of his former life – the fact that his own children had none of the qualities Mark Twain deplored – Franklin spoke little. But Abbé de la Roche reports that one day, while taking a walk in the Bois de Boulogne, the Doctor mentioned a little son, Francis, who had died of smallpox at the age of four. Forty years had passed, but his eyes were filled with tears. "I always fancy," Franklin said, "that he would have been the best of my children." [15]

But for this repressed sorrow, there is an immense difference between the sunny complacency of Franklin's recollections and the throbbing, self-lacerating quality of Rousseau's *Confessions*, which were being published posthumously in the 1780s. Yet at the time the French could not refrain from drawing parallels between the two. When Jacques Buisson published his pirated edition of the first part of Franklin's *Autobiography*, he claimed in his preface that the Doctor had decided to write the story of his life after reading the published installment of Rousseau's *Confessions*. An unsigned, undated note, unmistakably in the hand of Abbé de la Roche, vigorously protested such a notion. Nothing could be further from the truth, said the Abbé: "For reasons unnecessary to explain, Franklin never read Rousseau's *Confessions*, nor any other of his works. Franklin read little; and the cast of his mind would not have made him appreciate Rousseau's production in general, still less his *Confessions*." [16]

While Cabanis stressed the wisdom and self-discipline of the great man, Abbé Lefebvre de la Roche, in his "Note sur Franklin" published in 1790 shortly after Franklin's death, endeavored to pass on to posterity the fun and flavor of his friend. His relationship with Franklin, of course, lacked the master–disciple character it could not avoid with Cabanis. In some respects, the abbé played the role of the teacher: he revised Franklin's unpolished French and introduced him to the refinements of French bibliography. Together they went into the technicalities of first editions, precious bindings, rare etchings, and Franklin, who never forgot that he had started life as a printer ("Benjamin Franklin, Printer" was the epitaph he chose) must have enjoyed talking shop with such a connoisseur.

For all his admiration of the Doctor's straightforward wisdom, self-reliance, and manual ability, de la Roche had no higher opinion of American rusticity than John and Abigail Adams of French decadence. The Boston of Franklin's youth looked grim to the untraveled imagination of the sophisticated Parisian abbé:

Boston was no more than the gathering place of a few sailors and

European adventurers. . . . It had no private library, no public schools; religious quacks preached their absurd dogmas and fanatic morality, all the vices of superstitious ignorance created the greatest obstacles to the spreading of light. . . . The Bible was the only book known, and few colonists were able to read it.[17]

Hardly better than a village of savages. Yet, de la Roche realized that the poverty of his beginnings had been instrumental in making Franklin such a paragon of sobriety and endurance. Here was a man who could "work eight days running without any more rest than short naps in his armchair" and who would "find a new morning," as it were, after one or two hours of sleep; a man who, at the age of almost eighty, "would teach one of his grandsons how to swim by swimming himself across the Seine, at Passy, early in the morning."[18] More amazing still, in the abbé's eyes, was the fact that Franklin, Minister Plenipotentiary of America, never used more than one manservant at a time, feeling, as he said, "that with two you get only half of one, and with three hardly any at all."[19] In the same mood, the Doctor would quip good-naturedly about the French taste for superfluities:

Your most beautiful apartments are filled with the most uncomfortable kind of luxury. I see a profusion of marble, porcelain and gilding abounding to no purpose, elegant chimneys that smoke without giving any heat, tables where one cannot write except freezing and against the light, beds and alcoves lovely to sleep in when one feels well, but impossible to read in, write in, or be taken care of, in sickness.[20]

A born collector of books and literary tidbits, de la Roche collected the witticisms and anecdotes Franklin contributed to the general conversation at Auteuil. An endless source of amusement was provided by the flow of bizarre letters and requests Franklin never stopped receiving from everywhere in France during his eight years in Passy. People who thought they had a cure for dropsy, gout, the stone, and a host of other diseases; dreamers who had devised a brave new political scheme; lovelorn sailors, adventurers, abandoned wives, indigents, rebellious sons; distraught parents, poets, and poetasters – almost anybody who could wield a pen wrote to Franklin, and wrote again if left without an answer, imploring him for a word of recognition: thoughtful letters, pathetic letters, preposterous letters. De la Roche tells of the one sent by a provincial gentleman who reasoned that America needed a king, and since his own ancestors could be traced back to William the Conqueror, he offered his services to Congress for the post. Should Congress decline, he was willing to settle for a pension of 15,000 livres, promising in return that he would never leave his country seat and would allow the Americans to choose whatever form of government they wished.

Franklin laughed at the crackpots but was irked by the enormous number of people utterly unknown to him or at most introduced by someone he hardly knew, who wanted his recommendation to obtain a post or a favor. To relieve his feelings, he ended by composing a satirical document in which he parodied this procedure:

Sir, The Bearer of this who is going to America, presses me to give him a Letter of Recommendation, tho' I know nothing of him, not even his Name. This may seem extraordinary, but I assure you it is not uncommon here. Sometimes indeed one unknown Person brings me another equally unknown, to recom-

mend him; and sometimes they recommend one another! As to
this Gentleman, I must refer you to himself for his Character and
Merits, with which he is certainly better acquainted than I can
possibly be.[21]

To appreciate Franklin's irony, one must read the letters
of recommendation for, or self-recommendation by, career
officers who wanted desperately to jump onto the bandwagon
of America's Continental Army. Franklin had been instructed
to hire only a hand-picked number of specialists. Hundreds of
applications are preserved in his papers, and they describe a
pitiful group. Some of the petitioners were sincerely enamored
of American ideals, but a great number merely sought to
evade boredom and poverty at a time when the French army's
budget had been cut, and when, to put it in the blunt words of
a would-be volunteer, "peace has unfortunately been reign-
ing in Europe for a good many years."

What could one reply to that petty nobleman who offered
America the services of his five sons, making it clear that he
was in no position to equip them or pay for their travel, but
that he of course would make sure that they brought along
their *certificats de noblesse?* Franklin's favorite letter of the
kind, says de la Roche, was sent to him by a lady from the
Court who wrote the following: "Sir, If in your America
one knows the secret of how to reform a detestable subject
who has been the cross of his family, I beg you to send
hither the one who will bring you this recommendation. You
will thus accomplish a miracle worthy of you." [22] And
Franklin liked to add that the young man did, indeed, go to
America and died a brave death on the battlefield.

Such were some of the stories and remarks exchanged at
Auteuil. It was, it would seem, during such a moment –

listening to an anecdote, considering a better one to cap it with – that Franklin, who had been painted so many times, was painted once more, at the request of Madame Helvétius. De la Roche quotes him as telling his friends: "Cheer me up, or you will have of me the saddest of portraits."[23] In fact, it is perhaps the liveliest of the French series. Painted against a dark green background, in a green coat with a light brown fur collar, his silver spectacles on his nose, his grey locks carefully combed, his grey eyes twinkling with more malice than usual, Franklin seems about to say something. The name of the artist is not known, but it is a likely guess that he was Charles-Amédée Vanloo, whose relative, Louis-Michel Vanloo, had, years before, painted both Madame Helvétius and her husband. For more than 150 years, the portrait remained in Lumigny, the château Madame Helvétius had given as a dowry to her older daughter Charlotte, Marquise de Mun, but since 1948 it has been in Philadelphia.

To Cabanis, Franklin was a father, to de la Roche, a witty companion, but to Abbé Morellet, the best known of the Auteuil regulars, he was infinitely more. For the abbé, unlike Cabanis and de la Roche, who tended to live in ivory towers, was steeped in life. And so was Franklin.

They had met in England, in the spring of 1772, at a house party given by Lord Shelburne at his Wycombe estate. The party lasted five or six days: Franklin and David Garrick, the actor, shared the limelight. Franklin performed his famous trick of calming turbulent waters by scattering on them a few drops of oil concealed in his hollow magic cane. Morellet discovered with relief that the famous American did not limit his conversation to electricity, but that "public economy and government"[24] interested him just as much. They talked at length, in a mixture of Franklin's poor French and Morellet's shaky English, and understood each other perfectly. Back in London, Morellet rushed to see more of his new acquaintance, and they dined together frequently. He noticed Franklin's newly perfected stove, thought of the good such a model would do in France, bought it for twelve guineas, and started tinkering with it as soon as he got home.

Thus started between the two men a rich and hearty relationship, based on a variety of common interests. They shared a taste for food, wine, and singing, they were fellow putterers, fellow explorers of economic law, and fellow philanthropists endeavoring to improve the human lot. The abbé, who had known the hard school of poverty, was sensitive to the world's injustices and aggressive in wanting to relieve them. A two-month stay in the Bastille for his defense of the *philosophes* from an attack launched by the ultraconservative element had given him a halo in liberal circles. When he came out of jail, the editors of the *Encyclopédie* entrusted him with the writing of a number of articles; they must have just reached the letter F at that time, for Morellet signed "Fatalité," "Figures," "Fils de Dieu," "Foi," and so on.

The abbé was a good polemicist. Not endowed with outstanding originality himself, he was quick to sense greatness in others, absorb it, propagate it, and act as a cross-fertilizing agent between individuals and countries. He had the courage to translate and publish an explosive document discovered during a trip to Italy, a manual used by the Inquisition. And he had the foresight to introduce into France the humanitarian views of Italy's Cesare Beccaria, whose *Treatise of Crimes and Punishments* he was the first to translate. Along with Turgot, he fought the valiant battle against excessive tolls and taxes and contributed in no small measure to the suppression of the privileges hitherto enjoyed by the all-powerful *Compagnie des Indes*. At the time of Franklin's arrival in Paris, Morellet was battling Abbé Galiani and the group of economists then in power who maintained, with Necker, that the grain trade should indeed be regulated.

As their friendship deepened through almost daily contact, Franklin and Morellet embarked on a number of specific joint projects. Some were practical, such as working together on the famous stove. When Franklin left France, he gave Morellet his tool chest "with a drawer full of nails, to satisfy that taste for nailing and hammering that they had in common." [25]

Other projects were humanitarian. Franklin enlisted Morellet's help to get a former servant, Arbelot, admitted to the Hospital "des Quinze Vingt," a home for the indigent blind. In Arbelot's behalf, the abbé invoked no less an influence than that of the Prince-Cardinal Louis-René de Rohan, member of the Academy and Grand Almoner of the Kingdom. One might have thought that the Cardinal, already notorious for his love of intrigue, would have easily accommodated a protégé of the American Minister Plenipotentiary; but his scruples, for once, stood in the way of the unfortunate servant, who was almost blind, but not "perfectly blind." [26] To circumvent the strict requirements of the hospital, it was necessary, said the Cardinal's secretary, to obtain an affidavit from a certified surgeon outside Paris who would be willing to vouch for Arbelot's eligibility. While the bureaucratic wheels were grinding, Arbelot became the humble, unsuspected victim of the most clamorous court scandal of the century, the "affair of the diamond necklace."

Far from winning the Queen's favor by the gift of a fabulous necklace, as he had been led to believe, Rohan was tried and, though technically acquitted, fell into disgrace. In 1787, years after his first petition, poor Arbelot, as Le Veillard wrote to Franklin in Philadelphia, was now "perfectly blind" but still dangling, "all his hopes overturned," and begged to be recommended by his former employer to the new Grand Almoner, the Bishop of Metz.[27]

Some of the humanitarian ideas bandied about at Auteuil were to bear fruit a few years later. Thus, as a recent literary guide to the streets of Paris points out,[28] it was because he had met Franklin and his friends in Madame Helvétius' salon that a physician named Philippe Pinel realized how cruelly the lunatics were treated at La Salpêtrière. As soon as he was put in charge of that institution, in 1795, he freed them from their chains.

Morellet's interest in politics was strong, and he never stopped soliciting and recording Franklin's opinions on specific points. Did Franklin feel that, in America, a militia was more desirable than a standing regular army? Yes, he did. Did Franklin think that trade should be regulated? Of course not. "It must have taken quite a brainstorm for the Europeans to fancy that grain trade must be regulated by law."[29] How large a control did Franklin believe the state should exercise over economic affairs? As little as possible. The state's main function is to prevent violence. In all other matters, it should practice a policy of laissez faire.

Franklin, on his side, relied heavily on Morellet's political and critical judgment. The test came when Morellet, asked to read and translate a *plaisanterie sourde* which contained the sharpest of Franklin's attacks against the pretensions of hereditary aristocracy, advised the Doctor not to publish the "serious joke" in its original form. It had taken shape in Franklin's mind as a reaction to the founding of the Society of the Cincinnati, formed to bring together, with the blessing of both Washington and the French Government, the former officers of the American Army, including French and other foreign volunteers. In the original plan, membership was to be hereditary through the line of eldest sons, thus creating in free America something like a new nobility. This outraged Franklin, the self-made man, whose views were moving to the left as he grew older. As he had already pointed out in *Poor Richard* for 1751, any contemporary nobleman who traced his line back to the Norman conquest would be actually descended from 1,048,576 persons who had been living then. With the same kind of reckoning, he now figured that in "three hundred years . . . our present Chevalier of the Order of the Cincinnatus's share in the then existing knight will be but a 512th part." [30] Much better, he stated, was the Chinese system wherein honor does not descend but ascend, so that when a Chinese wins credit, it goes to his parents.

To Morellet, however, the idea of the Cincinnati was not repulsive at all. His profession placed him in one of the two privileged orders; furthermore, as the recent beneficiary of several small pensions (including one obtained from the French King at Lord Shelburne's request), he felt ever more closely connected to the Establishment. Without quite expressing his disapproval toward Franklin's outburst, he tried to tone it down:

I am sending you back, my respected friend, your original text and the translation. I believe I have preserved the accent of reason and of serious joke you have put in it. Check, however, whether I have caught your meaning everywhere. I have added the last line on my own, as a necessary correction, without which your sentence expressed some contempt for the officers who have served in America, a contempt which, no doubt, is not intentional. At any rate, if you permit me to say so, this paper, though excellent, may cause irritation to some people you do not want to antagonize; and for this reason you ought not to give it, unless you think otherwise, except to persons who have enough philosophy to know and feel all the absurdity and ridiculousness of the harmful bias you fight so well.

I presume I belong with them, but I also presume that I belong with those for whom you have shown some esteem and friendship and whom you regard as worthy enough to understand you. I embrace you with all the tenderness and respect I have devoted to you for life.[31]

Franklin was easily convinced. On the back of the same sheet, the same day, he answered:

Your Sentiments and mine, my dear Friend, are exactly the same respecting the Imprudence of showing that Paper; it has therefore, tho' written some Months past, never been communicated to anyone but yourself, and will probably not appear till after my Decease, if it does then. You see how much I confide in your Friendship and Discretion.[32]

The paper was never published in its final form, but some of its points reappear in Mirabeau's *Considérations sur l'Ordre de Cincinnatus*, that came out in London in September 1784, some time after Franklin had conversed at length with Mirabeau. Since Mirabeau's work was republished two years later in Philadelphia, Franklin's antinobility stand did get public exposure, if not under his own name. It has never been fully ascertained whether he changed his mind later and accepted membership in the Order; the document upon which this assumption is based is considered worthless by many scholars. That the Cincinnati did send an official delegation to Franklin's funeral does not prove anything either.

What was Madame Helvétius' part in these political conversations? She probably did not try to contribute actively to debates that were clearly beyond her blessed "ignorance," but she was far from indifferent. Later, when the excesses of the French Revolution pushed Morellet further to the right, she did not, as the abbé lamented in his *Memoirs*, "remain neutral among her friends and adopt a modest attitude of doubt on such lofty questions,'[33] but sided with the more progressive views of Cabanis and de la Roche And when the latter two, shocked by an antirevolutionary pamphlet that Morellet sprang on them as a surprise, decided to break all relations with him, Madame Helvétius, though plunged in grief, cast her lot with them and allowed Morellet to gather his books and furniture and quit her grounds forever.

Happily, there was no need to take sides during the years of Franklin's stay. Politics did not interfere with merrymaking and song. Music, though not as crucial as in the Brillons' home, played its part in Auteuil. Through Franklin's good offices, Madame Brillon's piano would be borrowed occasionally, and invitations for "good music and tea with ice" went back and forth. Morellet shared Franklin's fondness for Scottish songs and had a very pleasant voice. No man to underrate his own talents, the abbé never failed to interrupt the flow of his learned remembrances in order to quote himself in extenso any time he had composed a song or a poem for a special occasion. He seemed particularly proud of the drinking song for which Franklin had been the inspiration. In twelve lively stanzas, he submitted that the real reason for the American Revolution was Benjamin's wish to drink good French "Catholic" wine, no longer the drab beer of the English:

On ne combattit jamais
Pour de plus grands intérêts;
Ils veulent l'indépendance
Pour boire des vins de France,
    C'est là le fin
Du projet de Benjamin.

Le congrès a déclaré
Qu'ils boiraient notre claré
Et c'est pour notre champagne
Qu'ils se sont mis en campagne,
    De longue main,
Préparés par Benjamin.

L'Anglais sans humanité
Voulait les réduire au thé;
Il leur vendait du vin trouble
Qu'il leur faisait payer double,
    Au grand chagrin
De leur frère Benjamin.[34]

There was never any fight
For a greater, nobler right:
Independence, so they think

Will permit French wine to drink
    This goal I know
Of Benjamin.

Congress stated right away
They would drink France's claret;
For the sake of our champagne
They have started their campaign
    Planned long ago
By Benjamin.

The English lacked humanity
As they forced them to drink tea
And would sell them muddy wine
At the price of the most fine
    To the great woe
Of Benjamin.

Not to be outdone, Benjamin wrote down the words of a drinking song he had composed some forty years earlier and which had come back to his mind while he was reading a poem by Helvétius on happiness. It is in dialogue form between the Singer, who suggests various modes of reaching happiness (love, riches, power) and the Chorus, who invariably answers:

O No!
Not so!
For honest Souls know
Friends and a Bottle still bear the Bell.

(Franklin explains in a footnote that "to bear the bell"

Three Positions of the Elbow, illustration to Franklin's letter in praise of wine, drawn by Temple

means "to win the prize.") At the end, the Singer is convinced
and proclaims irreverently:

Then toss off your Glasses, and scorn the dull Asses,
Who missing the Kernel still gnaw the Shell.
What's Love, Rule or Riches? Wise Solomon teaches
They're Vanity, Vanity, Vanity still.[35]

Franklin had further thoughts about wine and set them
down in one of the gayest, maddest letters he ever wrote.
Addressed to Abbé Morellet, it was meant to bring laughter
to the whole Auteuil group, with its cascade of puns, at a
time when puns were still held in highest esteem. Unfortunately, since the punning is done on the French word
vin (facetiously linked to di*vin*, de*vin*er, etc.), much of the
fun is lost even in such a careful translation as Richard
Amacher's:

You have often enlivened me, my dear friend, with your excellent
drinking songs; in return, I desire to edify you by some Christian,
moral and philosophical reflections on the same subject.
　　"In vino veritas," says the wise man; "truth is in the wine."
　　Before Noah, men, having only water to drink, could not find
the truth. So they went astray; they became abominably wicked
and were justly exterminated by the water which they loved to
drink.
　　This good man Noah, having seen that all his contemporaries
had perished by this bad drink, took an aversion to it; and God,
to quench his thirst, created the vine and revealed to him the art
of making wine of it. With the aid of this liquor he discovered
more truth; and since his time the word to divine *has been in use,*

commonly signifying to discover *by means of* wine. .... *There-*
fore, since this time all excellent things, even the deities, have
been called divine *or* divinities.

Franklin (who signs himself "abbé Franklin") goes on to
say that the miracle of Cana is repeated for us every day as
rain falls upon vineyards and becomes wine. He then indulges
fully in his passion for twisting the Holy Scriptures to his own
slightly blasphemous purposes:

It is true that God has also taught men to bring back wine into
water. But what kind of water? Brandy (eau de vie), *in order*
that they might thereby themselves perform the miracle of Cana
in case of need, and convert the common water into that excellent
species of wine called punch.

Conclusion: don't offer your neighbor any water unless he
asks you.

I say this to you as a man of the world, but I will finish, as I
began, like a good Christian, by making a religious remark to
you, very important, and drawn from the Holy Writ, namely
that the Apostle Paul very seriously advised Timothy to put
some wine into his water for his health's sake; but that not one
of the apostles nor any of the holy fathers have ever recommended
putting water into wine.[36]

As an afterthought, Franklin reflected gratefully upon the
location Providence had given to the elbow. For if the long-
legged animals also have long necks to enable them to "reach
their drink without the trouble of falling on their knees,"
man, who was destined to drink wine, "ought to be able to
carry the glass to his mouth." A number of comically drawn
figures (the work, we are told, of one of his grandsons) shows

what calamities would befall the human race if the elbow had been placed too near the hand or too near the shoulder. But the human arm, in its capacity to carry glass to mouth, is perfection. "Let us adore then, glass in hand, this benevolent wisdom; let us adore and drink." [37] Let it be said that Franklin practised what he preached. His cellar in Passy was always well stocked; many friends sent him choice samples from their estates, and his household accounts mention no less than five kinds of champagne. When the Helvétius ménage ran out of Xeres (sherry), they asked Franklin for the loan of a few bottles, never doubting that he had them on hand.

It was, of course, with such apparent nonsense that the chains of friendship were kept bright and shiny. Friends had time for their friends. They wrote silly poems about each other as a means of telling each other how much they mattered. They warmed up their blood by drinking and singing – not just any traditional drinking song, but the ones they had composed in each other's honor. They paid that supreme tribute of making gentle, loving fun of each other's foibles.

Madame Helvétius was an easy, and willing, target. Morellet, who fancied himself a "slightly less bitter" [38] Jonathan Swift, was inspired by Franklin's *Petition of the Flies* to compose a much more elaborate, but equally whimsical *Petition of the Cats*. So good, indeed, was his pastiche of Franklin's sly humor that Temple erroneously attributed the piece to his grandfather and published it as such. Madame Helvétius, who loved every living creature under the sun, except women, had allowed her cats to multiply until the eighteen of them threatened to become thirty-six. Hearing that the abbés, their mortal enemies, are plotting their destruction by having them "put into a cask and rolled down to the river," the cats entreat their mistress to hear their side of the case – and in presenting it, provide an impudent description of life at Auteuil.

Here is the "Sieur Abbé Morellet, always thundering the most violent anathemas against the blackbirds and thrushes for plundering your vine, which they do with as little mercy as he himself." Here is the housekeeper, Mademoiselle Luillier, shuffling along so slowly that the mice, undisturbed by the lazy, overfed cats, nibble her slippers as she goes. Here is the "Sieur Cabanis, who makes an enormous consumption of sweetmeats in your house, and who is always ready to steal a lump of sugar when he thinks he can do it unobserved." Here is Abbé de la Roche, "whose speech at the Academy we just now read as it wrapped up a calf's lights which you had the goodness to give us," and who should be fully convinced, after so many years at Madame Helvétius', of the inutility of all knowledge. And here she is, Madame herself, in the glory of her uncultivated instincts, "good without the assistance of *Treatises upon Morals*, charming in manners without having read our historiographer Moncrief's *Art of Pleasing*, and happy without being acquainted with the *Treatise on Happiness* by the unfortunate Maupertuis." Her spelling is not much better than their own, say the cats, and her writing is very like the scratching of a cat's paw.[39]

But let her fall ill, and all irony vanished, while grim, panicky bulletins flew from Auteuil to Passy:

TUESDAY 7 A.M. *Mde. Helvetius has spent a good night. There has been profuse sweating, provoked and kept up by the use of camphor and saltpeter. Evidently the fever, which climbed still higher last night, has been helpful. There is very little coughing and sputum. . . . The lower abdomen is in good shape, urination quite easy, though with less sedimentation than yesterday, strength is coming back.*[40]

What other woman, even very sick, would allow such a bulletin to be communicated to the man who was or had been her avowed suitor? The news sent to Franklin the following day was still less sparing in physiological detail, but the eighteenth century, for all its refinement, was not squeamish.

It must be said, however, that Madame Helvétius was generally in excellent health and very active, as the Gout noted when she upbraided Franklin in the famous *Dialogue*:

Look at your friend in Auteuil, a woman who has received from nature more of truly useful learning than a half-dozen of you pretended Philosophers have been able to draw from all your books. When she wishes to do you the honor of her visit, she comes on foot; she walks from morning until night, and she leaves all the maladies of indolence for distribution to her horses. See how she keeps her health, even her beauty. But you, when you go to Auteuil, it is in the carriage. Yet it is no farther from Passy to Auteuil, you know, than from Auteuil to Passy.[41]

Not only did she walk, she organized little trips to the surroundings of Paris: Marly, Chaillot, Choisy, St. Germain, always including some young company for Temple – notably the pretty Alexander girls, one of whom had just married his cousin.[42] There survive a number of breathless, joyous little notes from various members of the group, as to who will bring what picnic basket, fill it "with the largest roast of veal to be found" or provide carriage and horses.[43]

Years passed in this pleasant way. Peace had long been concluded, and Madame Helvétius advised her friend "to remain in France, have a skilled surgeon operate him [for the gravel], and spend the rest of his days with her and other loving friends." [44] But by 1785, Franklin had decided that, no matter how agreeable life in Passy, he had to see his own kin once more and die at home. Of all his leave-takings, the most painful was at Auteuil. "Many honorable tears," says Cabanis, "were shed on both sides." [45] As for Morellet, there may have been a faint smile behind his tears, for it was in June 1785 that he was elected a member of the French Academy – surely the proudest moment of a life that was soon to know nothing but ruin and loneliness. Aside from the tool chest, Franklin gave Morellet his favorite armchair, on which the abbé promptly caused "Benjamin Franklin hic sedebat" to be inscribed. To Cabanis went the magic cane used to calm down the waters and the ceremonial sword worn by Franklin at Court.

Morellet's career was soaring, Cabanis and de la Roche still had exciting lives ahead of them, but for Franklin and Madame Helvétius, this was the end. In an unusual outburst of emotion, she tried to call him back after he had left: [46]

I cannot get accustomed to the idea that you have left us, my dear friend, that you are no longer in Passy, that I shall never see you again. I can picture you in your litter, further from us at every step, already lost to me and to your friends who loved you so much and regret you so. I fear you are in pain, that the road will tire you and make you more uncomfortable.

If such is the case, come back, my dear friend, come back to us. My little retreat will be the better for your presence; you will like it because of the friendship you will find here and the care we will take of you. You will make our life happier, we shall con-
.tribute to your happiness, such are the things that you must

know for sure, that you have read in my heart and that of our friends.

All I have left now is the pleasure of writing these things to you, of thinking of you, and of saying once more that I am your good friend   LIGNIVILLE-HELVETIUS

But nothing could stop Franklin. Feasted all along the way, cheered and acclaimed as he went, rising once more above his infirmities, thanks to the miraculous effect travel never failed to have on him, he arrived, after one week's journey, in Le Havre. And from that depressing port he unashamedly told his sadness, in rickety French:

We shall stay here a few days, waiting for our luggage, and then we shall leave France, the country that I love the most in the world. And there I shall leave my dear Helvetia. She may be happy yet. I am not sure that I shall be happy in America, but I must go back. I feel sometimes that things are badly arranged in this world when I consider that people so well matched to be happy together are forced to separate.

I will not tell you of my love. For one would say that there is nothing remarkable or praiseworthy about it, since everybody loves you. I only hope that you will always love me some. Visitors are pouring in . . .

He added a postscript in the afternoon. And he wrote again, from Southampton, only to her, but now he was the old Franklin once more, self-possessed, slightly ironical, looking ahead:[47]

Southampton, July 27, 1785
Our ship arrived here yesterday from London. We are sailing today. Farewell, my very, very, very dear friend. Wish me a

good crossing and tell the good abbés to pray for us, that, after all, being their profession. *I feel very well. If I arrive in America, you shall soon hear from me. I shall always love you. Think of me sometimes and write sometimes to your*

BENJAMIN FRANKLIN

The Parting of the Ways

*And now, even in my Sleep, I find that the Scenes
of all my pleasant Dreams are laid in that City,
or in its Neighbourhood.* ❧ FRANKLIN

This closing chapter should be told in a different style:
Franklin is no longer the buoyant, eager, half-gallicized envoy
of a country at war courting the friendship of a stronger,
richer country, using charm, humor, warmth – any tool at his
disposal. He is a venerable statesman in an established nation,
fully conscious both of his own status and of America's
power. Burdened by work and by infirmities, he writes less,
and what he writes sounds more dignified, more conservative,
more dogmatic. And no wonder. One month after his week-
long hero's welcome in Philadelphia, he found himself
President of the Executive Council of Pennsylvania, a post
to which he was reelected for three consecutive years. When
finally released from office, he spent four months laboring at
the Constitutional Convention. Only in his final months,
seriously ill, emaciated by the opium he took to dull his pain,
did he have leisure again to brood and to remember. Only
then, in occasional moods of fun and tenderness, did his days
in Paris come back to him in their full poignancy.

But his French friends, of course, remembered him as he
had been when among them, almost one of theirs. As the
American Ambassador to Paris, Gouverneur Morris,
observed:

*The Eagerness of Enquiry into every Thing which relates to
your Health and Situation shows better than any Expression
of Esteem can do it the deep Impressions you have made in this*

Opening of the *Etats Généraux*, 1789

Country. Many have asked me whether you did not intend to return, forgetting (in the Remembrance of what is past) your present Situation, the many Leagues of Ocean which separate America from Europe and in the Desire to repossess their friend they forget also that you are an American.[1]

France is approaching the hour of agony. Prepared by the philosophers, sparked by the middle classes, made inevitable by the Court, the Revolution is at the gates. Henceforth, the letters that cross the ocean so slowly and erratically, taking two months or more, tell two divergent, almost jarring stories: a serene, majestic dawn in the Western Hemisphere; mounting scandal and social convulsions in the Old World. The gap is bridged by memories, gestures of friendship, little gifts, but not by deep mutual understanding.

As always in times of political crisis, the men take over, making and interpreting the news. A woman is heard now and then, telling of children, of everyday life and nostalgia for past happiness, but the voice is faint, almost drowned in the coming tumult. As time went by and absence deepened, a few people emerged as trustworthy correspondents, relating news about the others and informing them of whatever Franklin, in his spaced-out answers, or Temple, in his disorganized way, had communicated.

Morellet carried the chief burden of intellectual give-and-take, fowarding the more or less facetious productions of the Auteuil Academy as well as his own worries about the direction of American economic policy, a direction far too protectionist for him. To his well-known hymn in praise of absolute freedom of trade, Franklin now replied that in theory, yes, economic freedom was still more important than political freedom; but in practice, America was justified in collecting duties on imports – as long, at least, as her system of direct taxation was not functioning efficiently:

I am of the same Opinion with you respecting the Freedom of Commerce, in Countries especially where direct Taxes are practicable. This will be our Case in time when our wide-extended Country fills up with Inhabitants. But at present they are so sparsely settled, often 5 or 6 Miles distant from one another in the back Counties, that the Collection of a direct Tax is almost impossible, the Trouble of the Collector's going from House to House amounting to more than the Value of the Tax.[2]

Franklin's explanation did not convince Morellet. As a matter of financial expediency, he said, tariffs might be justifiable; "but I fear that this system will come to be regarded among you, as it already is in all of Europe, as a clever political operation meant to increase national commerce and prosperity at the expense of the commerce and prosperity of foreigners, which is a great blunder."[3] In his straight-forward way, Morellet had hit a nerve, and Franklin dropped the issue.

He had become extremely touchy about anything that could be construed as criticism of America. To his friends' concern that divisive forces were at work in Pennsylvania, he curtly replied that they should not believe the fabrications of the English press:

The English Papers not only sent me gratis, as you observe, to Algiers,* but they are sending all the United States to Destruction.

---

* Rumors had circulated in France that Franklin had been captured on his return voyage and was a slave in Morocco. Le Veillard, who never gave them any credence, sent Temple some playful warning that he might not find the Muslim husbands as broad-minded as the French.

By their Accounts you would think we were in the utmost Distress, in Want of every thing, all in Confusion, as Government, and wishing again for that of England. Be assured, my Friend, that these are all Fictions, mere English Wishes, not American Realities. There are some Faults in our Constitutions, which is no wonder, considering the stormy Season in which they were made, but those will soon be corrected. And for the rest, I never saw greater and more indubitable Marks of public Prosperity in any Country. The Produce of our Agriculture bears a good Price, and is all paid for in ready hard Money, all the labouring People have high Wages, every body is well cloth'd and well lodg'd, the Poor provided for and assisted, and all Estates in Town and Country much increas'd in Value.[4]

This was the kind of picture that, with slight variations, he was to paint many times. His own estate, he had found "tripled in Value, since the Revolution."[5]

The French, for whom the exercise of one's critical faculties has always been an overpowering pleasure and necessity, frequently felt called upon to draw Franklin's attention to some flaw or other in the American political situation: there was "too much apathy among the population,"[6] said Le Veillard, the President's powers were too broad and his possibly indefinite tenure of office a real danger, the taxation system was woefully inadequate, and so on. To all these remarks, Franklin invariably replied that all was well. And in doing so he was in the American tradition that has always preferred consensus, be it imperfect, to a perpetual clash of views, be they brilliant:

Our Affairs mend daily, and are getting into good Order very fast. Never was any Measure so thoroughly discuss'd as our

*propos'd new Constitution. Many Objections were made to it in
the Public Papers, and Answers to those Objections. Much
Party Heat there was, and some violent, personal Abuse. . . . As
to the two Chambers, I am of your Opinion, that one alone
would be better, but, my dear Friend, nothing in human Affairs
and Schemes is perfect, and perhaps that is the Case of our
Opinions.*[7]

Franklin's own interest in French affairs was far less lively.
He was kept informed, in great detail, of the step-by-step
disintegration of absolutism: the tremendous loans floated
abroad by Finance Minister Calonne; the staggering figure
reached by the national debt; the convocation, in 1787, of the
Assembly of Notables and the high hopes raised by this first
consultation of the nation (however skimpily represented)
in one hundred and fifty years; the bitter frustration when it
proved a failure; the appointment of the Archbishop of
Toulouse (a friend of both Franklin and Morellet) to the
hopeless position vacated by Calonne's dismissal, his flounder-
ing, and the recall of Necker to that post; the floods and
hailstorms that ravaged France in 1788, making the price of
bread rise still higher; the national clamor for the convocation
of the Estates-General, another practice that had fallen into
disuse for one hundred and seventy-five years; the sudden
emergence of the Third Estate, the bourgeoisie, Franklin's
former friends and colleagues.

At every gust of wind that buffeted the people and
institutions he knew so well, Franklin's comment and advice
were solicited from overseas. But he remained extremely
cautious, not to say detached. He followed with bland benevolence the work of the Assembly of Notables (in which La

Rochefoucauld took an active part) and reacted to the first news of violence with noncommittal good wishes. To Countess d'Houdetot he wrote:

The Accounts I have heard of the Misunderstandings and Troubles that have arisen in the Government of that dear Country, in which I pass'd nine of the happiest Years of my Life, gave me a great deal of Pain; but I hope all will tend to its Good in the End. We have been laboring here to establish a new Form of Federal Government for all the United States. . . . If the Project succeeds our Government will be more energetic, and we shall be in a better condition of being serviceable to our Friends on any future Occasion.[8]

The man who has been credited, perhaps mistakenly, with the coining of the famous *Ça Ira* – "everything will turn out all right," in his mouth an optimistic expression of faith in time of stress, but in revolutionary days a sanguinary song of hate – did not grasp at once the implications of the fall of the Bastille. In a letter of October 18, 1789, to Pierre Samuel du Pont de Nemours, his comments were hardly more worried than those he had sent more than one year before to Countess d'Houdetot: "I am exceedingly sorry for the Troubles that have lately happen'd in France; but hope they are now at an End, and that they will eventually be productive of beneficial Consequences to the Nation."[9] One month later, however, writing to Jean-Baptiste Le Roy, he had a rather macabre flash of humor:

'Tis now more than a year since I have heard from my dear friend Le Roy. What can be the reason? Are you still living? Or have the mob of Paris mistaken the head of a monopoliser of

knowledge, for a monopoliser of corn, and paraded it about the streets upon a pole?

Great part of the news we have had from Paris, for near a year past, has been very afflicting. I sincerely wish and pray it may all end well and happily both for the king and the nation. The voice of Philosophy *I apprehend can hardly be heard among those tumults.*

Finally, in an outburst of national pride, he quipped: "Our new Constitution is now established, and has an appearance that promises permanency; but in this world nothing can be said to be certain, except death and taxes!" [10]

To be sure, few people, even among the French, had the vaguest inkling of the violence of the gathering storm. Practically the only note of anguish was sounded by that most perceptive and intelligent of men: Lavoisier. In a letter to Franklin in February 1790, he first recounted the latest developments in chemistry, then turned to politics:

Our revolution has happened, it has irrevocably happened, yet there is still an aristocratic party vainly struggling against it. The democratic party has on its side the greater number, and also education, philosophy, enlightenment. But the moderates who have remained cool-headed in the general effervescence believe that circumstances have carried us too far, that it is a pity one has been compelled to arm the people, to arm all citizens, and that it is not good politics to put power in the hands of those who must obey. . . . We do regret at this time that you should be so far from France; you would have been our guide and you would have shown us the boundaries that we should not have overstepped. [11]

The same theme – that Franklin should have been there to witness the great event – is struck not in a diffident, but in a triumphant mood, by Le Veillard:

How I regret you in the beautiful moment we are living! Why did you not stay in France? Oh, how happy we would be! How surprised you would have been to find both such energy and caution in this nation which to you appeared so sweet, so amiable, and perhaps so frivolous! You would have had, for the second time, the spectacle of an incredible revolution, more difficult and more surprising than yours, but just as complete ... the nation has shaken the yoke of priests, nobles and King, she is the absolute mistress of her fate.[12]

Both Lavoisier, the man of insight, and Le Veillard, the poor prophet, were to end on the scaffold. History is not discriminating.

Among Franklin's French friends, Le Veillard was un-questionably the champion letter-writer – at least two or three messages a month for five years, some of them five and six pages long. This enormous correspondence is divided about evenly among comments on public events, recrimina-tions about Franklin's and Temple's unsatisfactory answers, and a chatty chronicle of life in the Passy circle. He often stresses that Franklin's friends miss him and that their eyes fill with tears at the mention of his name; he quotes his wife as saying that "there is an element of piracy in making people love you so much and so faithfully, only in order to forget them."[13] (She is, nevertheless, embroidering him a purse.) He tells of their daily hopes and frustrations: they would all like to move to America (they never did); he would like to be elected to the American Philosophical Society (he was); his son's protector in Bordeaux suddenly died, leaving the young man jobless and hopeless; he often sees Jefferson and Madame Helvétius; otherwise Passy is empty, their friends having all left or died; he feels that with the suppression of packet boats, in 1788, Franklin is drifting further and further away: "You are now as far as China."[14]

Franklin answered all this in serene, measured tones. Le Veillard's deep concern over his health evoked nothing more than a shrug:

People who live long, who will drink of the Cup of Life to the very Bottom, must expect to meet with some of the usual Dregs; and when I reflect on the Number of terrible Maladies human Nature is subject to, I think myself favour'd in having to my share only the Stone and Gout.[15]

When, for once, he was the one to be left without news, he did not fret:

As you have so much leisure, and love writing, I cannot think you have been so long silent, you who are so good as to love me, and who know how much pleasure your letters always afford me. I therefore rather suspect you may probably have written too freely concerning public affairs, and that your letters may be arrested in your postoffice, and yourself lodged in the Bastille. You see I imagine any thing, however extravagant, rather than suppose, as your letters too often do, that my friends forget me.[16]

He may have indulged once in a while in a little ironic scolding, but on the whole Franklin was immensely grateful to Le Veillard for the lively accounts of the adventures and mis-adventures of his friends – particularly his women friends.

This chronicle started out in the jocular tone de rigueur in Passy. Having heard of Franklin's safe arrival in Philadelphia on September 14, 1785, and of the tumultuous welcome his fellow townsmen had given him, Le Veillard again played on the old themes:

You are far from blameless, you know. You had two good friends here, who lived rather in harmony since they hardly ever saw one another, and since you assured each one in private that she was the one you preferred. But now, you write to one of them and keep silent toward the other! The former does not fail to boast and show her letter everywhere; what do you expect the other one to do? Here are two women at daggers drawn, now, their friends take sides, the war spreads, and all that is your work! With a simple piece of paper, you set on fire one half of the world, you who had been of such help in bringing peace to the other half. And what position do you put us all in? Ah, let me tell you that if you came back now, you would not be greeted as one of the family anymore.

The favored one, we finally learn, was Madame Helvétius:

One lucky stroke, however: at the moment your letter arrived, Madame Brillon was busy with the marriage of her [second] daughter. Said daughter on the 20th of this month [October] married Mr. de Malachelle, counselor at the cour des aides. *He is rich, he is an only son, and we hope that he will make his wife happy; this affair, at least, has made Madame Brillon less aware of your ungratefulness, but from now on, watch out for her wrath, her nerves, her vengeance!* [17]

Thus, within three months of Franklin's departure, the Brillons had married off their second daughter, Aldegonde, the "demoiselle" Temple had been in love with and who had loved him. One cannot help feeling that such a timing was deliberate. After turning down Franklin's proposal about the older girl, Cunégonde (now Madame Pâris), they probably wanted to spare him and Temple the humiliation of seeing the younger one become Madame de Malachelle. Franklin's congratulations were cool and perfunctory – not even sent directly to the Brillons, but slipped in a letter to Le Veillard. Temple's reaction was bittersweet: he expressed the hope that the young lady had been allowed her own choice (he underlined the word *choice*) and would find the happiness she deserved.[18]

The story of the Brillons during the five years that Franklin spent in Philadelphia is told, at first, in many voices. Le Veillard and Chaumont report weddings, pregnancies, deaths, and other events, putting first things first, of course: income, dowries, inheritances.

The happiest voice is Monsieur Brillon's. He writes in the best Gallic tradition, bubbling with joie de vivre, pride in his descendants, and happy recollections of Franklin's earthier side:

Madame Paris is to be delivered next month. Her little girl is already thirteen months old, full of fun and strength. My second daughter is taking the necessary steps to catch up with her sister. Thanks to God, we have been given, my wife and I, sons-in-law endowed with huge appetites. And as you know, my dear Papa, he who eats well labors heartily!

His social comments are pungent:

Everybody wants to take up a lot of space, nowadays. The men wear hats that are just tremendous in height and width. The

women's hairdoes are like thick bushes; and they provide them-
selves with enormous bosoms, monstrous derrières. *If you think*
you saw some samples when you were here, I can tell you that
you saw nothing at all.[19]

Madame Brillon, of course, sounds more ethereal than her
husband. Not a word about her second son-in-law's position
or fortune. She stresses that he is twenty-seven, "doux et
aimable," that they are all living under the same roof in peace
and harmony. Were it not for Franklin's absence, their
happiness would be complete:

Though there is a tinge of sadness in the present and the future,
even our regrets have a certain sweetness, for we repeat: papa is
happy! We were happy! To have been, to still be, forever, the
friends of this amiable sage who knew how to be a great man
without pomp, a learned man without ostentation, a philosopher
without austerity, a sensitive human being without weakness, yes,
my good papa, your name will be engraved in the temple of
memory but each of our hearts is, for you, a temple of love.[20]

One more voice, the voice of Blanchette Caillot,* struck an
entirely different note. To her departed lover, a lukewarm
Temple, she tirelessly poured out the depth of her passion,
her frustration in her own marriage, and an astounding
amount of gossip, each tidbit of malevolent chitchat separated
from the others by dots and exclamation points. Passion lent
occasional dignity and, at times, tragic undertones to her

---

* Little is known about Blanchette. Her husband, the famous actor
Joseph Caillot, a protégé of the Comte d'Artois (future Charles X),
had been given an estate in Saint Germain. Blanchette, according to
Madame Vigée-Lebrun, became an ardent republican but was eventually overcome by despair and threw herself out of the window, in the
thick of the Revolution.

otherwise unattractive display of cynicism. Temple's negligence in leaving so many of Blanchette's letters unanswered more than once moved Le Veillard to upbraid him: "Aren't you ashamed? Here is an unfortunate woman who, besides all her other sorrows, has also had to endure the torment of letting her husband give her a child, and you do not even take the trouble of giving her a thought!" [21] A twisted morality, one would say; but Le Veillard knew that little Théodore, Blanchette's child by Temple, had caught smallpox and died in the country house where he had been put out to nurse. When announcing the sad news to Temple, Blanchette had moaned: "Oh, my God, must we be born only to suffer?" [22] But Temple, instead of offering sympathy, scolded her for not having taken proper care of the child. She replied: "Keep behaving like a Frenchman, be the fellow citizen of your tender friend; our virtue is not as stern as yours, but it has the sweet and humane quality of forgiving a friend even when he plunges a dagger in your heart." [23]

What Blanchette could not forgive was interference with her love; even though Temple had not married either of them, both the Brillon girls had been a threat to her, and she could not stand the thought that they might be happily married to others. She had been and still professed to be their friend, but when it came to the Brillon family there was a touch of Iago in her. She depicts Monsieur Brillon as going out frequently without his wife and daughters and "biting his thumbs" [24] for not having chosen Temple as a son-in-law; Monsieur Pâris, Cunégonde's husband, is described with burning hatred; Aldegonde is shown as miserably unhappy nine days before her wedding to Monsieur de Malachelle whom she does not love. A few months later, precisely when Madame Brillon tells Franklin of their joint happiness, Blanchette exclaims: "How that family has changed! Good God, how dangerous opulence can be, and how sad! If you could see what boredom, what solemnity in a house that used to be so gay!"[25] She has to admit that Malachelle is very handsome and as kind as possible to his bride, but Aldegonde "treats her husband with a coldness that approaches contempt. The dear girl was not made to get married; her heart, which needed only friendship, turns away from the other kind of love."[26] As for Pâris, he can do nothing right. When Cunégonde lost her infant son, Blanchette snickered that while the young mother was prostrate with despair, the haughty father was really more offended than grieved that death should dare touch an heir of his. The purchase of an estate in Normandy by the Pâris family drew equally acid comments: Blanchette "felt truly sorry" for poor Monsieur Brillon, afflicted once more with the gout, who sees the two young couples go off to the country, "leaving the mother-in-law to moan at his side, in a state of utter boredom."[27]

As a matter of fact, things were beginning to go wrong for the Brillons. Madame de Malachelle suffered a miscarriage due, said Le Veillard, to her recklessness in sailing off the Normandy coast in rough weather. Monsieur Brillon's gout was alarming. "The change in him is frightening," wrote Blanchette. "This really saddened me for I am very fond of him."[28] Madame Brillon confirmed in the last days of 1786 that her husband, ill since Easter, had fallen into a state of weakness and deep melancholia. He had decided to leave for Nice with a friend and two servants, but refused to be accompanied by any member of his family. Nice did not have the same miraculous effect it had on his wife five years earlier. Within three months, Brillon was dead. His funeral oration by Blanchette is another angry outburst against the lucky heir, Monsieur Pâris:

I hear that the house in Passy is to be sold. The butler has already been sent away. Oh! Now that despotic creature is going to have a free hand! He fancies himself a great lord, he will never be anything but a bourgeois, yes, by God, a real, a true bour-geois. . . .[29]

And then, the final blow. Madame Brillon's first and favorite grandchild died suddenly at the age of three. She was the little girl Franklin had seen nursing at her mother's breast, whose first sentence had been "*Voilà le bon papa Franklin,*" while looking up at his portrait. Lifted above herself by grief, Madame Brillon reveals extraordinary dignity:

Monsieur Brillon's death and that of my granddaughter who, at three, was a model of beauty, of sweetness and of grace, have so affected my soul that I had no capacity left but for grief. I took up my pen twenty times to seek refuge in your precious friendship, to seek help in your philosophy, but tears overwhelmed me every time and I had to postpone till a calmer moment my need to con-verse with you. How often have I looked at your portrait with a great, melting tenderness, my sorrow made worse by the distance between us! How much have I thought of Passy, of the short way I had to go to find the best of friends and the wisest of men! [30]

In a sad echo of the joyful fantasies of paradise they had built together, she sighs somewhat skeptically: "my friend will judge of the love I have devoted to him for this life if there is nothing beyond, and for eternity if we are to survive forever in the great whole." [31]

And Franklin, what words of comfort did he find for his "daughter" in her moment of distress? The fond papa, who had woven tales about sins and bishops, cupids and archangels, ephemeres and whistles, all to keep her happy and entertained, now sent a stiff little letter in English:

I am glad to hear that you continue well, with what is left of the amiable Family in whose sweet Society I pass'd so many happy Evenings while I liv'd in Passy. I sympathise with you in all your Losses and Afflictions, and hope the rest of your Life will be as tranquil and free from Trouble as it had been for some Years before we parted.

Whereupon he switched rather heartlessly to his own success story and to his happiness within his family:

I live in a good House which I built 25 Years ago, contriv'd to my Mind, and made still more convenient by an Addition since my Return. A dutiful and affectionate Daughter, with her Husband and Six children compose my Family. The Children are all promising, and even the youngest, who is but four Years old, contributes to my Amusement.

He told her about Benny, who had just completed his university studies and was about to enter the printing business, about Temple who "is settled 6 Leagues from me on his Plantation, which contains 600 Acres; but when in Town lives with me." He also informed her that his health was better than in Passy, and his financial situation quite sound – "I shall leave a handsome Estate to be divided among my Relatives." Only in the last paragraph, when his thoughts turn to death, does he seem to remember that it is to his dear Madame Brillon he is writing:

Being now in my 83d Year, I do not expect to continue much longer a Sojourner in this World, and begin to promise myself much Gratification of my Curiosity in soon visiting some other. Wherever I may hereafter travel, be assured, my dear Friend, that if I shall be capable of remembering anything, the Remembrance of your Friendship will be retained, as having made too deep an Impression to be obliterated, and will ever, as it always has done, afford me infinite Pleasure. Adieu. Adieu.[32]

Madame Brillon picked up the threads of her life. She sold her Passy house, settled in Paris, and, much to Blanchette's approval, announced that since unfortunately her husband's death had set her free, she was going to be her own mistress, "having been a slave all her life."[33] Her married daughters lived with her for a while, but as her guests. Then the Malachelles, whose tastes were too mundane "for such a dull household" (as Blanchette put it), left for a home of their own. The last of Blanchette's letters (March 8, 1788) directs an ultimate barb against Pâris, accused this time of exhausting his wife with repeated pregnancies – "four children in five years, isn't that a very bourgeois way to behave for such an aspiring nobleman?"[34] (of course she fails to mention that the unfortunate couple had lost two of those four children). Blanchette's own life was far from satisfying. She sighs for past joys, she glowingly recalls Franklin's fondness for her:

Does your papa remember me? Does he remember the pleasure he had, kissing his dear daughter? Holding her on his knees? Putting his arms around her neck? I remember the blessing he gave me upon his departure, the good and virtuous patriarch![35]

With Blanchette absent from the scene, the dialogue between Franklin and Madame Brillon reverted to its beginning. Since he found French too hard to handle, they communicated once more through Le Veillard. Franklin proudly sent to France the words and music of the first songs composed in America and asked Le Veillard to translate the lyrics for her. In March 1789, four months before the outbreak of the Revolution, Madame Brillon expressed the wish that her papa might live as long as Methuselah to see the glory of the America he had helped create; by that time, she speculated, France, too, might regenerate:

We are in a moment of crisis; evil has reached such a peak that it should (at least one must hope so) bring us finally some good if the new régime that they propose comes into being. Pray for us, my good papa, you love France and the French, be our saint, if our leaders resembled you I would become very devout! [36]

Her family is well. The younger daughter will obviously never have any children, which is all the better since she is frail. Madame Pâris and her husband now have two, and the baby girl already blows kisses to Franklin's portrait. Pâris is Madame Brillon's closest, most trusted friend. She and the young family spend half the year in Paris, the other half in the country, happily secluded from everything and everybody. The American songs that Franklin sent her fill her very last lines: "The engraving is clear but the paper too thin. There are, among them, one or two tunes that I would have played for my good papa who is fond of them, says Monsieur Le Veillard. What sweet regrets, what sweet memories!" [37] And thus, Franklin and Madame Brillon ended, as they had started, with music.

From a literary point of view, it is a disappointing ending, more like a sigh than the final chord of what had been a tight and vibrant relationship. But then, Madame Brillon had been seasoned by life, and Franklin, as friends and relatives could not help noticing, was no longer his old ebullient self. Temple remarked: "I left my grandfather in good health at the end of last month, but I did not find him as gay as he was in Passy. For that matter, neither am I." [38] Blanchette provided the only explanation that made sense to her: "It must be because your ladies are more serious than ours." [39]

Furthermore, situations about which he could do nothing were uninspiring to Franklin. In the case of the Chaumont family, which not only needed help but was represented right in Philadelphia by one of its members, his interest never flagged. We do not hear much about Madame Chaumont, except that her health is invariably said to be poor, or about two of Chaumont's daughters, pretty Madame Foucault and the young, unmarried girl who is only referred to anonymously as "mon enfant," though her name was Thérèse-Elisabeth. But the other daughters – Sophie, the one who knew English and accompanied Franklin part of the way to Le Havre, and "la mère Bobie," who had kept Franklin's household accounting, thus earning the nickname of Franklin's "wife" – are often mentioned, and their brother Jacques comes to the fore.

Franklin had not yet left Le Havre when Sophie, back home after her short journey with him, felt bold enough to expose her shaky English:

Your Letter my dear frend gave me infinite pleasure, you inform me of your good health; my joy est very great it is a proof of my heroic friendship for you in preferring you desires before mine for believe me my frend, I schould have a great satisfaction in seeing you again. [40]

While the Doctor was still at sea, Chaumont's fertile mind was already concocting new business ventures. Could the Americans build large flatbottomed ships, whose upper deck would be taken down in Rouen, leaving them free to sail on to Paris, be dismantled there, and sold as lumber? (Franklin's answer was lukewarm – the idea sounded interesting, but his part of the country was not rich in lumber.) Chaumont was also experimenting with various ways to whiten the green vegetal wax that Franklin had been toying with before departure. Since this green wax was cheaper, but the demand was for white candles, the idea seemed fruitful; Franklin, whose childhood had been spent helping his father in the candle business, applauded from afar.

No sooner had he set foot on American soil than young Chaumont was there to greet him. Jacques Leray's mission of collecting his father's credit from Congress was turning out to be much harder than expected, and it now looked as if his stay in America would be an extended one. After a while, he reconciled himself quite heartily to this state of affairs, having fallen in love with Grace Coxe, a girl from New Jersey. Aware that an American wife might provoke frowns in Passy, Franklin tried to pave the way for the young people. To la mère Bobie, his "wife," he sent one of his rare messages in French. He recalled her plea to come back to his old room, evoked the happy hours spent there, and sighed that those days would never return:

And as I am already in another world, you are free to choose a better husband, an event I wish with all my heart. Monsieur your brother seems anxious to deprive us of one of our best girls, to make her his wife and bring her to France. In all fairness, he must now send us one of his sisters as compensation. Better still, if the whole family came to settle in this good country.

As for the above-mentioned miss, she is a very sweet demoiselle, from one of the best families in the country. Her disposition is excellent, she will make you a good sister. As you love your dear brother, you would do well to win over his parents, as much as you can, so that they give their consent.[41]

On the same day (October 7, 1786), a letter in English went off to Chaumont *père*, with warm praise for the young lady's character and background. The marriage took place. A year later, feeling that his mission would soon be completed, Jacques asked Franklin for a certificate of good behavior. Franklin obliged, vouched that Chaumont junior "hath conducted himself in every respect not only unexceptionably but so commendably as to acquire the Esteem and Friendship of the best Families in the Place," and affixed to the document the seal of the President of the Supreme Executive Council of the State of Pennsylvania. Along with the official document went private greetings for the women in the family: affectionate respects to Madame Chaumont, "Love to Madame Foucault, to ma Femme [la mère Bobie], ma chere Amie [Sophie], et mon Enfant [Thérèse-Elisabeth]." Could "his wife" send him the music of "La Religieuse," which would give him pleasure, though less than when she herself played it for him?[42]

The music was sent, instead, by Sophie, for the "wife" had gotten married and gone to live on her husband's estates. Sophie's letter is unfortunately quite. mutilated, so that one can gather only that the new husband was the author of several esteemed works on politics, commerce, and finance;

that his fortune was "honnête" (read: fairly substantial); and
that her sister seemed happy. Other letters, written in mock
indignation at this betrayal, by Le Veillard and by the banker's
wife, Madame Grand, reveal the grimmer side of the picture:
Monsieur de Forbonnais who was, indeed, a well-known
economist, was also sixty-five years old and "accepting la
Mère Bobie without a dowry."[43] In truth, Chaumont's
affairs were taking a catastrophic turn. By the spring of 1789,
it was no longer possible to minimize the extent of the
disaster. Le Veillard wrote: "The Chaumont family is
scattered. Monsieur is in Chaumont with his two unmarried
daughters. Poor Madame is trying to obtain a *séparation de
biens** and in a few days will go to live in a convent. The house
in Passy is seized by their creditors."[44]

At this point, Franklin decided to take action, and much
as he hated to solicit, he felt that here was "a matter of
justice in which the honor of our country is concerned." On
June 3, he appealed to George Washington:

*Mr. Le Ray de Chaumont, father of the young gentleman who
will have the honor of waiting on you with this, was the first in
France who gave us credit, and before the Court showed us any
countenance trusted me with 2000 barrels of gunpowder, and
from time to time afterwards exerted himself to furnish the
Congress with supplies of various kinds, which, for want of due
returns, they being of great amount, has finally much distressed
him in circumstances. Young Mr. Chaumont has now been here
near four years, soliciting a settlement of the accounts merely,
and though the payment of the balance, to be sure, would be*

---

* Madame Chaumont's move, of course, does not mean that she was
divorcing but that she was taking the legal steps necessary to establish
that her property was not liable to her husband's debts.

acceptable, yet proposing to refer that to the time when it shall
better suit the convenience of our Government. This settlement,
if the father had it to show, would tend to quiet his creditors.[45]

A scribbled legal entry in the Archives of the Département
de la Seine informs us that on July 11 – three days before the
fall of the Bastille – Chaumont did manage to "quiet his
creditors" to the extent of obtaining a year's reprieve.[46]
Then, in September, Franklin wrote to the French Foreign
Minister, soliciting the post of consul of France in Philadelphia
for Jacques Leray, who had on various occasions helped the
retiring consul in his functions and knew the business and
language of America exceedingly well. But what could
Chaumont's private bankruptcy matter to a government
itself facing financial and political ruin? The King of France,
Franklin was told, was curtailing the number of his consuls
abroad.

In October, young Leray came up with a desperate proposal, based, as far as we know (his letter, which Franklin
calls "affecting," has disappeared), on an exchange between
Franklin's assets still in France and Chaumont's credit in the
United States. Franklin turned down the idea firmly: his
assets were grossly inadequate, he had incurred extraordinary
expenses, and France was in a state of chaos. He urged Leray
to postpone his departure for another two or three months and
await the next session of Congress when, in all probability,
he would be among the first paid: "Money, I think, will not
be wanting, as it is thought the immense Importation of
Goods lately made into this Port must produce at least one
fourth of the Impost expected from the whole of the United
States."[47]

Leray's answer, two days later, was drenched in misery. So sure had he been that Franklin would accede to his request that he had prepared to leave and reserved passage on a ship. The picture at home, he now revealed, was still more bleak than he had painted it. Yet he would submit: "I have taken your advice in all the most important acts of my life. At this critical juncture, I shall still take you as guide of my conduct."[48] More months passed, Chaumont's claims were aimlessly dragged from one American office to another, and Franklin became too ill to be of further assistance. Before sailing for France in March 1790, Leray wrote him despondently: "The affairs of my father in France are pretty much in the same situation they were when I had the honor to see you last. He is still at Chaumont, refusing to settle his business or to sell any of his properties before my arrival there."[49] But the reprieve was about to expire; though Leray's family managed to keep the château of Chaumont, the Hôtel de Valentinois, where Franklin had spent so many happy days, had to be sold in bankruptcy proceedings.* He never knew it: on April 17, 1790, while Leray was still at sea, the Doctor died.

He was fully prepared. The expectation of death had been for a few years almost a leitmotif in his letters to French friends. To Countess de Forbach, the dowager Duchess of Deux-Ponts, he had written in 1787:[50]

---

* The Hôtel de Valentinois no longer exists, but former rue Basse, at whose corner it stood, has been named avenue Franklin, and a plaque on a modern house of rue Raynouard commemorates Franklin's residence on that ground. As for Leray, he returned to the United States in 1802, became an American citizen, and built in upstate New York a replica of the Hôtel de Valentinois, known as LeRay Mansion in Leraysville. In the same region, the village of Chaumont still bears the name of his family.

MY DEAR FRIEND,

There is no one of that Character whom I left in Europe, that I think of so often as of you, and with great reason, the Instances of your Friendship to me while I resided there being innumerable, and having made the deepest Impression on my Mind. I am now past 81 Years of Age, and therefore tho' still in tolerable Health cannot expect to survive much longer. We are at a great Distance, and I can never again have the Pleasure of seeing you. I write this Line then to express my sincere Wishes of Health and Happiness to you and your good Children, and to take leave. Adieu, most respectable and most amiable of Women, and believe me while I live, Yours most affectionately

B.F.

In a postscript, he added: "I beg your amiable Daughter to accept a few of our Squirrel Skins, which I sent with this by Commodore Jones; to do me the honour of lining one of her Mantles with them for the ensuing Winter."

What did Frenchmen and Americans send to one another in the eighteenth century? What did they try to procure from each other's country? Since a sizable part of Temple's letters to Le Veillard is made up of requests, and a sizable part of Le Veillard's answers is taken up with lengthy explanations of his often frustrated efforts to satisfy them, it is easy to draw up a catalogue of the Parisian items in demand in Philadelphia.

The easiest orders to fill were for books. Franklin and Temple, drawing on funds left in Paris for that purpose, ordered quantities of them, on all topics, from "how to" literature, to travel in China. Next came wine. But the bottles from the estates of the Duchesse de la Rochefoucauld did not travel well, having been improperly corked.

Franklin's own wishes did not go beyond those two items. For Sally, who had greatly admired a coverlet sent by Madame Grand, the banker's wife, Franklin set out to procure French knitting patterns and equipment. Since he had previously sent squirrel skins to Madame Grand, the lady exclaimed: "Isn't it marvelous, the way we keep each other warm at such a distance without any other electricity than that of our friendship?"[51] She shipped all that Sally needed and even started the work, so that the Philadelphia ladies could follow instructions more easily. Not to be outdone, Madame Helvétius went shopping throughout Paris to find for Sally the latest model of a capelet that was all the rage in the capital, as well as "robes, hats, and bonnets."[52]

Temple's requests were more difficult to satisfy. One of them was for a frightening variety of fruit trees, vines, and even ordinary trees, such as poplars, to plant on his New Jersey estate. The trees proved an unending headache to Le Veillard because, on account of uncertain shipping schedules, they would leave France at the wrong season and be dead long before reaching Philadelphia, whereupon Temple would refuse to pay for them and put in a new, more elaborate order. He also imported wooden shoes, but in spite of his coaxing, the New Jersey farmers would have nothing to do with the *sabots* so dear to the French peasant. For himself, he requested six pairs of elegant custom-made shoes, but Le Veillard, whose efficiency did not always match his zeal, got into such a fight with the shoemaker that he felt impelled to forward to Temple the impertinent letter that the cobbler, a

Monsieur Mazzar, had written him – a letter so impertinent, indeed, that it leaves little doubt as to the imminence of a revolution in France. Nor was this all: Temple wanted a hunting dog, but by the time Le Veillard had consulted the proper authorities and found the right dog, he did not want it anymore.

The most involved, by far, was the saga of the deer. It covered fifteen months, took up countless hours of Le Veillard's life, and had a tragicomic element of frustration. Before leaving France, Temple had procured a variety of deer (*chevreuil*) unknown, he maintained, on the American continent and asked Le Veillard to keep them until the following spring when he would be ready for them. Two of the deer died while Temple was still at sea, but the others were "royally treated in the King's zoo."[53] However, suggested Le Veillard, was it really necessary to go to such trouble? Monsieur de Bougainville had just assured him that he had hunted exactly the same kind of deer in Canada. Not at all, answered Temple. People who had gone to Canada vouched that deer did not exist there. Could Le Veillard send him a boy to take care of the animals aboard ship and later work for him as a carpenter or a gardener? There followed a quest for the right boy, but then as now, as Le Veillard soon found out, most Frenchmen do not leave France willingly, and of all those he interviewed, the only one who seemed suitable did not want to go.[54] At this point (March 1786), Le Veillard was working on the problems of the deer, the hunting dog, books, various kinds of seed, the second shipment of saplings, the shoes and the gardener-carpenter. But, as he never tired telling Temple, none of this was too much trouble to please his friend, a friend who would, wouldn't he, secure the longed-for Memoirs from the good Papa?

By the time there was a boat ready to take the deer in April and a friend willing to put them up at Le Havre – so that they should be available as soon as the sailing date was set – they had fallen ill.[55] Only three were left, and on advice from Madame Helvétius it was decided to let them breed, and send the young by the first opportunity in the fall. Crates were built for their transportation. By May, four more had died and the other three were sick,[56] and when they were all in fine shape again there was no ship. To all this, Temple replied a little impatiently that his appetite for deer was growing and that he hoped he would be able to teach his cook how to prepare them properly.[57] In the fall, one more occasion had to be passed up, for the animals were all dying. Finally, the whole project was given up.[58]

Did Le Veillard ask for anything in return? Yes. He, too, wanted some trees that were on the botanist Bartram's list of American specialties. He was also interested in importing mahogany but found the price too high.

On the whole, the only presents the French received were sent by Franklin himself, mainly homemade soap and Virginia ham. The soap was a matter of his particular delight, having been for many years his family's specialty: "The Soap is thought to be the best in the World, for Shaving and for washing Chinzes, and other things of delicate Colours." Along with the cask shipped to the Grand family, Franklin sent the list of friends to whom he wanted the cakes remitted, while prudently adding: "This kind of Soap is not for sale in this Country at present, and perhaps I may not be able to procure any more of it."[59]

Alas, soon after shipping it, he discovered that the soap, which had been made expressly for the purpose by his sister Jane Mecom, started crumbling as it dried. A number of worried letters were exchanged. Both Jane and Sally experimented with remedies, but without much success. The only hope left was that the moist heat of the boat might, somehow, restore the cakes to normal. What state they were in upon arrival in France, we shall never know. Franklin's friends were too polite to send any comment beside their thanks.

As for the Virginia ham, it already commanded the national pride it so deservedly retains: "The Hams are in a Cask, and have Labels to denote who they are for. I send them because Strangers here admire them for their good Taste and the Sweetness of their Fat, which is all made by their feeding on Maize [Corn], and I hope they will come to Hand." [60] This feeling about American ham was shared by George Washington who, while sending a barrel of it three months later to Lafayette, wrote ambiguously: "You know that the ladies of Virginia peg their self-esteem to the quality of their hams." [61] The ham did, indeed, elicit great praise from all its recipients and was favorably compared to its French rival, the jambon de Bayonne.

The only one for whom there was a different, additional present was, of course, Madame Helvétius. And what else would she want but an American bird for her aviary, a cardinal? This too, presented difficulties:

It is rare that we see the Cardinal Bird so far north as Pennsylvania. Those sent here from Virginia generally perish by the Way, being a tender Bird, and not well bearing the Sea. . . . Mr.

Alexander has, I understand, sent several for our Dame in his Tobacco Ships to France, which never arriv'd; and unless a Friend was going in the Ship who would take more than common Care of them, I suppose one might send an hundred without landing one alive. They would be very happy, I know, if they were once under her protection; but they cannot come to her and she will not come to them.

At this point, he could not repress one little taunt:

She may remember the offer I made her of 1.000 Acres of Woodland out of which she might cut a great Garden, and have 1.000 Aviarys if she pleased. I have a large tract on the Ohio, where Cardinals are plenty. If I had been a Cardinal myself, perhaps I might have prevailed with her.[62]

It seems to have been the mode, in Paris too, to tease Madame Helvétius for not having married Franklin and thus fixed him in France for good. As Monsieur Brillon put it:[63] "Every time the talk turns to you, Madame Helvétius exclaims: 'Ah, that great man, that poor dear man, we shall not see him anymore!' 'Certainly through your fault, Madame,' says I."* The Comte d'Estaing, another Passy friend, also reports some gentle chiding:

Madam Helvétius has just had a second fit of Vekness, tho not so bad as ye first. We tell her 'tis your absence and love, that are ye cause of it: of which she does not blush, but only answers, friendship and true regrets hurt full as much.[64]

The friends may have smilingly pretended to believe in a romantic game, but Franklin and Madame Helvétius knew

* This letter of December 30, 1785, has been hitherto wrongly attributed to Madame Brillon; it was undoubtedly written and signed by her husband.

better. The few letters they exchanged are straight, gripping regret – no false pretense, no vain hope. Something irreplaceable had been lost. True, Abbé de la Roche, after evoking the old image of the paradise on earth that Auteuil with Madame Helvétius had been, added with resignation: "another Paradise was waiting for you in America. Providence could not, without you, make that country free and happy; we respect its designs too much to complain that it has given happiness to others at our expense."[65] But Franklin was not entirely resigned. To Madame Helvétius he wrote, as late as April 23, 1788: "I often think of the happiness I so long enjoyed in your sweet society. When we meet in paradise, as I trust we shall, the Pleasures of that place will be augmented by our recollection of all the circumstances of our acquaintance here below."[66] This is a far warmer response than the hazy recollection ("if I shall be capable of remembering anything") he promised Madame Brillon. And whereas for Madame Brillon he could not manage French any more, he would still struggle with it for Notre Dame d'Auteuil.

He remembered her hospitality:

It was Wednesday yesterday. At ten in the morning, I thought of you, of your house, your table, your friends. At this hour, said I to myself, they are all dining, M. Le Roy, the abbés de la Roche and Morellet, M. Cabbanis [sic], maybe some of the little stars [her daughters and granddaughters]. Madame serves the whole company, with as much ease as pleasure. – But, alas, I was not there to take my share in the lovely, sensible talk, the wit and the friendship with which her meals are always seasoned! [67]

She remembered his kindness:

*What happiness you have spread in my little retreat, my dear
Franklin! We all gathered to read and reread your sweet letter,
to remember once more the days you spent with us and the light
you poured into my soul. I never left you that I did not feel a little
worthier the next day. And now your letter has the same effect,
for it brings out, powerfully, all your qualities, the simple and
noble disposition that I so admired. We are not fated to meet
again in this world. Well, my good friend, let it be in the next. . . .
I am getting old, my dear, but I don't mind it, I am coming
closer to you, we will meet again all the sooner.*[68]

The final words were his – and they were in French. A laborious
French, rusty and often wrong, but that conveyed exactly
what it wanted to convey – a last message of longing:

*Je ne peux pas laisser partir cette Occasion, my chere Amie,
sans vous dire que je vous aime toujours, et que je me porte bien.
Je pense continuellement des Plaisirs que j'ai joui dans la douce
Société d'Auteuil. Et souvent dans mes Songes, je dejeune avec
vous, je me place au coté de vous sur une de votre mille sofas, ou
je promène avec vous dans votre belle jardin.*[69]

*I cannot let this chance go by, my dear friend, without telling you
that I love you always, and that I am feeling well. I think
endlessly of the pleasures I enjoyed in the sweet society of Auteuil.
And often, in my dreams, I dine with you, I sit beside you on one
of your thousand sofas, or I walk with you in your beautiful
garden.*

Chronology of Franklin's Dealings with France: 1767–1790

1767

August 28–October 8: Franklin's first journey to France (presented to Louis XV, September 1767).

1769

July 14–August 23: Franklin's second journey to France.

1772

August 16: Franklin elected to French Academy of Sciences.

1773

Jacques Barbeu-Dubourg publishes *Oeuvres de M. Franklin.*

1775

May 5: Back in Philadelphia from England, Franklin learns of battles of Lexington and Concord.

May 10: Attends opening session of Second Continental Congress (subsequently appointed to committees on manufacture of gunpowder, "Secret Correspondence," i.e. foreign affairs, etc.).

1776

June 11: On committee to prepare Declaration of Independence.

September 26: Appointed one of three commissioners to the court of France, ostensibly to negotiate a treaty of commerce (the other two commissioners are Silas Deane and Thomas Jefferson, the latter replaced at his request by Arthur Lee, October 22).

October 10: Arranges for reception of French aid through Beaumarchais (France and Spain secretly advance 2,000,000 livres).

October 26: Sails for France on Congress warship *Reprisal,* accompanied by two grandsons, William Temple Franklin and Benjamin Franklin Bache.

December 3: Lands at Auray, Brittany (reaches Paris, December 21).

December 26: Washington crosses Delaware.

December 28: The three commissioners received for the first time by French Foreign Minister Vergennes.

1777

January 14: They obtain a secret subsidy of 2,000,000 livres from France.

April 26: Lafayette sails to America.

September: The commissioners ask Vergennes to recognize the independence of America and to grant a loan of 14,000,000 livres.

September 26: Howe takes Philadelphia; news reaches Franklin in November.

October 17: Saratoga; news of Burgoyne's surrender reaches Franklin by December 4.

1778

January 28: The commissioners report a French grant of 6,000,000 livres, payable quarterly.

February 6: Treaties of Alliance and of Amity and Commerce with France signed; ratified by Congress, May 4.

March 20: Commissioners formally presented to Louis XVI.

April 9: John Adams in Passy, to replace Silas Deane as commissioner.

July 8: French fleet, commanded by Comte d'Estaing, arrives at the mouth of the Delaware (with Gérard, accredited Minister Plenipotentiary of France, on board).

September 14: Congress appoints Franklin sole Minister Plenipotentiary; news of appointment reaches Franklin on February 12, 1779.

1779

March: The first exchanges of prisoners of war between England and America, arranged by Franklin.

March 23: Franklin formally presents credentials as Minister Plenipotentiary.

June 21: Spain declares war on England.

July 10: Congress sends France a request for military supplies worth about 12,000,000 livres; invoice received by Franklin in September.

December: Franklin obtains a grant of 3,000,000 livres for military supplies and other needs.

1780

February 9–July 27: Adams again in France with powers to negotiate peace with Great Britain and to secure a loan and a treaty from Holland; the mission fails.

May 2: French fleet, commanded by de Ternay, sails from Brest to America (with Rochambeau's expeditionary force on board).

May 12: The British take Charleston; news reaches France by July.

December 2: Franklin announces to Congress a plan, approved by Chaumont and Vergennes, to repay a debt of 2,000,000 livres to France by supplying provisions to the French forces in America.

1781

March 10: Vergennes informs Franklin of a proposal by Russia and Austria to act as mediators for peace.

March 12: Franklin asks Congress to relieve him as Minister, pleading age and ill health.

March 27: The largest cargo of military supplies, gathered by Franklin, Jonathan Williams, and Chaumont, and worth more than 6,000,000 livres, is shipped from Lorient, Brittany, on the *Lafayette*. (The ship is captured by the British, May 3; news reaches Franklin in June.)

June 13 and 14: Congress takes no formal action on Franklin's request to retire and appoints him, Jay, Laurens, and Jefferson to join with Adams as commissioners to negotiate peace; news reaches Franklin on August 15.

October 19: Yorktown; news of Cornwallis' surrender reaches Franklin by November 19.

1782

March 21: Lord Cholmondely, carrying letters of introduction from Madame Brillon, begins informal peace negotiations with Franklin.

July 10: Franklin suggests to Oswald, British negotiator, "necessary" terms for peace, without communicating them to Vergennes.

November 30: Oswald, Franklin, and other American commissioners sign preliminary articles of peace.

December: Franklin appeases Vergennes' complaints of American neglect and obtains a loan of 6,000,000 livres.

1783

January 20: Franklin and Adams present at signing of Anglo-French and Anglo-Spanish preliminary articles of peace.

April 3: Treaty of amity and commerce with Sweden.

September 3: Definitive treaty of peace between Great Britain and United States is signed (ratifications exchanged on May 12, 1784).

1784

May 13: Franklin renews his request for release from post as Minister Plenipotentiary. He is writing Part Two of his autobiography.

December 2: "Polly" Stevenson Hewson and her children arrive to spend winter with Franklin.

1785

May 2: Jefferson appointed Minister Plenipotentiary to France.

July 12: Franklin leaves Passy on his way home, arrives at Southampton on July 24, and sails from there, July 28.

September 14: Franklin lands at Philadelphia, greeted by cannon salutes, pealing bells, and a large crowd.

October 11: Elected member of Supreme Executive Council of Pennsylvania, then its president (October 18), and re-elected annually until 1788.

1787

February 22: French Assembly of Notables meets; dissolves, May 25; meets again, November 1788, and dissolves again, December 12.

May 28–September 17: Franklin, Pennsylvania delegate to the Federal Constitutional Convention.

1788

July 17: Franklin makes last will and testament (adds codicil, June 23, 1789).

October 14: Franklin ends service as President of Supreme Executive Council of Pennsylvania and retires to private life.

1789

May 4: French Estates-General meet; fall of Bastille, July 14.

November: Franklin sends Parts One, Two, and Three of autobiography to friends in England and France.

1790

February 3: Franklin signs, as President of Pennsylvania Abolition Society, a petition to Congress against slavery and the slave trade.

April 17: Franklin dies.

June 11: On a motion of Mirabeau, seconded by Lafayette and La Rochefoucauld, the French National Assembly votes by acclamation to wear mourning during three days for Benjamin Franklin.

Bibliographical Note to Franklin's Years in Paris: 1777–1785

The story of Franklin's papers

Whether because of his innate thrift or a sense of his place in history, Franklin – just as he always cherished a good story – seems to have preserved most of the letters he received, no matter how unimportant. The saga of his papers is as chaotic as their owner was methodical. If, as it unfolds, Temple appears in the role of the grasping and negligent villain, it should be borne in mind that his life was ruined, albeit unwittingly, by his grandfather. Between the ages of sixteen and twenty-four, when young men complete their education and choose a career, he served in Paris as Franklin's aide, confidant, and secretary, thus acquiring a taste for the niceties of urban, diplomatic life, but no real preparation in any field. Franklin had always assumed that Congress would continue his grandson in public service, allowing him to put to good use his polish, his connections, and his fluency in French. But Franklin's enemies prevailed in Congress after his return, and Temple, completely ignored by his country, drifted bitterly from gentleman-farming to whatever occupation came his way.

It was perhaps to make amends that his grandfather, when he died in April 1790, bequeathed to Temple all his papers, with permission to make any profit he could from them. The letters and manuscripts accumulated in France alone formed an enormous bulk of more than 15,000 items. From these, Temple selected a few thousand which seemed more interesting because of their public or scientific character and took them with him to London in 1791, with a view toward publication. The remainder he left with his friend, Dr. George Fox, of Champlost, near Philadelphia, first as a deposit, later, in his will, as a gift. For about half a century, these papers remained in a stable owned by the Fox family. Some 1,100 of them were given as a souvenir to one of Franklin's grandsons, Dr. Franklin Bache; others were casually offered to friends and visitors. In 1837, the Harvard historian Jared Sparks used them for his edition of Franklin's writings, and in 1840, at his urging, some 13,000 of them were presented to the American Philosophical Society in Philadelphia. But at that time a whole batch of manuscripts escaped detection and remained undiscovered for many more years; some of them were destroyed along with other papers in the Fox family stables; the rest, miraculously saved by a keen-eyed visitor, eventually made their way in 1903 to the University of Pennsylvania.

After a delay of twenty-six years, Temple published part of the papers he took to London in 1791. He then lost all interest in the manuscripts, which disappeared, only to turn up about 1840 in a London tailor's shop where they were being cut up for use as paper patterns. An American bookseller in London, Henry Stevens, bought them, but had to pledge them as security for a loan; it was not before many further vicissitudes that this portion of the papers found shelter in the Library of Congress.

Whereas Franklin's official correspondence with the French Government has been carefully preserved in the files of the Ministère des Affaires Etrangères in Paris, private letters to and from his French friends survived erratically. Thus it is often difficult to gauge his various attachments by the number of messages we have, or even to be certain that what looks like a sudden cooling off is not due to a sudden increase in that London tailor's business.

The publication of Franklin's papers

In a major effort to bring together for publication (in the full text or, at least, in abstract) every line that has been written by Franklin or to him, the editors of the Franklin Papers have endeavored to assemble at the Yale University Franklin Collection photocopies of all the relevant material that could be tracked down throughout the world. The work was undertaken in 1954, under the joint sponsorship of the American Philosophical Society and Yale University. With the assistance of about three hundred private owners and numerous institutions, belonging to thirty-two states and fifteen foreign countries – documents came from Honolulu as well as Moscow – a collection of more than twenty thousand items (not counting duplications) was assembled. A detailed description of the material and its provenance has been given by Leonard W. Labaree, the man in charge of the project from its very beginning, in "The Papers of Benjamin Franklin," *Daedalus 86* (1954), 57–62. On other aspects of the same question, one should see William E. Lingelbach, "Benjamin Franklin's Papers and the American Philosophical Society," APS, *Proceedings, 99* (1955), 358–80; Leonard W. Labaree and Whitfield J. Bell, "The Papers of Benjamin Franklin: A Progress Report," APS, *Proceedings, 101* (1957), 532–34; and the preface to volume *1* of *The Papers of Benjamin Franklin* (New Haven, Yale University Press, 1959).

This new edition, launched in 1959, has covered so far the years 1706 through 1761. Thus, in its chronological unfolding, it is still sixteen years short of the French period of Franklin's life, which will not see the light for quite some time. While awaiting its completion, we still must rely on the earlier printings, the most important of which are: Jared Sparks, *The Works of Benjamin Franklin* (10 vols. Boston, 1840); John Bigelow, *The Complete Works of Benjamin Franklin* (10 vols. New York, 1887–89); Albert Henry Smyth, *The Writings of Benjamin Franklin* (10 vols. New York, Macmillan, 1905–07), is the best so far. Sparks published less than 1,400 items, Bigelow less than 1,600 and Smyth 1,806. The current edition will publish about 20,000 items: its magnitude is therefore apparent.

Smaller collections and isolated pieces are listed in the Introduction to *The Papers of Benjamin Franklin*, *1*; I. Minis Hays' *Calendar of the Papers of Benjamin Franklin in the Library of the American Philosophical Society* [and in that of the University of Pennsylvania] (5 vols. Philadelphia, 1908), which lists almost two thirds of the surviving manuscripts, is of limited usefulness because the dates are often wrong and the identification of senders not always correct.

Franklin's printed works and iconography

The *Bagatelles*, so many of which were written to or for French women, deserve particular mention. The Yale Library collection of Franklin's original printings contains several rare and some unique pieces. Two modern editions include not only these but also a few papers and excerpts which, although written in the same mood, were not called "*Bagatelles*" by Franklin himself: P. McPharlin, *Satires and Bagatelles* (Detroit, Fine Book Circle, 1937), and Richard E.

Amacher, *Franklin's Wit and Folly* (New Brunswick, N.J., Rutgers University Press, 1953), useful also for its bibliography (the translations of French originals are generally good, though not always flawless).

Of Franklin's own *Autobiography*, a new, annotated edition has been published by the editors of *The Papers of Benjamin Franklin* (New Haven, Yale University Press, 1964). Those who wish to see the variants of the different versions of the *Autobiography* still use the parallel text edition by Max Farrand: *The Autobiography of Benjamin Franklin, a Restoration of a "Fair Copy"* (Berkeley and Los Angeles, University of California Press, 1949).

For Franklin iconography, Charles Coleman Sellers, *Benjamin Franklin in Portraiture* (New Haven, Yale University Press, 1962), is indispensable. He gives a wealth of information on Franklin and his circle in connection with the portraits.

General Background

Contemporary Memoirs

Of memoirs and correspondence by Franklin's American contemporaries, John Adams' *Diary and Autobiography*, ed. L. H. Butterfield (4 vols. Cambridge, Mass., Harvard University Press, 1961), is by far the most valuable and entertaining, a running criticism and downgrading of everything Franklin tried to do. Since the new edition of the Adams papers, like that of the Franklin papers, is still in progress, one has to use an older edition for other writings: Charles Francis Adams, ed., *The Works of John Adams* (Boston, Little Brown, 1856). More vitriolic and less informative are the papers of the Lee brothers: Richard Henry Lee, *Life of*

Arthur Lee, LL.D. (Boston, Wells and Lilly, 1829), and William Lee, *Letters* (Brooklyn Historical Printing Club, 1891). Both Silas Deane and Thomas Jefferson wrote little that is relevant to the present book. Even Jefferson's biographical sketch of Franklin – Thomas Jefferson, *Writings* (20 vols. Washington, Jefferson Memorial Association, 1903–04), *18*, 168 ff. – contains anecdotes mostly of dubious authenticity. There is more to draw from a less famous author, W. C. Watson, ed., *Men and Times of the Revolution, or Memoirs of Elkanah Watson* (2nd ed. New York, Dana, 1857).

Virtually every French memoir or collection of letters of the period had something to say about Franklin, but only a minority said anything worth noting. Those concerning individual Parisians are mentioned under separate headings below. Here are some others: Duc E. de Croy, *Journal inédit*, E. H. Grouchy and P. Cottin, eds. (4 vols. Paris, Flammarion, 1907), *4*; Horace Walpole, *Correspondence with Madame du Deffand* (New Haven, Yale University Press, 1939). See also Madame du Deffand, *Correspondance complète* (3 vols. Paris, Michel Lévy, 1866–77); Louis P. de Bachaumont, *Mémoires secrets pour servir à l'histoire de la république des lettres ...* (36 vols. London, 1784); Louise Elisabeth Vigée-Lebrun, *Souvenirs* (Paris, Arthème Fayard, n.d.); Madame de Campan, *Mémoires sur la vie de Marie-Antoinette* (Paris, Firmin Didot, 1858). The last two are strongly tinged by a royalist point of view.

Modern Scholarship

"A complete bibliography of Franklin would be almost a bibliography of the eighteenth century," says the author of his best biography, Carl Van Doren, *Benjamin Franklin* (New

York, 1938, and many later editions; we quote from the paperback edition of the Viking Press, first issued in 1964). Nevertheless, Van Doren proceeds to offer a long and substantial list of books which, in addition to his own work, will give more than a start for any research in the field. A hurried reader will value Verner W. Crane's shorter, but still very good *Benjamin Franklin and a Rising People* (Boston, Little, Brown, 1954), with its useful bibliography. As a general assessment of Franklin's impact and personality, Carl Becker's entry in the *Dictionary of American Biography* (New York, Scribner's, 1931), *6*, 585–98, is superb.

Among the scholars who have dealt with the relation between Franklin and the women of France, Gilbert Chinard occupies the first place. His knowledge of both the French and English literature and history of the period, his command of eighteenth-century French, his talent as critic and writer are displayed in a large number of papers and small monographs, the most important of which are listed under the relevant headings. Unfortunately, he has not brought together the remarks and conclusions reached in his individual articles into a single major work.

The most important book on Franklin and his personal relationships with French men and women – more particularly, Franklin's image as reflected in the contemporary writing of France – is Alfred Owen Aldridge, *Franklin and his French Contemporaries* (New York, New York University Press, 1957); its French translation by the author, *Benjamin Franklin et ses contemporains français* (which we cite) (Marcel Didier, Paris, 1963), contains some additional material.

On the more general image of America in French society, one should consult Durand Echeverria, *Mirage in the West*

(Princeton, Princeton University Press, 1957). Its bibliography and that of Aldridge are excellent guides to further reading. Insights into Franklin's stylistic proficiency are provided by Bruce Ingham Granger, *Benjamin Franklin, an American Man of Letters* (Ithaca, Cornell University Press, 1964).

On a still broader scale, there is the classic work of Daniel Mornet, *Les Origines intellectuelles de la révolution française* (Paris, Colin, 1933), but the chapter concerning Franklin relies almost exclusively on Bernard Faÿ, *Franklin, the Apostle of Modern Times* (Boston, Little, Brown, 1929). Faÿ's style is vivacious, but his is not a reliable book, mixing, as it does, fact and fancy. On the other hand, the chapter devoted by Albert Henry Smyth to Franklin's "Social Life in France" (*Writings, 10*, 405–56) is loosely organized and suffers from the editor's inadequate knowledge of the French language and background.

There is vast literature on the private life and status of women, beginning with Edmond and Jules de Goncourt's classic (but old-fashioned) *La Femme au XVIIIe siècle* (Paris, Charpentier, 1862). Charles Kunstler, *La Vie quotidienne sous Louis XVI* (Paris, Hachette, 1950), is one of the liveliest and most instructive books in this field, enhanced by an excellent bibliography. Somewhat older but no less valuable is Louis Ducros, *French Society in the Eighteenth Century* (New York, London, Putnam, 1927). Georges May, *Le Dilemme du roman au XVIIIe siècle* (New Haven and Paris, Yale University Press and Presses Universitaires de France, 1964), devoted primarily to the reflection of life in the French novel, has penetrating vistas on private life itself and a valuable bibliography.

The political, economic, and philosophical aspects of Franklin's story in France are generally beyond the scope of the present book. It will be enough to cite Edward Everett and E. E. Hale, *Franklin in France* (2 vols. Boston, Roberts, 1888), old, but still useful; Henri Doniol, *Histoire de la participation de la France à l'établissement des Etats-Unis* (10 vols. Paris, 1886–92), documents; André Lasseray, *Les Français sous les treize étoiles* (2 vols. Macon, Protat Frères, 1935); and, for additional information, to refer to the bibliographies of Van Doren and Crane.

Individual Portraits

Madame Brillon

She is both the most famous and the most elusive figure in our gallery of portraits. Every biographer of Franklin speaks of her at some length; Franklin's fondness for her has been stressed in the popular magazines; yet nothing precise is ever said about her personality except that she inspired the great man and must have been worthy of his admiration – by her beauty, her wit, or both.

A large proportion of her correspondence with Franklin (though by no means all of it) has been published more than once, notably by Albert Henry Smyth in *Writings*, and in *Putnam's Monthly* (October 1906–07). Some of the letters and *Bagatelles* dedicated to her are famous, but no one so far has attempted to put the mass of undated materials into chronological order, and, hence, logical sequence. The author of the present book has tried to do so, through internal evidence, by cross-reference with letters of other correspondents who mention Madame Brillon, and by reference to episodes related in the journals of the time. It has been a trying work, and no doubt some of the clues may have been misinterpreted, but it was indispensable preparation to a reconstruction of Madame Brillon as an interesting human being in her own right, not merely as a mirror of Franklin's moods.

What has been written previously about Madame Brillon herself is of help only on a few specific points. As usual, Charles Van Doren's flair and poetic talent have enabled him to write the most convincing characterization. But there has been some useful work in connection with several of the *Bagatelles* inspired by her, and we have made progress in establishing their dates. Luther S. Livingston, *Franklin and his Press at Passy* (New York, the Grolier Club, 1914), has made the most thorough study. Other works are listed in Richard Amacher's *Wit and Folly*, mentioned above. The best study, not limited to practical problems of dates but exploring the literary and psychological circumstances, is that of Gilbert Chinard, "Random Notes on Two Bagatelles," APS, *Proceedings, 103* (1959), 740–60.

To Gilbert Chinard we also owe an interesting discovery concerning music, admittedly Madame Brillon's personal claim to fame. We knew of her talent as a performer through the expert opinion of Charles Burney, *An Eighteenth-Century Musical Tour in France and Italy*, P. A. Scholes, ed. (2 vols. London, Oxford University Press, 1959), but her own compositions, so often mentioned in the correspondence, remained hidden in the private archives of her descendants. Professor Chinard obtained the musical manuscripts, acquired them for the library of the American Philosophical

Society, and commented on them briefly in "Music Enjoyed by Franklin," APS, *Proceedings*, *100* (1956), 331–37. The "Marche des Insurgents" was performed in Philadelphia, on the 250th anniversary of Franklin's birth. Thanks to the courtesy of the American Philosophical Society, we reproduce the manuscript, for the first time, in this book.

The Chaumont and Le Veillard Families

Not only does the literature lack any study of the ladies in the Chaumont and Le Veillard families, but the men themselves have never been given the attention they deserve. The author's "Benjamin Franklin, Lafayette and the *Lafayette*," APS, *Proceedings*, *108* (1964), 181–223, tells for the first time in full detail the complicated story of the largest shipment of supplies ever sent from France to the Continental Army, through the joint efforts of Franklin, Jonathan Williams, and Chaumont. Most of the supplies were held over because of a squabble between John Paul Jones, Pierre Landais, and Chaumont himself; the balance was sent in a large ship, the *Lafayette*, which was unfortunately captured by the British. This failure led to the most galling charges leveled at Franklin by his enemies in Congress. The episode is not relevant to the present book, but the paper discusses certain points concerning the rent paid by Franklin to Chaumont, which had not been clarified in J. Bigelow, "Franklin's Home and Host in France," *Century Illustrated Monthly Magazine*, *35* (1888), 741–54, and lists the scant bibliographic material on Chaumont (p. 186, notes 28, 29).

All the information on the women in Chaumont's household is gathered from the mostly unpublished correspondence.

I had previously accepted without question the assumption of Samuel Eliot Morison, *John Paul Jones* (Boston, Little, Brown, 1959), pp. 123, 184 ff., that Madame Chaumont had a love affair with the famous commodore. On closer scrutiny, I find no scrap of evidence in Morison or in any other sources to support this claim. Surely Jones' collection of broken hearts (and raped girls) does not need the addition of mature Madame Chaumont.

On the American ventures of Chaumont's son, James Leray, one can read the somewhat fanciful but exciting book by T. W. Clarke, *Emigrés in the Wilderness* (New York, Macmillan, 1941).

On Le Veillard, there is a fairly good article by C. Leroux-Cesbron, "Un Ami de Franklin: Le Veillard," *Bulletin de la Société Historique d'Auteuil et de Passy, 10* (1921), 32 ff. In the same journal one can find other papers on aspects of life at Passy in Franklin's time, for instance, Louis Madelin, "Franklin à Passy, 1777–1785," *Bulletin, 12* (1933–34) 75–85. Nevertheless, the story of Le Veillard and his family, too, must be pieced together mostly from the correspondence, the larger part of which is still unpublished. A thorough study of it would bring much needed light on the composition and fate of Franklin's *Autobiography*.

Comtesse d'Houdetot

The most thorough biography, overflowing with praise, is that of Hippolyte Buffenoir, *La Comtesse d'Houdetot, une amie de Jean-Jacques Rousseau* (Paris, Calmann Lévy, 1901); see also his *La Comtesse d'Houdetot, sa famille, ses amis* (Paris, H. Leclerc, 1905). Almost all the correspondence between the Countess and Franklin has been published, with a learned commentary, by Gilbert Chinard, *Les Amitiés américaines de Madame d'Houdetot, d'après sa correspondance inédite avec Benjamin Franklin et Thomas Jefferson* (Paris, E. Champion, 1924).

The biography of the Countess, however, needs to be supplemented by that of the men in her life, most particularly Rousseau, Saint-Lambert, and Saint-John de Crèvecoeur. On the latter, one can see Robert de Crèvecoeur, *Saint-John de Crèvecoeur, sa vie et ses ouvrages* (Paris, Librairie des Bibliophiles, 1883), and Julia Post Mitchell, *St. Jean de Crèvecoeur* (New York, Columbia University Press, 1916). We shall not undertake to offer here a short bibliography of Rousseau.

The Aristocrats

On the personal and social aspects of Franklin's relationship with the King and Queen, the best comments are in the memoirs and correspondence of Franklin himself; of some help are the Duc de Croy, Madame du Deffand, the Lee brothers, and most notably Madame de Campan – in spite of her royalist bias, or indeed because of it. Elkanah Watson, on the contrary, draws an unrealistically rosy picture of Franklin's dealings with the Court. Saul Padover, *The Life and Death of Louis XVI* (New York, Appleton-Century, 1939), with bibliography, is useful for the general background.

Franklin's eulogy by La Rochefoucauld is printed in Gilbert Chinard, *L'Apothéose de Benjamin Franklin* (Paris, Librairie Orientale et Américaine, 1955), but on the duke's mother, the main source is her own, mostly unpublished, correspondence. The same can be said about Comtesse de

Forbach. In both cases, the correspondence, full of cryptic allusions to interesting conversations and lost letters, is quite frustrating.

Two papers by Gilbert Chinard, "Benjamin Franklin et la Muse Provinciale," APS, *Proceedings*, *97* (1953), and "Benjamin Franklin and the Mysterious Madame G——," *APS Library Bulletin* (1946), offer lively profiles of Baroness Bourdic and Countess Golowkin, while publishing most of their correspondence with Franklin.

André Maurois, *Adrienne ou la vie de Madame de la Fayette* (Paris, Hachette, 1960), is the most recent, compassionate biography of the unfortunate Marquise de Lafayette; it contains a number of unpublished letters and a valuable bibliography.

Reams of speculation have been written about the Chevalier d'Eon; among others: M. Coryn, *The Chevalier d'Eon* (New York, Frederick Stokes, 1932), and Jean-Jacques Brousson, *La Chevalière d'Eon* (Paris, Flammarion, 1934).

The Bourgeoisie

Biographical information on Marie-Pierrette Lavoisier can be found especially in Edouard Grimaux, *Lavoisier (1743–94) d'après sa correspondance* (Paris, F. Alcan, 1888); other works are cited in Claude A. Lopez, "Saltpeter, Tin and Gunpowder: Addenda to the Correspondence of Lavoisier and Franklin," *Annals of Science, 16* (1960), 83–94.

The last letter from Madame Le Roy to Franklin has seen print more than once, but the rest of her correspondence is unpublished, and so is the larger part of the voluminous correspondence of her husband, Jean-Baptiste Le Roy. On this man, a famous scientist in his day and one of Franklin's best friends, there is unfortunately no adequate work; the only biographical sketch is a short article in the *Grand dictionnaire universel*, by Pierre Larousse.

On women artists one can see Pierre de Nolhac, *Madame Vigée-Lebrun* (Paris, Goupil, 1912), John Theodore Tussaud, *The Romance of Madame Tussaud's* (New York, Doran, 1920), not always reliable, Félix Bouvier, "Une Concierge de Passy en l'An II," *Bulletin de la Société Historique d'Auteuil et de Passy*, 5 (1905–06), 110–28, "Biheron" in the *Grand dictionnaire universel*, by Pierre Larousse; in the *Biographie universelle, ancienne et moderne* (Paris, Michaud, 1811); Sellers, *Benjamin Franklin in Portraiture*, pp. 84 ff., and Elkanah Watson, *Memoirs*, pp. 142 ff. Most of our information, however, comes from letters in the Franklin Collection.

Unpublished letters, too, supplement the general information on the Fournier family in F. B. Adams Jr., "Franklin and his Press at Passy," *Yale University Library Gazette, 30* (1956), 133 ff. Madame de Baussan and the beggars are totally unknown except for the unpublished letters used in the present book.

Madame Helvétius

Though her place in Franklin's life was at least as important as that of Madame Brillon, Madame Helvétius is poorly represented in the correspondence. One has to rely heavily on the letters between Franklin and her friends Morellet, de la Roche, and Cabanis, whose lives were closely linked with hers, and messages from more casual acquaintances, such as the Alexander family living in nearby St. Germain.

Two biographical studies, both partial to Madame Helvétius but written with grace and altogether reliably, are: Antoine Guillois, *Le Salon de Madame Helvétius* (Paris, Calmann Lévy, 1894), and Jules Bertaut, *Egéries du XVIIIe siècle* (Paris, Plon, 1928). Some interesting comments will also be found in the essay on Franklin by Charles-Augustin de Sainte-Beuve, *Causeries du Lundi* (3rd ed. Paris, Garnier Frères, n.d.), *7*, 127 ff., and in Gilbert Chinard, "Random Notes on Two '*Bagatelles*'," APS, *Proceedings*, *103* (1959), 727–40.

Of the men in Madame Helvétius' life, her famous husband (who died long before Franklin went to Paris) does not have a direct bearing on our story. But there are interesting sidelights to be gained from Gustave Schelle's preface to Anne-Robert Turgot, *Œuvres* (5 vols. Paris, Alcan, 1913–23), from Turgot's own letters in the fifth volume of that edition, as well as from Jean Gaulmier's biography of "L'Idéologue Volney, 1757–1820," Doctoral Dissertation, Beyrouth, 1951.

Far more important are the three profiles of Franklin by his three closest friends of the "Académie d'Auteuil." André Morellet, *Mémoires inédits* (2 vols., Paris, Baudouin, 1823); Martin Lefebvre de la Roche, in Gilbert Chinard, "Abbé Lefebvre de la Roche's Recollections of Benjamin Franklin," APS, *Proceedings*, *94* (1950); Pierre J.-G. Cabanis, *Œuvres philosophiques* (2 vols. Paris, Presses Universitaires, 1956), *2*, 342 ff. Some other anecdotes from unpublished papers of de la Roche and Morellet are cited in Aldridge, *Contemporains*, chapt. 12. See also André Morellet, *Lettres à Lord Shelburne* (Paris, Plon, 1898).

Notes

Chapter 1, pp. 1 – 27

1. William Temple Franklin, *Memoirs of the Life and Writings of Benjamin Franklin* (3 vols. London, 1818), *1*, 309.

2. Albert Henry Smyth, *The Writings of Benjamin Franklin* (10 vols. New York, Macmillan, 1905–07), *7*, 55.

3. *The Letters of Benjamin Franklin and Jane Mecom*, edited with an introduction by Carl Van Doren (Princeton, Princeton University Press, 1950), p. 191.

4. Smyth, *Writings*, *7*, 132.

5. Charles Francis Adams, ed., *The Works of John Adams* (Boston, Little Brown, 1856), *1*, 660. Extract from *The Boston Patriot*, May 15, 1811.

6. L. H. Butterfield, ed., *The Adams Papers: Diary and Autobiography of John Adams* (4 vols. Cambridge, Mass., Harvard University Press, 1961), *4*, 118.

7. Pierre J.-G. Cabanis, *Œuvres complètes* (5 vols. Paris, Bossange, 1823–25), *5*, 267.

8. Smyth, *Writings*, *7*, 347–49.

9. Ibid., *7*, 290.

10. C. F. Adams, ed., *The Works of John Adams*, *1*, 660.

11. Butterfield, ed., *Adams Papers*, *2*, 389. A. O. Aldridge, *Benjamin Franklin et ses contemporains français* (Paris, Didier, 1963), p. 103. See also Maurice Cousin, *Les Souvenirs de la Marquise de Créquy*, Eng. trans. Colquhoun Grant, *The French Noblesse of the XVIII Century* (New York, Dutton, 1904), pp. 188 ff.

12. Aldridge, *Contemporains*, p. 220.

13. Butterfield, ed., *Adams Papers*, *2*, 391.

14. Gilbert Chinard, "Abbé Lefebvre de la Roche's Recollections of Benjamin Franklin," APS, *Proceedings*, *94* (1950), 219.

15. Smyth, *Writings*, *7*, 393–94.

16. Chinard, "Abbé de la Roche," APS, *Proceedings*, *94* (1950), 219. C. F. Adams, ed., *The Works of John Adams*, *1*, 661.

17. Carl Van Doren, *Benjamin Franklin* (New York, Viking, 1964), pp. 297 ff.
18. American Philosophical Society, Philadelphia [1779?].
19. Smyth, *Writings*, 2, 361.
20. Bruce Ingham Granger, *Benjamin Franklin, An American Man of Letters* (Ithaca, N.Y., Cornell University Press, 1964), p. 109.
21. Bibliothèque de l'Institut, Paris; Library of Congress, Washington, D.C.
22. BF to Abbé Morellet, April 22, 1787. Nathaniel E. Stein Collection.
23. Butterfield, ed., *Adams Papers*, 4, 57–60.
24. Winslow C. Watson, ed., *Men and Times of the Revolution: Memoirs of Elkanah Watson* (2nd ed. New York, Dana, 1857), pp. 303–304

Chapter 2, pp. 29 – 53

1. Charles Burney, *An Eighteenth-Century Musical Tour in France and Italy*, ed. P. A. Scholes (2 vols. London, Oxford University Press, 1959), *1*, 27 f.
2. American Philosophical Society, Philadelphia (hereafter APS), LXXI, 123b. Many of the letters quoted below appear in Smyth, *Writings*, but not always in their full text or in chronological order. Since in every case a fresh translation has been supplied from the French original, our reference will be directly to the original French letters.
3. APS, no date.
4. APS, July 30 [1777].
5. APS, XLIII, 103. See Gilbert Chinard, "Music Enjoyed by Franklin," APS, *Proceedings*, *100* (1956), 331–37.
6. Smyth, *Writings*, *8*, 99 f.
7. APS, XLIII, 19.
8. APS, XLIII, 19½.

9. APS, XLIII, 20.
10. Butterfield, ed., *Adams Papers*, *4*, 46 f.
11. Smyth, *Writings*, *8*, 100.
12. APS, XLIII, 97.
13. APS, XLVI (i), 47.
14. APS, XLIII, 56.
15. APS, XLVI (i), 46.
16. APS, XLIII, 94 and 95.
17. APS, XLIII, 100.
18. APS, XLVI (i), 50.
19. Louise-Elisabeth Vigée-Lebrun, *Souvenirs* (Paris, Arthème Fayard, n.d.), pp. 80–83.
20. Pierre de Nolhac, *Madame Vigée-Lebrun peintre de Marie-Antoinette* (Paris, Goupil, 1912), pp. 90 f.
21. Cicero, *Tusculan Questions*, I, c. 39. See Gilbert Chinard, "Random Notes on Two 'Bagatelles'," *APS, Proceedings*, *103* (1959), 740–60.
22. Richard E. Amacher, *Franklin's Wit and Folly* (New Brunswick, N.J., Rutgers University Press, 1953), pp. 48–52.
23. APS, XLIII, 111.
24. APS, XLIII, 96.
25. APS, XLIII, 112.

Chapter 3, pp. 55 – 87

1. APS, XLIII, 73.
2. APS [May 1778?].
3. APS, XLIII, 49.
4. APS, XLIII, 37.
5. Ibid. See also APS, XLIII, 41.
6. APS, XLIII, 25.
7. APS, XLIII, 115.
8. APS, XLIII, 68.
9. APS, XLVI (i), 52.

10. APS, XLIII, 26.
11. APS, XLVI (i), 45.
12. APS, XLIII, 78.
13. APS, XLIII, 13.
14. APS, XLIII, 23.
15. APS, XLIII, 24.
16. APS, XLVI (i), 43.
17. APS, XLIII, 2.
18. André Maurois, *Adrienne ou la vie de Madame de La Fayette* (Paris, Hachette, 1960), p. 55.
19. APS, XLIII, 25.
20. APS, LXX, 35b.
21. APS, XLVI (i), 42.
22. APS, XLIII, 35.
23. Amacher, *Wit and Folly*, pp. 42–47.
24. APS, XLIII, 44.
25. APS, XLIII, 87 and $87\frac{1}{2}$.
26. APS, XLIII, 64.
27. APS, July 10, 1780.
28. APS, LX.
29. APS, XLIII, 80.
30. *Le Sage et la Goutte*, in *Bagatelles*, Yale University copy; reprinted in Luther S. Livingston, ed., *Benjamin Franklin's Dialogue with the Gout* (Cambridge, privately printed, 1917).
31. Smyth, *Writings*, *8*, 37.
32. APS, XLVI (i), 44.
33. APS, XLIII, 3.
34. Smyth, *Writings*, *8*, 159 f.
35. APS, L (i), 36.
36. APS, XLIII, 57.
37. APS, November 23, 1780.
38. APS [November 29, 1780].
39. APS, XLIII, 77.

40. APS [November 29, 1780].
41. APS, XLVI (i), 42.
42. APS, XLIII, 82.
43. APS, XLVI (i), 42.
44. APS, XLVI (i), 44.
45. APS, XLIII, 82.
46. APS, XLVI (i), 42.
47. Smyth, *Writings*, *10*, 339 f.
48. APS, XLII, 15.
49. APS, February 16, 1781.
50. APS, XLIII, 16.
51. APS, February 16, 1781.
52. Smyth, *Writings*, *8*, 217 ff.

Chapter 4, pp. 89 – 121

1. Amacher, *Wit and Folly*, pp. 70–71.
2. APS, XLIII, 67.
3. *Deane Papers* (New York, New-York Historical Society), *4*, 445.
4. Smyth, *Writings*, *7*, 344–46.
5. Library of Congress, no date [before April 20, 1781].
6. APS, XLIII, 6.
7. Library of Congress.
8. APS, XLIII, 6.
9. APS, XLIII, 6a.
10. APS, XLIII, 7.
11. APS, CIV, 97.
12. APS, CV, 75.
13. APS, CV, 98.
14. APS, CVI, 76.
15. APS, CVIII, 115.
16. APS, XLIII, 39.
17. APS, XLVI (i), 51.

18. APS, XLIII, 74.
19. APS, XLIII, 28.
20. APS, XLIII, 29.
21. APS, XLIII, 30.
22. APS, October 1, 1781.
23. APS, XLIII, 30.
24. APS, XLIII, 44½.
25. APS, October 12, 1782 [correctly, 1781].
26. APS, October 30, 1781.
27. APS, XLIII, 43.
28. APS, XLIII, 30.
29. APS, October 30, 1781.
30. APS, XLIII, 30.
31. APS, XLIII, 45.
32. APS, XLIII, 42.
33. APS, XLIII, 43.
34. T. Smollett, *Travels through France and Italy* (London, 1766). See Eugene Schuyler, *Italian Influences* (New York, Scribner's, 1901), pp. 237 ff.
35. APS, XLIII, 42.
36. APS, XLIII, 48.
37. APS, XLIII, 43.
38. APS, December 12, 1781.
39. APS, XLIII, 43.
40. APS, October 30, 1781.
41. Ibid.
42. APS, XLIII, 44½.
43. APS, December 12, 1781.
44. APS, XLIII, 44.
45. APS, XLIII, 44½.
46. APS, LVI, 79.
47. APS, January 6, 1782.
48. APS, XLIII, 46.

49. APS, XLIII, 48.
50. APS, XLIII, 47.
51. XLIII, 116.
52. APS, December 12, 1781.
53. Ibid.
54. APS, XLIII, 44½.
55. APS, XLIII, 1.
56. APS [ca. 1784?].
57. APS, XLIII, 48.
58. Smyth, *Writings, 8*, 459–61.
59. Ibid.
60. APS, XLIII, 46 and 47.
61. APS, CIV, 34.
62. APS, XLI, 141.
63. APS, XLIII, 33.
64. APS. XLIII, 114.
65. APS, XLIII, 17.
66. APS, XLVI (i), 49.
67. APS, XLV, 180.
68. APS, XLV, 181.
69. Ibid.
70. APS, XLIII, 113.

Chapter 5, pp. 123 – 49

1. *Adams Papers, 4*, 109.
2. *L'Espion Anglais*, quoted in Aldridge, *Contemporains*, p. 58.
3. H. Lüthy, *La Banque protestante en France de la révocation de l'Edit de Nantes à la Révolution* (2 vols. Paris, 1959–61), *2*, 613 n.
4. Samuel Eliot Morison, *John Paul Jones* (Boston, Little Brown, 1959), pp. 123, 184 ff.
5. *Adams Papers, 4*, 64.
6. APS, XLIV, 50.

7. APS, XLIV, 51.
8. Duc de Croy, *Journal inédit* (4 vols. Paris, Flammarion, 1907), *4*, 167 f.
9. Bibliothèque Nationale, Paris, and Library of Congress. BF to Madame Helvétius, July 19, 1785.
10. APS, October 20, 1785.
11. APS, XXIII, 16.
12. APS, LXX, 1.
13. APS, XLIII, 119.
14. Thomas Jefferson, *Writings* (20 vols. Washington, Jefferson Memorial Association, 1903–04), *18*, 168 f.
15. APS, XLVI (i), 78a, 78b.
16. Library of Congress. BF to Madame Chaumont, June 12, 1785.
17. APS, XLI, 40.
18. Van Doren, *Benjamin Franklin*, p. 723.
19. Yale University Library. BF to Madame Le Veillard, July 22, 1785.
20. APS, XXXIII, 184b.
21. Ibid.
22. Smyth, *Writings*, *9*, 495.
23. Pierpont Morgan Library, New York. BF to Le Veillard, April 15, 1787.
24. APS, LXXI, 84b.
25. APS, XVI, 113.
26. APS, XVII, 33.
27. Smyth, *Writings*, *10*, 69 f.
28. The fact that Benjamin Vaughan's manuscript disappeared without leaving any trace would point to it as a possible source. But when, in 1793, two English versions of Franklin's *Life* appeared, they were retranslations from Buisson's French text, not printings of Vaughan's English text. So the mystery remains.

29. Pierpont Morgan Library, New York (Temple to Le Veillard, Feb. 28, 1792).
30. C. Leroux-Cesbron, "Un Ami de Franklin: Le Veillard," *Bulletin de la Société Historique d'Auteuil et de Passy, 10* (1921), 32 ff.

Chapter 6, pp. 151 – 77

1. Hippolyte Buffenoir, *La Comtesse d'Houdetot, une amie de Jean-Jacques Rousseau* (Paris, Calmann Lévy, 1901), pp. 272 ff.
2. Marquise d'Epinay to Melchior Grimm, in Buffenoir, *Comtesse,* p. 289.
3. Buffenoir, *Comtesse,* pp. 16 ff.
4. Ibid., p. 200.
5. Ibid., pp. 15, 139–40.
6. Gilbert Chinard, *Les Amitiés américaines de Madame d'Houdetot, d'après sa correspondance inédite avec Benjamin Franklin et Thomas Jefferson* (Paris, Librairie de la Société de l'Histoire de France, 1924), p. 51.
7. Jared Sparks, *The Works of Benjamin Franklin* (10 vols. Boston, 1840), *9,* 22–24.
8. Ibid.
9. Robert de Crèvecoeur, *Saint-John de Crèvecoeur, sa vie et ses ouvrages* (Paris, Librairie des Bibliophiles, 1883). See also Julia Post Mitchell, *St. Jean de Crèvecoeur* (New York, Columbia University Press, 1916).
10. Louis P. de Bachaumont, *Mémoires secrets pour servir à l'histoire de la république des lettres en France depuis 1762 jusqu'à nos jours* (31 vols. London, J. Adamson, 1777–89), *11–12,* 155.
11. Crèvecoeur, *Crèvecoeur,* p. 71.
12. From Jean-Pierre Brissot de Warville, *Mémoires, 2,* 409, as quoted in Crèvecoeur, *Crèvecoeur,* p. 71 n.
13. APS, XXIV, 137.

14. Smyth, *Writings*, *9*, 20 f.
15. Crèvecoeur, *Crèvecoeur*, p. 77.
16. Smyth, *Writings*, *9*, 147–49.
17. Franklin Bowditch Dexter, ed., *The Literary Diary of Ezra Stiles* (3 vols. New York, 1901) *3*, 161.
18. APS, XXVIII, 155.
19. APS, XXXI, 193.
20. Collection du Vicomte Foy. BF to Countess d'Houdetot, June 9, 1784.
21. APS, XII, 15.
22. APS, XLIII, 35.
23. APS, XVI, 138.
24. Smyth, *Writings*, *9*, 182 ff.
25. APS, XXXI, 190.
26. APS, XLIII, 138.
27. Smyth, *Writings*, *9*, 268.
28. Denis I. Duveen and Herbert S. Klickstein, "Benjamin Franklin and Antoine Laurent Lavoisier," *Annals of Science*, *2* (1955), 295.
29. APS, XXXII, 205$\frac{3}{4}$.
30. Smyth, *Writings*, *9*, 166 f.

Chapter 7, pp. 179 – 205

1. Mrs. Paget Toynbee, ed., *Lettres de la Marquise du Deffand à Horace Walpole (1766–1780)* (London, Methuen, 1912), *3*, 422 f.
2. Duc de Croy, *Journal inédit*, *4*, 78.
3. Richard Henry Lee, *Life of Arthur Lee, LL.D.* (Boston, Wells, and Lilly, 1829), *1*, 403. William Lee, *Letters (1766–1783)* (Brooklyn Historical Printing Club, 1891), *2*, 417.
4. Smyth, *Writings*, *5*, 53 f.
5. Ibid., *5*, 47.
6. Twenty-five of these cancellation notes are extant in the Franklin Papers.

7. APS, LXXIII, 27–30.
8. Smyth, *Writings*, *10*, 339–40.
9. APS, XLVI (i), 80.
10. Smyth, *Writings*, *8*, 128.
11. Chinard, "Recollections of Benjamin Franklin," APS, *Proceedings*, *94* (1950), 221. The same story is told, in a more biting (and less credible) way by Cabanis, in *Œuvres philosophiques* (2 vols. Paris, Presses Universitaires, 1956) *2*, 359 n.
12. Madame Vigée-Lebrun, *Souvenirs*, p. 118.
13. Madame de Campan, *Mémoires sur la vie de Marie-Antoinette* (Paris, Firmin-Didot, 1858), p. 177.
14. Vigée-Lebrun, *Souvenirs*, pp. 118 f.
15. Toynbee, ed., *Marquise du Deffand*, pp. 547, 549.
16. APS, VIII, 199.
17. Bibliothèque Municipale, Mantes. Franklin to Duc de la Rochefoucauld, February 18, 1778.
18. Ibid., March 31, 1781.
19. Ibid., February 6, 1778.
20. Butterfield, ed., *Adams Papers*, *4*, 41 f.
21. Ibid., 66 f.
22. APS, XXXIII, 252.
23. Chinard, *L'Apothéose de Benjamin Franklin* (Paris, Librairie orientale et américaine, 1955), pp. 93 ff.
24. APS, XXXVI, 16.
25. Smyth, *Writings*, *10*, 493–501. The stick is now in the Smithsonian Institution, Washington, D.C.
26. APS, XIV, 195.
27. University of Pennsylvania. BF to Countess de Forbach [June 1779].
28. APS, IX, 141.
29. APS, XIV, 29.
30. APS, CII, 45.
31. APS, XXIII, 75.

32. *Journal de Paris* (July 5, 1784). See also Chinard, "Benjamin Franklin et la Muse Provinciale," APS, *Proceedings*, *97* (1953), 500. He quotes from a later edition.

33. Chinard, "Benjamin Franklin and the Mysterious Madame G——," *APS Library Bulletin* (1946), 49–72.

34. APS [ca. 1780].

35. APS, February 1, 1781.

36. APS, LXX, 63a.

37. Collection of the Duc de Duras.

38. Lafayette to BF, Sept. 17, 1786. University of Pennsylvania.

39. Smyth, *Writings*, *8*, 595 f.

40. Maurois, *Adrienne*, p. 107.

41. Butterfield, ed., *Adams Papers*, *4*, 171.

42. Smyth, *Writings*, *7*, 26.

43. Jean-Antoine de Condorcet, *Œuvres* (Paris, Firmin-Didot, 1847–49), *5*, 70.

44. C. Kunstler, *La Vie quotidienne sous Louis XVI* (Paris, Hachette, 1950), pp. 238 f.

45. Smyth, *Writings*, *7*, 16.

46. Ibid., p. 290.

47. Amacher, *Wit and Folly*, pp. 77 ff., 156.

Chapter 8, pp. 207 – 41

1. Claude A. Lopez, "Saltpeter, Tin and Gunpowder: Addenda to the Correspondence of Lavoisier and Franklin," *Annals of Science*, *16* (1960), 91–92.

2. Duveen and Klickstein, "Franklin and Lavoisier," *Annals of Science*, *2* (1955), 123.

3. Douglas McKie, *Antoine Lavoisier, Scientist, Economist, Social Reformer* (New York, Henry Schuman, 1952), pp. 404, 407.

4. APS, XXXIV, 95$\frac{1}{2}$; XXXV, 50.

5. APS, LXX, 67.

6. APS, LXXI, 36a.

7. APS, LXXI, 43b.

8. APS, XXX, 121.

9. L. B. Bachaumont, *Mémoires secrets*, p. 65.

10. Gaston Tissandier, *Histoire des ballons et des aéronautes célèbres, 1783–1800* (Paris, H. Launette, 1887), pp. 33 f.

11. Tissandier, *Histoire des ballons*, p. 45.

12. APS, XLIV, 146.

13. APS, IX, 33.

14. APS, IX, 31.

15. Tissandier, *Histoire des ballons*, pp. 33 f.

16. Smyth, *Writings, 9*, 113–18.

17. APS, L (i), 51.

18. APS, XXXIV, 106½.

19. APS, XLIV, 295.

20. Library of Congress. BF to Mme. Le Roy [April 1787].

21. APS, XXXV, 85.

22. Daniel Mornet, *Les Origines intellectuelles de la révolution française* (Paris, Colin, 1933), p. 427.

23. John T. Tussaud, *The Romance of Madame Tussaud* (New York, Doran, 1920), pp. 66 f. C. C. Sellers, *Benjamin Franklin in Portraiture* (New Haven, Yale University Press, 1962), pp. 150 f., casts doubt on the entire Tussaud tradition.

24. APS, III, 101. Dubourg to BF, May 31, 1772.

25. APS, XLII, 8.

26. APS, III, 121.

27. Félix Bouvier, "Une concierge de Passy en l'an II," *Bulletin de la Société Historique d'Auteuil et de Passy, 5* (1905–06), 110–28.

28. APS, LXXI, 72a, and 72b; XLIII, 174, etc.

29. Sellers, *Portraiture*, p. 122.

30. APS, CVII, 15.

31. F. B. Adams, Jr., "Franklin and his Press at Passy," *Yale University Library Gazette, 30* (1956), 133 ff.

32. APS, XVIII, 72; XIX, 67.
33. Smyth, *Writings*, *7*, 347.
34. Sellers, *Portraiture*, pp. 136–37.
35. Smyth, *Writings*, *8*, 62–63.
36. APS, XVIII, 72.
37. APS, XXI, 95.
38. APS, XLIII, 134.
39. APS, XLI, 141.
40. Kunstler, *La Vie quotidienne sous Louis XVI*, p. 262.
41. Christian Guy, *Une Histoire de la cuisine française* (Paris, Les Productions de Paris, 1962), p. 34.
42. APS, VIII, 58.
43. Aldridge, *Contemporains*, pp. 108 ff.
44. APS, 1777–85.
45. APS, XII, 31.
46. APS, XII, 52.
47. APS, XL, 29.

Chapter 9, pp. 243 – 71

1. Smyth, *Writings*, *10*, 439.
2. Georges Poyer, *Cabanis* (Paris, Louis-Michaud, n.d.), p. 222.
3. APS, XLIII, 109.
4. APS, XLIII, 42.
5. Jules Bertaut, *Egéries du XVIIIᵉ siècle* (Paris, Plon, 1928), pp. 139 f.
6. Georges May, *Le Dilemme du roman au XVIIIᵉ siècle* (New Haven, Yale University Press, 1963), p. 175.
7. André Morellet, *Mémoires inédits* (2 vols. Paris, Baudouin, 1823), *1*, 141.
8. Antoine Guillois, *Le Salon de Madame Helvétius* (Paris, Calmann Lévy, 1894), p. 16.
9. Guillois, *Salon*, p. 28 n.
10. Ibid., p. 126.

11. Ibid., p. 38.
12. Smyth, *Writings*, *10*, 441 f.
13. Amacher, *Wit and Folly*, pp. 60–62; Yale *Bagatelles*.
14. Butterfield, ed., *Adams Papers*, 2, 301 f.; *4*, 58 f.
15. Ibid., *4*, 58 f.
16. Ibid.
17. Morellet, *Mémoires*, *1*, 381.
18. APS, XXXV, 96.
19. Bibliothèque Nationale, Paris; Duke University, Durham, N.C. BF to Abbé de la Roche (no date).
20. C. F. Adams, ed., *Letters of Mrs. Adams* (2nd ed. 2 vols. Boston, Little Brown, 1840), 2, 55–56.
21. APS, LXXI, 100a.
22. APS, LXXI, 100b.
23. Smyth, *Writings*, *7*, 375.
24. Smyth, *Writings*, *10*, 438 f.
25. BF to Cabanis. In *Curious and Facetious Letters* (1898), pp. 15–16.
26. APS, Bache Collection.
27. APS, XIII, 214.
28. For instance, in Paul McPharlin, ed., *Satires and Bagatelles* (Detroit, Fine Book Circle, 1937), pp. 32–34; and in Cabanis, *Œuvres philosophiques*, 2, 348.
29. Amacher, *Wit and Folly*, pp. 57–59; Yale *Bagatelles*.
30. APS, XL, 91.
31. Anne-Robert Turgot, *Œuvres*, Gustave Schelle, ed. (5 vols. Paris, Alcan, 1913–23), 5, 584.
32. That Franklin actually proposed to Madame Helvétius is believed by Van Doren, pp. 651 f; Guillois, pp. 43 ff.; Schelle, *Vie de Turgot*, in Turgot, *Œuvres*, *1*, 38 f.; and many others. The "highly dramatized presentation of the case" by Bernard Faÿ," *Franklin, the Apostle of Modern Times* (Boston, Little Brown, 1929), pp. 461–62, is rightly questioned by Gilbert

Chinard, "Random Notes on two 'Bagatelles'," APS, *Proceedings, 103* (1959), 740; on the other hand, Chinard seems to lean toward the opposite extreme by discounting the whole incident as a mere joke.

33. Turgot, *Œuvres, 5*, 609.
34. Sainte-Beuve, *Causeries du lundi* (Paris, Garnier Frères, n.d.), *7*, 136–38.
35. Yale University. BF to Abbé de La Roche, March 29, 1781.
36. Parallel texts in Chinard, "Random Notes," APS, *Proceedings, 103* (1959), 727 ff.
37. Morellet, *Mémoires, 1*, 300.
38. Sainte-Beuve, *Causeries, 7*, p. 138.
39. APS, XLII, 87 and 87$\frac{1}{2}$.
40. APS, XL, 189.
41. Morellet, *Mémoires, 1*, 300.
42. John Bigelow, ed., *The Life of Benjamin Franklin Written by Himself* (5th. ed., rev. 3 vols. Philadelphia, 1875), *2*, 496b–496c.
43. Turgot, *Œuvres, 5*, 628.
44. Ibid., p. 629.
45. BF to Mme. Helvétius, no date. Bibliothèque Nationale, Paris, and Library of Congress, Washington, D.C.

Chapter 10, pp. 273 – 301

1. Morellet to BF, no date. Historical Society of Pennsylvania, Philadelphia.
2. Amacher, *Wit and Folly*, p. 127.
3. Letter of Constantin Volney to F. Besnard, in Jean Gaulmier, "L'Idéologue Volney," Doctoral Dissertation, Beyrouth, 1951, pp. 39 f.
4. Cabanis, *Œuvres, 2*, 365.
5. Ibid., p. 345.
6. Ibid., p. 342.

7. Ibid., p. 346.

8. Ibid., p. 345; *1*, 118 n.

9. Ibid., *2*, 348.

10. Ibid., p. 350.

11. Mark Twain, "The Late Benjamin Franklin," *The Galaxy, 10* (1870), 138–39.

12. Cabanis, *Œuvres, 2*, 363.

13. Ibid., p. 364.

14. Ibid., p. 365.

15. Chinard, "Recollections," APS, *Proceedings, 94* (1950), 221.

16. Bibliothèque de l'Institut, Paris,

17. Chinard, "Recollections," p. 218.

18. Ibid., p. 220.

19. Ibid., p. 218.

20. Ibid., p. 219.

21. Smyth, *Writings, 7*, 36.

22. Chinard, "Recollections," p. 221.

23. Ibid., p. 219.

24. Morellet, *Mémoires, 1*, 203.

25. APS, XXXV, 99.

26. APS, CVIII, 65 and 74.

27. APS, CVII, 24.

28. *Guide littéraire de la France* (Paris, Hachette, 1964), pp. 106 ff.

29. Morellet, *Mémoires, 1*, 386.

30. Smyth, *Writings, 9*, 164. See also Van Doren, *Benjamin Franklin*, pp. 707 ff.

31. APS, XL, 89b. See also Bernard Faÿ, "Franklin et Mirabeau, Collaborateurs," *Revue de Littérature Comparée, 8* (1928), 5–28.

32. APS, XL, 89b.

33. Morellet, *Mémoires, 1*, 382.

34. Ibid., p. 296 ff.

35. Amacher, *Wit and Folly*, pp. 130 ff.

36. Morellet, *Mémoires*, *1*, 303 ff.
37. Ibid., p. 306.
38. APS, XXXV, 99.
39. Amacher, *Wit and Folly*, p. 127.
40. APS, XLIII, 194. See also APS, XLIII, 195.
41. APS, L(i), 36.
42. "One of them is as beautiful as Helen of Troy, two more are very lovely." Morellet, *Lettres à Lord Shelbourne* (Paris, Plon, 1898), p. 147.
43. APS, XLI, 156; XL, 94 and 140; CVIII, 2.
44. Chinard, "Recollections," p. 221.
45. Cabanis, *Œuvres*, *2*, 359.
46. APS, XLIV, 274a.
47. Library of Congress, Washington, D.C.; Bibliothèque Nationale, Paris. BF to Madame Helvétius, July 27, 1785.

Chapter 11, pp. 303 – 34

1. Library of Congress. Gouverneur Morris to BF, February 23, 1789.
2. Nathaniel E. Stein collection. BF to Morellet, April 22, 1787.
3. APS, XXXV, 99.
4. Library of Congress. BF to Ferdinand Grand, March 5, 1786.
5. Ibid., January 29, 1785.
6. APS, CVII, 23.
7. Harvard University. Franklin to Le Veillard, October 24, 1788.
8. Collection of Vicomte Foy. BF to Comtesse d'Houdetot, February 16, 1788.
9. Library of Congress. BF to P. S. du Pont de Nemours, October 18, 1789.
10. William Temple Franklin, *Memoirs*, *2*, 123.
11. Duveen and Klickstein, "Benjamin Franklin and Antoine Laurent Lavoisier," *Annals of Science*, *13* (1957), 39–40.
12. APS, XXXVI, 160.

13. APS, XXXIV, 154.
14. APS, CVII, 45.
15. Pierpont Morgan Library, New York. BF to Le Veillard, April 15, 1787.
16. Sparks, *Works, 10*, 337.
17. APS, XXXIII, 232.
18. APS, XLV, 207.
19. APS, XLIII, 119.
20. APS, XLIII, 9.
21. APS, CVII, 37.
22. APS, CVIII, 126.
23. APS, CVIII, 125.
24. APS, CVIII, 114.
25. APS, CVIII, 123.
26. APS, CVIII, 126.
27. APS, CVIII, 117.
28. APS, CVIII, 133.
29. APS, CVIII, 137.
30. APS, XLIII, 10.
31. Ibid.
32. APS, April 19, 1778.
33. APS, CVIII, 138.
34. APS, CVIII, 142.
35. APS, CVIII, 139.
36. APS, XLIII, 12.
37. Ibid.
38. Pierpont Morgan Library, New York. Temple to Le Veillard, January 18, 1886.
39. APS, CVIII, 133.
40. APS, XXXIII, 163.
41. Library of Congress. BF to Chaumont's daughter, October 7, 1786.
42. Smyth, *Writings, 9*, 620.

43. APS, CVII, 37.
44. APS, XXXVI, 129.
45. John Bigelow, "Franklin's Home and Host in France," *Century Illustrated Monthly Magazine*, *35* (1888), 741–54.
46. Archives de la Seine, Paris, DC⁶¹, 32, fol. 126v.: "Lettres de Surceance Générale obtenues au conseil d'Etat du Roy le onze Juillet 1789 signées Laurent de Villedeuil pour un an à comter du jour du présent arrêt en faveur de M. Le Ray de Chaumont maitre honoraire des eaux et forêts de France."
47. Yale University. BF to Leray, October 31, 1789.
48. APS, XXXVI, 183.
49. APS, XXXVI, 196.
50. Library of Congress. BF to Madame de Forbach, July 13, 1787.
51. APS, XXXIV, 49.
52. Library of Congress. BF to Abbé de la Roche, April 22, 1787.
53. APS, CVI, 207.
54. APS, CVIII, 5.
55. APS, CVII, 7.
56. APS, CVII, 8.
57. APS, XLIX, 76.
58. APS, CVII, 16.
59. Library of Congress, BF to Ferdinand Grand, March 20, 1786.
60. APS, CVII, 4.
61. Maurois, *Adrienne*, p. 159.
62. New York Public Library. BF to Abbé de la Roche, April 22, 1787.
63. APS, XLIII, 119.
64. APS, XXXIV, 23.
65. APS, XXXV, 96.
66. Library of Congress; Bibliothèque Nationale. BF to Madame Helvétius, April 23, 1788.
67. Library of Congress. BF to Madame Helvétius, October 20, 1785.

68. APS, XL, 189.
69. Library of Congress; Bibliothèque Nationale. BF to Madame
    Helvétius, October 25, 1788.

Index

Italicized page numbers refer to illustrations

Acacia tree: Comtesse d'Houdetot and Rousseau under, 155–56; BF plants, 156–58

Académie française. *See* French Academy

Academy of Sciences (Paris). *See* Royal Academy of Sciences

Acadia (Halifax) campaign (*1746*), 187 n.

Adam, 276

Adams, Abigail: opinion of French mores, 257–58, 280; quoted, 257–58

Adams, John: criticism of BF as Ambassador, 6–9, 183; criticism of BF's life in France, quoted, 7–9, cited, 20, 211; cited and quoted on BF's prestige, 13; criticism of BF's friends, 18; quoted on BF's conversation, 21–22; criticism of BF's French quoted, 26; French lessons, 26; description of Brillon ménage, quoted, 41–42, cited, 60–61, 253; shocked by French mores, 42–43, 253–55, 280; criticism of BF's residence, 124; quotes Mme. Chaumont's quip on BF, 129; opinion of La Rochefoucaulds quoted, 187; on difficulty of pronouncing "George Washington" in French, 200; attends dinner at Mme. Helvétius', 253–55, 257–58; description of Mme. Helvétius' ménage quoted, 253–55

Alembert, d' (mathematician and secretary of the Royal Academy of Science), 187, 246

Alexander, Mr., 332

Alexander girls, 298

Alleghenies, 34

Almanachs des Muses, 194

Amacher, Richard, translation of BF's letter on drinking quoted, 294–96

American Philosophical Society, 212; founded by BF, 277; Le Veillard elected to, 310; BF's papers given to, 342; publication of BF's papers by, 343

American Revolution, 159; effect on Franklins, 1, 11; in *1776*, 3–4; English view of, 3–4, 115–16; effect on American economy, 11; spies, 12–13, 114, 133, suspected, 159; Saratoga campaign, 36, conclusion of, 109–10, 115, 192; relation to French Revolution, 184, 310; capture of BF portrait during, 210; BF's role in, according to Morellet, 291–92. *See also* Continental Army

Ancaster, Duchess of, 112

Anet, 49, 52

Animal magnetism. *See* Mesmer, theory and practice

Annonay, balloon launching at, 215

Arbelot, BF's aid to, 286–87

Arlandes, Marquis d', 218, 221

Armonica, 74; described, 22–23; popularity of, 23; method of playing described by BF, 23, 25; virtues of described by BF, 23; virtues of listeners described by BF, 83; BF plays, 83, 117; Mesmer's use of, 170

Arnold, Benedict, 3
Artists, women, 227, bibliographical note on, 355
Artois, Comte d' (Charles X), 168, 314
Assembly of Notables (*1787*), 188–89, 307–08
Astrology, 169
Atlantic coast of Europe, 116
Auray, 1
Austria, 244
Auteuil, 12; Mme. Helvétius' estate in, 247–48, 250, 331, 334
Auteuil Academy, 84, 108, 115, 244; music and politics at, 108, 287, 290–92, 294, 296; basis of, 248–51; role of Mme. Helvétius in, 249, 273, 297, BF quoted on, 251, 270, 271; BF's description of not eating breakfast at, 252–53, 333; BF's conversations in, 273–79, 281, 284; effect of French Revolution on, 290, 299; drinking songs, 291–92, 294, 296; picnics, 298; BF's leave-taking from, 299; correspondence with BF after his return to America, 304, 333; bibliographical note on, 355–56. *See also* Cabanis; Franklin, Benjamin; Helvétius, Anne-Catherine; La Roche; Morellet; Turgot, Anne-Robert; Voltaire
Autobiography of BF: BF writes second part, 145–46, 278; original copy rediscovered, 148; Twain's description of as an "affliction," 278–79; relation to Auteuil reminiscences, 279; bibliographical note on, 345. *See also* Memoirs
Avignon, 103

Ayen, Adrienne d'. *See* Lafayette, Adrienne
Ayen, duc d', 197

Bachaumont, Louis P. de, quoted, 161
Bache, Benjamin, 15, 168; comes with BF to Paris, 1, 2; education in Europe, 5, 12; quoted, 138; copy of BF's Memoirs by, 149; learns printing trade in France, 233–34; receives swimming lessons from BF, 281; after return from Europe, 318
Bache, Dr. Franklin, 342
Bache, Richard, 318; letter from BF quoted, 92
Bache, Sarah, 1, 56, 92, 318; BF's reply to request for French pins, lace, and feathers, quoted, 10–11; BF's letter to on vices of the American eagle and virtues of the turkey quoted, 177; BF's letter to on being "i-doll-ized" quoted, 232; gifts from BF's French friends to, 328
Bagatelles by BF: purpose of, 26–27; preparation, 26–27; collection given to Mme. Brillon, 118–20; typography, 230; bibliographical note on, 344–45.
    Champs Elysées, Les, 119 n.
    Conte (on religious tolerance): popularity, 89; quoted, 89–90
    Dialogue Between the Gout and Mr. Franklin, 75, 119 n.; inspiration for, 77–79, 90; editing of, *76*, 79, 81–82; quoted, 81–82, 298
    Elysian Fields: analyzed, 264–65, 268; quoted, 265–67; publication, 268

Ephemera, The, 119 n., 318; composition of, 50; sources, 50; quoted, 50–52
   Franklin à Madame la Fr[et]é, 119 n.; quoted, 252–53
Handsome and Deformed Leg, The, 83, 119 n.
Information to Those who would Remove to America, 119 n.; anti-nobility views in, 203, 205; quoted, 205
   Morals of Chess, The, 119 n.
Mouches à Madame He[lvétius], Les (Petition of the Flies), 119 n., 296; quoted, 262–63
Parabole contre la Persécution, 119 n.
Remarks Concerning the Savages of North America, 119 n.
Sage et la Goutte, Le (Fable by Mme. Brillon), 77–79; quoted, 77–78; BF's apology for using quoted, 119
Story of the Whistle, The, 119 n., 275, 318; composition of, 69; quoted, 69–70, 71; publication, 70
To the Royal Academy of ——— [Brussels], 119 n.
Bailly, M. (first mayor of Paris), 171
Baker Street, 225
Balloons: first ascensions, *206, 215–19, 217;* BF's interest in, 216–20 passim; BF quoted on, 220–22; Mme. Le Roy's ascent in, 223–24
Bancroft, Edward, 12–13, 133
Banks, Sir Joseph, correspondence with BF on balloon development, quoted, 216, 220–21, cited, 220
Barbé-Marbois, François: criticism of BF, 13; memoirs, 13–14

Barbeu-Dubourg, Jacques, 226
Bartram, John (botanist), 330
Bassora, consul of the French King at, 196–97
Bastille, 311; fall of, 240, 325, French reaction to, 18, BF's reaction to, 308–09; Morellet in, 285
Bathtubs, eighteenth-century, 29
Baussan, Mme. de, letters on attempts to have BF to dinner quoted, 116–17, 235–36
Bavaria, 191; Elector of, 211
Bayonne, jambon de, 331
Beaumarchais, Pierre-Augustin Caron de, 238; support of U.S., 5, 128, 167; posthastiness, 36
Beccaria, Cesare, *Treatise of Crimes and Punishments,* 285
Beethoven, Ludwig von, 28, 31; "Fidelio," 248
Benedictine Fathers, boarding school, 130
Bermuda, 159
Bertaut, Jules, quoted, 244
Bible, The, 281; according to "abbé Franklin," 294–95
Bien Aimé (disciple of Deslon), 173
Bigelow, John, 140
Biheron, Mlle.: anatomical models, 225–26; relationship with BF, 226–27
Bitaubé, Paul-Jérémie, translator of *Iliad,* 59
Boccherini, Luigi, 30, 31
Bocquet, Blaise, 227, 229
Bois de Boulogne, 247, 279
Bonaparte, Napoleon, 248; as student, 194
Bordeaux, 98, 116, 193, 311

Bossuet, *Funeral Orations*, 26

Boston, 166, 257; of BF's childhood, 275, 280–81

Boucher, François, 85

Bougainville, M. de, 329

Bouilly, Jean-Nicolas, *Les Oiseaux de Madame Helvétius*, 248

Bourbon, Duchesse de, chess game with BF, 135

Bourdic, Baroness de, 194–95; poems by, 194; poems about, 195; bibliographical note on, 354

Bourgeoisie: women known by BF, 224–29; BF's friends in, 307; bibliographical information on, 354–56

Brandy, 295

Breget, M. de, cured by Deslon, 172–73

Brest, 193

Breuer, 169

Brickland, Ester, 239

Brienne, 194

Brillon de Jouy, M., 34, 101, 152; friendship with BF, 29, 60, 67–68, 72, 77, 83–84, 121; described, 31, by Adams, 42, by BF, 43, 68, by Mme. Brillon, 66; affair with governess, 31, 41, 42–43, 61–65, 67, 68, 107; personality, 67–68; refusal of BF's offer to have Temple wed his older daughter, 92, 93, 313, 315; career, 94–95, 99, 100–01; attitude toward Temple's romance with younger daughter, 99, 100–01, 313; accompanies wife to Nice, 102, 107; postscripts and letters to BF, 107, quoted, 29, 67, 121, 134, 313–14, 332; letters from BF quoted, 107;

attacks of gout, 116, 316–17; death, 317–19

Brillon de Jouy, Aldegonde. *See* Malachelle, Aldegonde

Brillon de Jouy, Anne-Louise d'Hardancourt (Madame Brillon), 9, 138, 168, 227, 228, 235, 236, 258; reclines in bathtub while BF plays chess, 29, 59; complains of gossips and withdraws "favors," 29, 57–60, 64; correspondence with BF, size, 29, 116, dating, 33, language and editing, 39; nature of relationship with BF, 29, 32, 33, 46, 48–49, 55–59, 81, 113–14, 117–20, 256; husband, 29, 60 (*see* Brillon de Jouy, M.); daughters, 29–30, 36, 42, 60, 73, 75, 84, 102, 111, 112 (*see also* Malachelle, Aldegonde; Pâris d'Illins, Cunégonde); described, 29–32, by Adams, 42; as musician and composer, 30–31, 34, 37 n., 42, 44, 60, 73, 111, 186, 290; garden steps, 30, as BF's cure for nervous illness, 75, as BF's cure for gout, 80, as BF's barrier, 83, 84; personality, 31–32, 37, 47, 62, 94, 244; relationship with Le Veillard, 33 (*see* Le Veillard, Louis-Guillaume); campaign of *1777* to win BF's *amitié amoureuse*, 33-37, 41; letters to BF quoted, 35–36, 38–39, 40–41, 43–44, 46–48, 52–53, 55–63, 65–66, 68, 71, 74–75, 79, 81, 83–86, 90, 94, 95, 97, 101–07, 109, 111–12, 117, 120–21, 170, 314, 317, 319, 320; BF's evenings with, 35, 36, 37, 80–81, 117; "Marche des Insurgents" composed by 36, *37*, 37 n., 112,

117, 118; BF's campaign of *1778* to make the *amitié* more *amoureuse*, 37–53, 58–59, 72; ménage, 37, 117, described by John Adams, 41–43, 60–61, 253, taken to Nice, 102; correspondence with BF on fantasy of paradise, 37–38, 41, 68, 69, 71, 72–74, 90–91, 170, 268, 317, 319, 333 (see also *Bagatelles, Conte*); flirtation with BF in terms of sins, salvation, and twelve commandments, 38–41, 43–44, 104; letters from BF quoted, 39–40, 44–46, 47, 48, 56, 58, 59, 63–65, 67–68, 69–71, 72, 73, 75, 79, 82, 83, 84, 86, 92–94, 95–96, 102, 103–06, 107–13, 118–19, 268, 318–19; cited, 29, 91, 107, 108–09; possessiveness, 43–48, 85–86, 101–02, 312; BF's letter requesting nourishment for his cupid and setting forth a peace treaty to, 44–46, 318; excursion with BF to Moulin-Joli, 49–52; BF writes *The Ephemera* for, 50–52, 318; expresses her feelings for BF, 52–53, 56–57; aquatint of Passy by, *54*; establishes father–daughter relationship with BF, 55–59, 64–65, 92; mother, 60 (*see* Hardancourt, Mme. d'); distressed by discovery of husband's infidelity and receives solace from BF, 60–72, 74, 113, 224; nervous illness, 61, 74–75, 77, 83, 85, 101–03, 116, BF's remedies for, 75, 79, 82; criticism of husband, marriages "by weight of gold," 66–67, 94, 95; BF writes *The Whistle* for, 69–71, 318; reaction to *The Whistle*, 71; as

editor of BF's *Dialogue Between the Gout and Mr. Franklin*, *76*, 79, 81–82; writes *Le Sage et La Goutte* for BF, 77–79, letters on, 79, 85; letters on isms and instincts, 81–82; comments on *The Handsome and Deformed Leg*, 83; reunion with BF after their illnesses (*1780*), 84–85; becomes *la famille Brillon* to BF, 84; writes *The Four Seasons* for BF, 85, BF's comment on, 85; view of religious tolerance in paradise, 90–91, 94; BF's letter asking for marriage between Cunégonde and Temple, 91–94, 156, refusal, 94–95, 313, 315, BF's acceptance of, 95–96; view of religious tolerance on earth, 94, 95; as grandmother, 96–97, 117, 317, 320; letters on sorrows and pleasures, 102, 314, 317; trip to Nice to regain health, 102–08, 111–16, 117; correspondence with BF on her absence, 103–14; describes BF's character, 106, 314; hears of Yorktown and hears from BF, 109–10; plays "Marche des Insurgents" for English, 112; BF's gradual separation from, 113–14; return to Paris, 116–18; is happy, 117; BF gives collection of *Bagatelles* to, 118–20; sends adieus to BF, 120–21; portrait of BF owned by, 120, 317, 320; visit with BF to see Mesmer, 170; life after BF leaves France, 312–21; final correspondence with BF, 317–21; bibliographical note on, 349–51
Brillon de Jouy, Cunégonde. *See* Pâris d'Illins, Cunégonde

Brittany, 1

Buffon, Georges, 14, 162

Buisson, Jacques, pirated edition of BF's *Autobiography*, 148, 279–80

Burgundy wine, 237

Burgoyne, General, 36

Burney, Charles, quoted, 30

Cabanis, Pierre-Georges: opinion of BF quoted, 9–10; translates *The Handsome and Deformed Leg*, 83; poem on Mme. Helvétius quoted, 243; as medical theorist, 250, 274–75, 299; relationship with Mme. Helvétius, 250, 297, 333 (*see also* Auteuil Academy); relationship with BF, 252, 273–80, 284, 299; letters from BF on Mme. Helvétius, quoted, 259–60, 268–69; *Works*, 274, cited, 275; "Notice sur Benjamin Franklin," cited, 275–80; quoted, 277; political views, 290

Caen, Normandy, 158

Caillot, Blanchette: affair with Temple, 101, 235, 276, 315; letters to Temple, 314–15, quoted, 101, 315–17, 319, 321

Caillot, Joseph, 235, 276, 314 n.

Calonne (French Finance Minister), 307

Camasse, Marianne. *See* Forbach, Comtesse de

Camembert cheese, 236

Campan, Henriette de: quoted, 184, cited, 184

Canada, 3, 158, 329

Carolina, 199

Castries, Maréchal de, 165

Catherine II, 226

Chaillot, 12, 298

Champagne. *See* Brienne

Champ de Mars, balloon launching at, 215–16

Champlost, Pa., BF papers at, 342

Champs Elysées, Les. See under *Bagatelles*

Charcot, 169

Charles, Jacques: invention of hydrogen balloon, 215–16, *217*, 217, 218–19; quoted on flight, 219; as scientist, BF quoted on, 220

Charles X. *See* Artois, Comte d'

Charleston, 270

Charlotte Sophia, Queen of England, 112

Chastellux, Chevalier de, 109, 195–97; letter from BF quoted, 197; *Voyage en Amérique septentrionale*, 197

Chateaubriand, 194

Châtelet, M. du, 153

Châtelet, Mme. du, 153

Chatelguyon, mineral waters, 141

Chaumont (village), 326

Chaumont, Jacques-Donatien Leray de, 73, *148*, 259; nature of relationship with BF, 123, 128–29, 186; as BF's landlord, 123–24, 126, 135–36, BF's memo to, 135–36; financial and trade contributions to American cause, 124, 126–28, 322, 324; fate in French Revolution, 126; career, 126–28, 324–26; ceramics factory, 126, 127; painting of BF commissioned by, 127, 209, 233; financial disaster caused by aid to U.S., 128, 135, 321–22, 324–26; family, 238 (*see* Foucault, Mme.; Leray, Jacques

(James); and Chaumont *below*), bibliographical note on, 351–52; letters to BF, 313, 322; BF's aid to, 321–26; letter from BF, 322

Chaumont, Mlle. "mère Bobie," 321; as BF's household manager, 123–24, 131–34; reply to BF letter on his departure, quoted, 138; letter from BF quoted, 322–23; marriage, 322, 323–24

Chaumont, Sophie, 137, 323; letters to BF, quoted, 321, cited, 323–24

Chaumont, Mme. Thérèse, 9, 321, 323; relationship with BF, 9, 123, 137; Nini medallion of, *122*, 129; witticism on BF, 129; letters to BF, 129–31, quoted, 129, 130; letter from BF quoted, 137; children, 123–24, 131, 137, 321 (*see also* Chaumont, Mlle. "mère Bobie," Sophie, Thérèse-Elisabeth; Foucault, Mme.; Leray de Chaumont, Jacques); retires to convent, 324

Chaumont, Mlle. Thérèse-Elisabeth, 321, 323

Chaumont-sur-Loire (château), 126, 134, 326; exploitation of, 126; Mme. Chaumont's attempts to lure BF to, 130–31

Chess: BF's passion for, 9, 78, 80, 134–35; Mme. Brillon left in bathtub while BF plays, 29, 59; games played by BF and Mme. Brillon, 35, 36, 68; BF's style at life and, 110, 135; *Bagatelle* on, 119 n.; anecdotes about BF and, 134–35; as BF's "best Christian deed," 192; Mme. Le Roy left out in rain while BF plays, 213–14

China: dinnerware, 236; honor system, 288; books on, 328

Choisy, 298

Cholmondeley, Lord: described by Mme. Brillon, 111, 114; visit to BF and role in peace negotiations, 115

Cicero, 50

Cincinnati, Society of the, BF's stand against, 288–90

Compagnie des Indes, 286

Condorcet, 142, 187, 246; *Letters from a New Haven Burgher*, 167, cited, 202

Confessions. See Rousseau

Congress, 12; Committee of Secret Correspondence, 3; appointment of commissioners to France, 3, 124 (*see also* Adams, John; Deane; Franklin, Benjamin; Lee); BF's difficulties with, 85; BF sends resignation to President of (*1781*), 86–87; refuses to accept BF's resignation, 101; refusal to honor claims of French entrepreneurs, 128, 135, 322–26; offer of king to, 282; BF's opinion of, 307; refusal to appoint Temple, 341

Connecticut, 199

Constitution, BF's opinion of, 306–09

Constitutional Convention, BF's work at, 304

Constitutions of the American States, 167; French translation of, 167, 186

Conte. See under *Bagatelles*

Continental Army: Frenchmen in, 109, 191–94 passim, 196, 205, 283, 289 (*see also* Chastellux; Lafayette); hereditary society for officers in, 288–90

Conway, Mr., 116
Cook, Captain, 131
Corday, Charlotte, 29
Cornwallis, 109, 192
Correspondance littéraire, 268
Corrèze, 275
Court, French. *See* Versailles
Coxe, Grace, 322–23
Crèvecoeur, Frances-America, 166
Crèvecoeur, Michel-Guillaume de (Normannus Americanus; St. Jean; Saint John): returns to France after living in America, 158–59; *Letters from an American Farmer*, 159, 164; pamphlet on growing potatoes, 160; correspondence with BF quoted, 160; introduced into French society by Turgot, 160–61; relationship with Comtesse d'Houdetot, 162–67; *Memoirs*, quoted, 162, 165; report on America, packet boats, 165; as French consul in New York, 165–67; gives "freedom of the city" of New Haven to French friends, 166–67
Croy, Duc de, 131, 179–80

Daily Advertiser, 70
Daubigny, drawing by, *28*
Dauphin. *See* Louis
David, Jacques-Louis, 209, 228–29
Deane, Silas, 5–6, 124, 180; quoted, 91
Declaration of Independence, 3, 4; translated into and banned from français, 186
Deffand, Marquise du, letters to Walpole on BF, quoted, 179, 184, cited, 180

De Lon, M., 114
Départment de la Seine, Archives, 325
Deslon, Dr. Charles: relationship with Mesmer, 169, 171, 173; practices investigated by BF's commission, 171–74, reports on, 174–75
Deux-Ponts (Zweibrücken), 190–91; regiment from in American Revolutionary War, 192, 193
Deux-Ponts, Dowager Duchess of. *See* Forbach, Comtesse
Deux-Ponts Birkenfeld, Duke Christian de, 191
Dialogue Between the Gout and Mr. Franklin. See under *Bagatelles*
Diderot: *Encyclopédie*, 246, 285; praise of Mme. Helvétius, 247
Didot, Pierre F., 119 n.
"Dieu d'Amour," favorite aria of BF, 117, 196
Dogwood, Mrs. Silence, letter by BF under name of, 221
Dreux, Normandy, 143
Dublin, 159
Ducreux, J. N., *261*
Dumay, Ignace Adolphe, 239
Dupin, Antoine, 211
Duplessis, Joseph-Siffrède: Chaumont portrait of BF by, 127, 209, 233; Le Veillard portrait of BF by, 140
Du Pont de Nemours, Eleuthère Irénée, 210, 211
Du Pont de Nemours, Pierre Samuel, 15, 211, 264, 270; letter from BF quoted, 308
Du Pont de Nemours, Victor, 210, 211

Eagle, *176*; falls in BF's garden, 176; BF's disapproval of, 177

Eaubonne, 154, 155, 156

Elbow, BF on placement of, *293*, 295–96

Electricity, BF's theory of, 212, 220

Elizabeth, Empress of Russia, 237

Elysian Fields. See under *Bagatelles*

Empire period, 250, 274

Encyclopédie, 246, 285

England, English, 23, 159, 164, 174, 237; relations with France, 3 (*see* France); view of American Revolution, 3–4, 115–16; peace treaty with U.S., 4, 145 (*see also* U.S.); Ambassador to, 5; in Mme. Brillon's paradise, 68; defeat at Yorktown, 109–10, 115, 192; vacationers at Nice, 111–12, 114–16; House of Commons, 115; Ambassador to France, 124, 180 (*see also* Stormont); rule of American colonies, 164, 200, 291, 292; packet boat service to U.S., 165–66; blockade of France, 193; in clockmaking, 212; press, BF's letters to, 221; reports on U.S., 305–06; rivalry with France over balloon development, 216–17, 221; BF meets Morellet in, 284–85

English Channel, 139, 159, 208

Eon, Chevalier Charles-Geneviève-Louise-Auguste d': life, 237–39; letter to BF cited, 238; gross tale linking BF and, 238–39; bibliographical note on, 354

Ephemera, The. See under *Bagatelles*

Epinay, Marquise d', 154; quoted, 152–53

Ermitage, L', 154

Espion Anglais, L', quoted, 128

Estaing, Comte d', letter quoted, 332

Etats Généraux (*1789*), 189, *302*, 307

Europe, 180, 283, 304, 305; gets potato and gold from Peru, 161; importance of birth in, 205; grain laws, 287

Farmers-General, 207–08, 211, 245, 254

Figaro, 128

Filleul, Louis, 227, 228

Filleul, Mme. Rosalie, 227–29; letters to BF, 228; portrait of BF, 229, *230*; self-portrait, *231*

Finck, Jacques, BF's malcontent majordomo, 132–33

Fontenelle, 247

Forbach (town), 192

Forbach, Comtesse, Duchesse Douairiere du Duc de Deux-Ponts, 194, 260; gives presents to BF, 189–90; letters to BF, 189–92, 256, quoted, 190, 191; letters from BF quoted, 190, 327; title, 190–91; children, 191, 192, 193, 327; nephew, Fontevieux, 191–92; pro-Americanism, 191; private secretary of, 192–93; bibliographical note on, 354

Forbonnais, M. de, 324

Foucault, Mme., 124, 134, 321, 323

Fourier, Baron, eulogy of Jacques Charles, 220

Fournier family (typefounders), 229; foundry, 233

Fournier le Jeune, Simon-Pierre: designs and sells type to BF and requests BF to pose, 229, 232–34;

Fournier le Jeune—*cont.*
letter from BF quoted, 233; letter
to BF quoted, 234

Fournier, Mme., wants to own a portrait of BF, 229, 232–34

Fox, Dr. George, 342

France, French, in eighteenth century: BF's return to, 1–3; BF's
adulation and prestige in, 2, 5–7,
13–18, 90, 99, 127, 161, 220, 232–
33, 239; women, BF comments on,
2, 19, 181, 202–03, BF's appeal for,
16–17, described, 20–22, 203, 314,
personalities, 31–32, 152, signatures, 124, effect of animal
magnetism on, 175, careers of,
224–27; hair styles and dress, 2,
12, 21, 104 n., *178*, 313–14, BF
quoted on, 12, 202–03; relations
with England, 3–4, 179, 184; relations with U.S., 3–4, 179–81, 184;
U.S. Treaty of Alliance with, 4,
200; Treaty of Amity and Commerce with U.S., 4, 179, economic
effect, 16; BF's opinion of, 12, 310;
interest in American experiment,
14–16, 157; mores, 18, 19, 152,
BF's acceptance of, 5, 10–12,
according to Adams, 254–55; conversation, 21, 210, 259; epistles,
24; marriages, arranged by parents,
66, 92, 94, 99, 244, 245, 247,
mixed, 92, 94, 99; Army, 126, 127,
283; packet boats between U.S.
and, 127, 165–66, 311; entrepreneurs' unrepaid aid to America,
128, 135, 167, 322–26; formal
dinners and gastronomy, 131, 161,
181, *201*, *204*, 236–37; BF's
departure from, 133, 135–41, 299–
301; importance of potato to, 161;
Minister of the Navy, 165; consuls
in U.S., 166, 325; memory of BF,
188, 304–05; BF's advice on
emigrating to U.S. to, 205 (see
also *Bagatelles*, *Information*);
nobility, BF's view of, 202–03,
205, 288–90; rivalry with England
over balloon development, 216–
17, 221 (*see also* Balloons);
excitement over balloon travel,
219; press, BF's letters to, 221,
letters about BF, 239 (see *Journal
de Paris*); ubiquity of BF's image
in, 232–33; Americans in, 235;
Minister Plenipotentiary to England, 237; gardens, 247; medicine
in, 274, 298; beliefs about noble
savages, 278; passion for memoirs,
279; furnishings, BF's criticism of
quoted, 281; in American Revolution, 283 (*see* Continental Army);
grain trade regulation, 286, 287;
Government, 288 (*see* Versailles);
coming of revolution to, 304, 307–
10, 320, 329; Foreign Minister
(*1789*), 325; exchange of goods
with Americans, 327–32. *See also*
French Revolution

Franco-German border, 190–91

Franklin, avenue, 326

Franklin, Abiah, 275

Franklin, Benjamin: trip to Paris,
1–3; use of relatives as assistants,
1–2, 9–10, 12 (*see also* Bache,
Benjamin; Franklin, William
Temple); prestige in France, 2
(*see* France); dress, 2–3, 11, 17,
127, 179, 182, 183, 184, BF quoted
on, 202; mission in France, 2–5,

9–10, 12–13, 85, 124, 126, 179–85, 193 (*see also* Versailles), BF quoted on, 4, 6; acceptance of French ways, 5, 10–12, 281; relations with other commissioners, 5–9, 113; as Minister Plenipotentiary, 6, 126, 281, 286; role in peace negotiations, 6, 114–16, 117, 253; "Life of . . . continual discipation," described by John Adams, 7–9, 211; visitors and dinner invitations, 8–9, 18–19, 116–17, 131, 142, 192, 200, *201*, 202, 215, 219, 234–36; relationships with French women, 8–9, 18–20, 27, quoted on, 25–26; "art of living" described by Cabanis, 9–10; daily life and residence in France, 12 (*see* Passy, BF's residence in); disabilities, 13, 133; French criticism of, 13–14; as symbol of America, 13–16, 127, 195; attacks of gout and stone, 13, 32, 67, 68, 69, 77–87, 117, 131, 141, 168, 209, 311 (see also *Bagatelles, Dialogue, Le Sage et la Goutte*); contributions to physiocrats' *Journal*, 15; circle of friends, 18 (*see* Auteuil Academy; Passy); stepniece, 19; difficulties with French language, 19, 20–21, 25–27, 36, 39, 68, 71, 73–74, 112–13, 142, 186, 280, BF quoted on, 25, 73, 81, 91, 112, 139, Mme. Brillon quoted on, 74, 80, 113; musical preferences, 22, 25, 34–35, 68, 290; inventions, 22–23, 25, 285, 286 (*see also* Armonica; Lightning rod); writes and publishes *Bagatelles*, 26–27 (see *Bagatelles*); life

in Paris described by a young American, 27; relationship with M. Brillon and Mme. Brillon, 29–121 (*see* Brillon de Jouy, M.; Brillon de Jouy, Anne-Louise); American critics of, 64, 85 (*see also* Adams, John; Lee, Arthur); illness (*1780–81*), 67, 68, 77–87; at seven, as viewed by BF at seventy, 70; at seventy, as viewed by BF at seventy, 78; lack of moderation, according to Mme. Brillon, 78–79; lack of exercise, according to BF, 79–81; sketch of a Passy garden, *86*; resignation to Congress, quoted, 87; desire to die in France, 87, 92, 101; religious tolerance, 89–91, 93–94; attempt to marry Cunégonde Brillon to Temple Franklin, 91–96, 156, 313; anxiety about dying in France, 91–92; papers, publication and editing of, 93, 146–49, 341–44, loss of, 116, 342–43, bibliographical note on, 343–56 (see also *Autobiography*; *Bagatelles*; Memoirs; *Poor Richard*); Congress refuses resignation of, 101; personality, 261–62, 264–65, 276–81, assessed by Mme. Brillon, 106, 314, assessed by BF, 110, 135, assessed by Mme. Helvétius, 334; portraits, owned by Brillons, 120, 317, 320, Duplessis oil commissioned by Chaumonts, 127, 209, 233, Duplessis pastel commissioned for Le Veillards, 140, by Mme. Lavoisier, 209–10, taken by British, 210, by Rosalie Filleul, 229, *230*, Judlin miniature for

Franklin, Benjamin—*cont.*

Fourniers, 232–33, Vanloo oil for Mme. Helvétius, *272*, 284; placets to, 110–11, 239–41; plans to return to U.S., 113; medallions of, 114, *125*, 127, 232; journal on peace negotiations quoted, 114–15; illness (*1782*), 117, 168; Polly Hewson visits, 118; relationship with Chaumonts, 123–24, 127–38, 186 (*see also* Chaumont, Jacques-Donatien); Finck's efforts to blacken, 133; departure from France, 133, 135–41, 299–301; passion for chess, 134–35 (*see* Chess); attempts to get Congress to repay French merchants, 135, 322–26; relationship with Le Veillards, 138–49 (*see also* Le Veillard, Mme.; Le Veillard, Geneviève; Le Veillard, Louis-Guillaume); verse dedicated to, 142; continues work on Memoirs (*Autobiography*), 145–46, 278; sends Le Veillard copy of Memoirs, 145–46; will and bequests, 146–47, 189, 341; relationship with Comtesse d'Houdetot, 151 (*see* d'Houdetot, Comtesse Sophie); aid to escapees, 159–60, 167; aid to Crèvecoeur, 159–60, 164; pet projects, 161, 186, 239, 274–75, 285, 286; role in French acceptance of potato, 161; comment on *Life of an American Farmer* quoted, 164; comments on packet boats quoted, 165–66; on King's commission to investigate Deslon and mesmerism, 168, 171–74, 208, reports on, 174–75, BF quoted on, 174–75; interest in Mesmer's use of armonica, 170; letters on mesmerism and hypochondriacs quoted, 172, 174–75; at court, 179–85 (*see also* Versailles); comments on kings and queens, 181; relationship with La Rochefoucaulds, 184–88 (*see also* La Rochefoucauld d'Enville, Duchesse de; La Rochefoucauld d'Enville, Louis-Alexandre); in Royal Academy of Sciences, 188; eulogies on, 188; relationship with Comtesse de Forbach, 189–94; intelligence work and propaganda for, 193; has medals made, 193; relationship with Baroness de Bourdic, 194–95; relationship with Countess Golowkin, 195–97; relationship and correspondence with the Lafayettes, 198–202; anti-nobility views, 202–03, 205, 287–90; relationship with Lavoisiers, 207–10; scientific investigations, 202, 212; scientific friends and colleagues, 207, 208, 210, 212, 213 (*see also* Lavoisier; Le Roy, Jean-Baptiste); memories of Paris quoted, 210; relationship with Le Roys, 211–15, 222–24 (*see also* Le Roy, Mme.); interest in development of balloon travel, 215–22; anonymous letters to the press, 221–22; bourgeois women of note known by, 224–29; wax sculpture of, 225; works translated into French by Barbeu-Dubourg, 226; relationship with Mlle. Biheron, 226–27; unwillingness to pose, women who overcame, 227–33; likeness of as status symbol, 229, 232–34, ubiquity of, 232–33; relations with French of the lower classes, 239; relationship with Chevalier d'Eon, 237–39; relationship with Mme. Helvétius, 243–44, 251–70 (*see* Helvétius, Anne-Catherine); as member of l'Académie d'Auteuil, 249 (*see* Auteuil Academy); relationship with Morellet, 249 (*see* Morellet); relationship with Turgot, 251 (*see* Turgot, Anne-Robert); relationship with Cabanis, 252 (*see* Cabanis); reminiscences, 275–80; relationship with his children and grandchildren, 275, 279, 318 (*see also* Bache, Benjamin; Bache, Sarah; Franklin, William; Franklin, William Temple); agenda of progress in virtues, 277; epitaph, 280; relationship with de la Roche, 280–81 (*see* La Roche); bizarre letters and requests for recommendations to, 281–83; parody of letter of recommendation quoted, 282–83; political and economic views, 286, 287, 304–09; paper against hereditary nobility and societies in the U.S., 288–90; fondness for wine, 291–92 (*see also* Passy, BF's residence in), Morellet's drinking song about, 291–92; drinking song by, 292, 294, letter in praise of wine, *293*, 294–96; decision to leave France, 299, 300; health and spirits after return to Philadelphia, 304, 311, 318, 321; French memory of, 304–05; defense of U.S. on French

friends' criticisms, 304–07; opinion of the Constitution, 306–09; estate, 306, 318, 325; disinterest in French affairs, 307–09, 311; *83*d year, 318–19, 321; fondness for Blanchette Caillot, 319; expectation of death, 319, 326–27; exchange of gifts and goods with French friends, 327–28, 330–32; chronology of BF's dealings with France (*1767–90*), 335–40

Franklin, Deborah: death, 1; marriage, 19, 32, 78, 191, 267, 277, BF quoted on, 82; portrait of, 210; spelling, 214; in *Elysian Fields*, 265–67

Franklin, Francis, 279

Franklin, William, 1, 174, 181; relationship with BF, 275

Franklin, William Temple, 86, 87, *88*, 105, 124, 131, 132, 252, 254, 258, 260, 298; life before France, 1; trip to Paris with BF, 1–2; as BF's secretary, 9–10, 12, 79, 235, 341; interest in Brillon daughters, 84, 315; BF's attempt to marry Cunégonde Brillon to, 91–96, 156, 313; relationship with BF, 91–93, 275; personality and career, 91, 93, 95, 99, 100–01, 133, 341; as BF's editor, 93, 146–48, 276, 296, 341–42; wild life, 97, 98, 111; romance with Aldegonde Brillon, 97–101, 118; letters from Le Veillard junior, 97–98, 116, quoted, 98–100; affair and correspondence with Blanchette Caillot, 101 (*see* Caillot, Blanchette); M. Brillon's feeling for, 107, 313; appointment book for *1785*, 118; relationship

Franklin, William Temple—*cont.*
with Chaumonts, 130, 134; correspondence with BF quoted, 134, 174–75; bequeathed BF's papers, 145–46; relations with Le Veillards, 145, 146, 327–30, letters from, 305 n., 327, letters to, 327; request to Le Veillard for a live deer, 146, 329–30; letter to Le Veillard on BF's papers quoted, 147–48; joins Mesmer's secret society, 174; BF's letter to on Mesmer report, 174–75; illustrations to BF's letter on drinking wine, 293; correspondence from U.S. with French, 304, 327; letter on Aldegonde's marriage, 313; as gentleman farmer, 318, 328, 341

Franklin family, soap, 330–31, BF's praise of, 330

Frederick, 7

French Academy, 81, 153, 286, 297, 299

French Revolution, 155, 188–89, 225, 240, 290; fate of BF's friends in, 18, 126, 148–49, 152, 171, 189, 192, 197–98, 210–11, 224, 228–29, 274, 310, 314 n.; Terror, 152, 211, 229, 250; relation to American Revolution, 184, 310; French social thought contributing to, 246; coming described by participants, 307–10, 320

Freté, Mme. de la, letter to. See under *Bagatelles*

Freud, 169

Friseurs, BF's army of, 202–03

Galiani, Abbé, 246, 286

Garonne, river, 116

Garrick, David, 284

Geller, W. O., *xv*

George III, 200; bond between Louis XVI and, 180

Georgia, 199

Gerard, placets to BF quoted, 240–41

Germany, 161, 191, 245; BF's contacts with, 191, 194, 195

Glasspiel, 22

Gluck, 22, 49; BF refers to, 51

Golowkin, Count Alexander, 195

Golowkin, Countess Wilhelmina: relationship with Chastellux, 195–97; relationship with BF, 195–97; personality, 196, 198; letters to BF quoted, 196, 197; letter from BF quoted, 196; bibliographical note on, 354

Gonesse, 216, 219

Gottingen, 195

Gout: works inspired by, 77–81; BF's attacks of, 77. *See also* Franklin, Benjamin

Graffigny, Mme. de, 244–45; *Les Lettres d'une Péruvienne*, 245

Grand, Ferdinand, 123

Grand, Mme., 330; letters to BF, 324, quoted, 328

Greece, Greeks: building, 212; philosophy, as used by Mme. Brillon, 47–48

Grimaldi family, 124

Grimm, editor, *Correspondance littéraire*, 268

Grosholtz, Marie. *See* Tussaud, Mme.

Guide littéraire de la France, cited, 287

Guillotin, Docteur, guillotine named for, 171

Gulf Stream, BF's chart of, 166

Gunpowder manufacture, Lavoisier's and BF's interest in, 207–08, 210

Halifax, Nova Scotia. *See* Acadia
Hambourg, Hôtel d', 12
Hancock, Governor (Mass., *1782*), 164
Handel, 23
Handsome and Deformed Leg, The. See under *Bagatelles*
Hardancourt, Mme. d' (Mme. Brillon's mother), 60; relationship with BF, 72, 73, 74, 84, 268
Hardancourt, Anne-Louise d'. *See* Brillon de Jouy, Anne-Louise
Harmonica. *See* Armonica
Helvétius, Anne-Catherine de Ligniville (Madame Helvétius), 9, *242*, 311, 328, 330; as rival to Mme. Brillon, 84, 108, 244, 268, 312, 333; as link between Lord Shelburne and BF, 116; *Bagatelles* written for, 119, 252–53, 264–68 (see also *Bagatelles, Elysian Fields, Mouches à Madame He[lvétius]*); Cabanis' poetic tribute to, 243; personality, 243–44, 245, 247, 252, 257–58, BF quoted on, 251, Morellet quoted on, 246, 297; BF's proposal of marriage to, 243, 260, 264–68, 270–71; life before BF, 244–51; Turgot's courtship of, 245, 249–50, 264; letters, 245, 256–57, 297, 333, to BF, quoted, 258, 260, 268, 298–300, 334; salon (*1750–71*), 246–47; daughters, 247, 252, 270, 284, 333; déshabillées, 247, 253, described by Abigail Adams, 257–58; love of animals and people, 248, 270, satirized by Morellet,

296–97; l'Académie d'Auteuil, 248–51 (*see* Auteuil Academy); ménage, 248–53, 259–60, 263, 270, 333, inside jokes about, 252, 255, 267, 297, John Adams' description of, 253–55, described by de la Roche and Morellet, 255–56, 296–97, 333, BF accepted as member of, 252–53, and not more, 270–71 (*see also* Cabanis; La Roche; Morellet); BF's courtship of, 256, 256–60, 262–68, 270–71, 298, 332; BF's view of paradise and, 256, 268, 333; painting of BF for, 284; political views, 290; health, 297–98, 332; picnics and visits to BF, 298; asks BF to remain in France, 298–300; letters from BF, 312, quoted, 133, 251–52, 258–59, 262–63, 271, 300–01, 331–34; BF unable to send cardinal to, 331–32; French regret at her not marrying BF, 332; shared remembrances and regrets with BF, 332–34; bibliographical note on, 355–56
Helvétius, Claude-Adrien, 245–47, 248, 249, 257; *De l'Esprit*, 247; career, 254; tomb, 254; BF's identification of himself with, 265; in BF's *Elysian Fields*, 266–68; poem by, 292
Hewson, Polly Stevenson, 19, 118, 123, 226
Hippocratic Oath, 274
Holbach, Baron d', 246
Holland, 245, 248
Homer, 274; *Iliad*, 59
Hopkinson, Mr., 232
Hospital "des Quinze Vingt," 286
Hôtel-Dieu, Paris hospital, 275

Houdetot, Comte, d', 152, 155–56, 162; quoted, 153

Houdetot, Comtesse Sophie de la Live de Bellegarde d', *150*; described, 151–52; influence, 151, 156, 258; personality, 151–52, 162; marriage, 152–53; children, 152, 156; love affairs with Saint-Lambert, Rousseau, 153–56; letter to Rousseau quoted, 154; BF plants acacia and endures party for, 156–58, 167; aid to America, 156, 158, 166–67, 186; poetry recitation for BF quoted, 157, 158; nature of relationship with BF, 158, 167, 175; aid to Crèvecoeur, 158–67; letters to BF, 159–60, 167–68, 256, quoted, 164, 167–68, 173, 176; receives "freedom of the city" of New Haven, 166–67; pleased by BF's gift of *Constitutions of the American States*, 167; BF's letters to, quoted, 168, 308; consulted by BF on Mesmer's cures, 168, 172–73, 175; poem on eagle falling in BF's garden, 176–77; bibliographical note on, 352–53

Hume, David, 246, 265

Hypnotism, Mesmer's work in, 169, 171. *See also* Deslon; Mesmer

Idéologues, 250

Ile St. Louis, 141, 160

Indians, 45; BF's view of, 16, 45, 277–78

Information to Those who would Remove to America. See under *Bagatelles*

Ingenhousz, Jan, 226

Inquisition, 285

Invalides, Hôtel des, 126

Ireland, Irish, 159; music, 22; importance of potato to, 161

Iroquois Indians, 200

Issy, 223

Italy, Italians, 106, 285; Risorgimento, 250

Jacobins, 256

Jamaica, 159

Jardin des Dames et des Modes, Le, 70

Javelle, 223

Jay, John, 135

Jefferson, Thomas, 151, 155, 311; quoted on BF chess anecdote, 135

Jolly, Baron, *xv*

Jones, John Paul, 91, 128, 327; relationship with Chaumonts, 129

Jones, Tom (character), 276

Journal de Paris, letters and poems on BF, 17, 90, 147, 195, 239

Journal des Affaires de l'Angleterre et de l'Amérique, 186

Judlin, Alexis, miniature of BF by, 233–34

Jupin, Mlle.: affair with M. Brillon, 31, 41, 42–43, 60–61, 107, discovery by Mme. Brillon, 61–65, 67, 68, 224, 253; description by John Adams, 42, cited, 60–61

Keralio, Chevalier Agathon de, 192–94, 260; as BF's propagandist and intelligence agent, 193

Laclos, Choderlos de, quoted, 151

Lafayette, Adrienne, Marquise de: escape from guillotine, 197–98; personality, 198; as wife, 198–200,

207; letters to BF, 198; letters from BF, 199; bibliographical note on, 354

Lafayette, George Washington, 200

Lafayette, Kayenlaha, 200

Lafayette, Marie Joseph Paul Yves Roch Gilbert de Motier, Marquis de, 91, 109, 128, 135, 191, 331; support of Mesmer, 169, 173; cited, 173–74; described, 198; family, 198–200; letters to BF, 199, quoted, 198; letter from BF quoted, 199; dinner parties, 200, *201*, 202

Lafayette, Virginia, 199, 200

La Fontaine, 77

La Freté, Madame de, BF's letter to. See under *Bagatelles*

La Live de Bellegarde, Sophie de. *See* Houdetot, Sophie

La Roche, Abbé Martin Lefebvre de, 21, 79, 279, 299; *Memoirs* quoted, 18–19; comes to live with Mme. Helvétius, 248–49, 252; as part of Helvétius ménage, 252, 253, 254–56, 265–67, 273, 290, 297, 333; letter to BF quoted, 255–56, 333; letters from BF quoted, 256, 262–63, 265; note on BF quoted, 280; "Note sur Franklin," quoted, 280–81, 283–84, cited, 282; relationship with BF, 280–81, 284

La Rochefoucauld's maxims, 185

La Rochefoucauld d'Enville, Duc de (father of BF's friend), 187

La Rochefoucauld d'Enville, Duchess de (mother of BF's friend), 189; is first in Paris to invite BF, 185; letters from BF quoted, 185; liberalism, 186–88; John Adams'

opinion of, quoted, 187; sends BF wine, 328; bibliographical note on, 353

La Rochefoucauld d'Enville, Louis-Alexandre, Duc de, 203; BF gives copy of Memoirs to, 146, 188; letters to BF quoted, 184–85, 188; letter from BF quoted, 185; relationship with BF, 185–86, 188; translates American political documents, 186; patriotism and liberalism, 187–89, 307–08; eulogy of BF, 188; death in French Revolution, 189

La Tour, Quentin de, 247

Lavoisier, Antoine-Laurent, 142, 161, 169; on Mesmer Commission, 171, 208; fate in French Revolution, 171, 210–11, 309; relationship with BF, 207–10; career, 207–08; letter to BF quoted, 309

Lavoisier, Marie-Pierrette: marriage, 207–11, assists her husband in laboratory, 207, *209*; portrait of BF, 209–10; letter from BF quoted, 209–10; life after French Revolution, 211; bibliographical note on, 354

Lee, Arthur, 180; hostility to BF and Deane, 5–6; letter from BF quoted, 6; accuses BF of nepotism, 12; quoted, 180

Lee, William, quoted, 180

Le Havre, 330; BF departs from, 133, 137, 139, 300, 321

Leibnitz, 7

Leray de Chaumont, Jacques (James Leray), 321; in America, 124, 135, 326 n.; attempts to collect his father's credit from Congress,

Leray de Chaumont—*cont.*
322–26; BF's aid in marriage, 322–
23; certificate of good behavior
from BF, 323; letters to BF, 325,
quoted, 326; letter from BF
quoted, 325

Leray, Jacques-Donatien. *See* Chaumont, Jacques-Donatien

Leray, Vincent, cited, 134–35

Leraysville, N.Y., 326 n.

Leroux-Cesbron, C., quoted, 149

Le Roy, Mme., 9; as BF's pocket
wife, 211, 213–15, 223–24; marriage, 211, 213, 214, 224; personality, 213, 223, 224; letter to
BF on being shut out quoted,
213–14; letters to BF quoted,
214–15, 223–24; ascent in balloon,
222–24; letter from BF quoted,
223; bibliographical note on, 254

Le Roy, Charles, 212

Le Roy, Jean-Baptiste, 170, 220, 227;
friendship with BF, 211–14, 265,
333; marriage, 211 (*see* Le Roy,
Mme.); family, 211–12; Benny
Bache boards with, 234; correspondence with BF, 212–13;
letters to BF quoted, 219, 223; as
BF's collaborator, 275; letter from
BF quoted, 308–09; bibliographical note on, 354–55

Le Roy, Julien, 212

Le Roy, Julien-David, 212

Le Roy, Pierre, 212

Letters from an American Farmer. See
Crèvecoeur

*Letters from a New Haven Burgher.
See* Condorcet

Lettres d'une Péruvienne, by Madame
de Graffigny, 245

Le Veillard, Mme.: love of church
and BF, 108, 139, 140, 310; BF
visits, 108, 109; curé of, 108, 143;
letters from BF quoted, 139, 143;
children, 139; dowry, 141; letters
to BF, 143, quoted, 139–40; BF's
opinion of quoted, 143

Le Veillard, Geneviève, 140; letters
to BF quoted, 143–45; on what
goes on in a French girl's head,
144, 149; saves BF's *Autobiography*,
149

Le Veillard, Louis-Guillaume, 48,
79, 117; as liaison between BF and
Mme. Brillon, 33, 34, 35, 39, 52,
138–39, 142, 313, 320; relationship with Mme. Brillon, 35, 42, 43;
chess game with BF in Mme.
Brillon's bathroom, 59; family, 97–
98, 139, bibliographical note on,
351–52 (*see also* Le Veillard, Mme.,
Geneviève, Louis, "le jeune");
correspondence with Mme. Brillon, 103, 108, quoted, 34; accompanies BF to Southampton, 138–
40; as mineral-water entrepreneur,
140–42; aid to BF in writing
French, 142; devotion to BF,
142–43; part in writing and publication of BF's Memoirs, 145–48,
329–30; in French Revolution,
149, 310; letters to BF, 310, 313,
quoted, 35, 287, 306, 310–12,
cited, 228, 316, 324; letters from
BF, 313, quoted, 140–41, 311,
cited, 320

Le Veillard, Louis, "le jeune," 143;
correspondence with Temple, 97–
99, quoted, 98–99, 116; career, 98,
311

Liaisons dangereuses. See Laclos

Library of Congress, BF papers in, 342

Lightning rods, 129, 137, 177, 195, 213; chorus in honor of, 157; installed in France, 164

Ligne, Prince de, quoted, 49–50

Ligniville d'Autricourt, Anne-Catherine de. *See* Helvétius, Anne-Catherine

Locke, John, 276

Lodge of the Nine Sisters. *See* Masonic Lodge of the Nine Sisters

London, 115, 148, 185, 226, 289; BF in, 22; BF's friends in, 253; publication of *Letters from an American Farmer* in, 159; wax museum, 225; fate of BF's letters in, 341–43

London Academy, *Philosophical Transactions*, 196

Long Island, N.Y., 3

Lorient, 137, 160

Lorraine, 153, 244

Lorry, Dr. Anne-Charles, 102, 106

Louis XIV, women in the era of, 20

Louis XV, 102, 212, 237; women in the era of, 20–21; reception of BF (*1767*), 181; parties at la Muette, 228; gastronomy in age of, 236

Louis XVI, 109, 225, 228, 288, 325, 329; court, 5 (*see* Versailles); court painters for, 127, 183–84, 227; ice reserve, 133; miniature for BF, *136*, 138; use of Passy mineral waters, 141; in French Revolution, 148; aid to development of potato, 161; commissions to investigate Mesmer, 171–74, reports on, 174–75, quoted, 180; attitude toward

U.S. and BF, 180–81, 183, 184; watches balloon ascension, 216; gastronomy in reign of, 236–37; wife, 244 (*see* Marie-Antoinette)

Louis, dauphin, 225; birth, 21, 108, BF's letter about, 182–83

Louvre, 212

Luchet, Marquis de, 14

Luillier, Mlle., 297

Lumigny (château), 284

Lyons, 103, 215

Magalhaens (Magellan), Joachim de, 208

Magna Carta, 157

Malachelle, M. de, 101, 312, 314, 315–16, 319

Malachelle, Aldegonde Brillon de Jouy de, 107; romance with Temple, 97–101, 313, 315; marriage, 101, 312–13, 315–16, 319, 320. *See also* Brillon de Jouy, Anne-Louise, daughters of

Marat, Jean-Paul: death in bathtub, 29; as amateur scientist, 213

Marathon, 189

"Marche des Insurgents." *See* Brillon de Jouy, Anne-Louise

Maria Leczinska, wife of Louis XV, 181, 228

Maria Theresa, mourning for, 182

Marie-Antoinette, 21, 25, 85, 225, 229, 244; reception of BF, 181–84; parties, 227–28; affair of the diamond necklace, 286–87

Marly, 298

Marmontel, Jean François, 249, 265

Marseilles, 103

Masonic Lodge of the Nine Sisters, 15, 249

Massachusetts, 199

Mather, Cotton, 37

Maupertuis, *Treatise on Happiness*, 297

Maurois, André, quoted, 66; Adrienne cited, 198, quoted, 199

Maximilian, King of Bavaria, 191

Mazzar, M. (cobbler), 328–29

Mecom, Jane, 331

Memoirs of BF: quoted, 2; discovered, 145; writing of, 145–46, 278; publication, 146–49; copies given to Le Veillard and Duc de La Rochefoucauld, 146, 188; pirated edition in French published, 147, 279–80; thought lost, 279. See also *Autobiography*

Memoirs of the Marquise de Créquy, quoted, 14

Mesmer, Friedrich Anton, 274; debate over, 168–69; relationship with Deslon, 169, 171, 173; theory and practice, *163*, 169–73, report on, 174–75; BF's visit with, 170; letters to BF, 170, 173–74, quoted, 170; Sociétés de l'Harmonie, 173–74 n.; effect of Mesmer report on, 174–75

Metastasio, 23

Metropolitan Museum of Art (N.Y.), Duplessis painting of BF in, 127

Metz, Bishop of, 287

Milly, Comte de, 213

Mineral water, 140–42

Ministère des Affaires Etrangères, BF papers held by, 342

Mirabeau, 142; death, 274; *Considérations sur l'Ordre de Cincinnatus*, 289–90

Molière, *Misanthrope*, cited, 79

Monaco, 124

Moncrief, *Art of Pleasing*, 297

Montalembert ladies' ascent in balloon, 223

Montesquieu, *Lettres persanes*, 245

Montgolfier, Joseph Michel, 217, 218, 220; and brother, Jacques Etienne, launch first balloons, *206*, 215–16, 217–18

Montmorency, Vallée de, 156

Morals of Chess, The. See under *Bagatelles*

Moreau the younger, J. M., *204*

Morellet, Abbé, 307; songs by, 108, 290–92, 294, on BF, quoted, 291–92; as part of l'Académie d'Auteuil, 246, 248–49, 252, 254–55, 266–67, 273, 290, 299, 333, according to Morellet, 297; *Memoirs* quoted, 246, 255, 267, 290, cited, 249; relationship with BF, 249, 252, 263, 265, 273, 284–92, 299, 304–05; letters to BF, 304, quoted, 273, 288–89, 305; political and humanitarian work and views, 285–90, 304–05; letters from BF quoted, 286, 289, 294–96, 305; editing of BF's antinobility paper, 288–89; *Petition of the Cats*, quoted, 296–97; elected to French Academy, 299

Morison, Samuel Eliot, cited, 129

Morocco, BF thought to be slave in, 305 n.

Morris, Gouverneur, 197; quoted on BF's continuing popularity in France, 304–05

Morris, Robert, 3

Mosheim, Wilhelmina von. *See* Golowkin, Countess

Mouches à Madame He[lvétius], Les.
See under *Bagatelles*
Moulin-Joli, *28*, 52; described, 49–
50; as setting for *The Ephemera*,
50–51
Mozart, 23
Muette, Château de la, 213, 227–29
Mun, Charlotte, Marquise de, 284
Music: controversy over Gluck and
Piccinni, 22, 49, BF refers to, 51;
BF's preferences in, 22, 25, 34–35,
68, 290; BF's knowledge of, 25;
eighteenth-century parlor, 117;
Mesmer's use of, 170; American,
320. *See also* Armonica; Glasspiel;
Pianoforte

Nanterre, 137
Nantes, 12, 126; reception of BF at,
2, BF quoted on, 203
Nantucket, 159
Napoleon. *See* Bonaparte
Necker, Mme., 249
Necker, Jacques, 307; economic
theory, 249, 286
Née, Denis, engraver, *28*
New Haven, Conn., gives "freedom
of the city" to Parisian friends,
166–67
New Jersey, 322
Newton, Isaac, 7
New York (state), 159, 326 n.
New York (city), 3, 159; Public
Library, portrait of BF, 140
Nice, 316; Mme. Brillon's journey
to, 102–04; described, 106–07;
Mme. Brillon at, 106–08, 111–15,
317; political views of Niçois,
111; carnival, 111; Governor of,
112; English at, 111–12, 114–15

Niédrée (bookbinder), 119 n.
Nini, Giovanni-Battista, 126; his
medallions, of BF, *125*, 127, of
Mme. Chaumont, *122*, 129, of M.
Chaumont, *148*
Noailles (family), 197
Nogaret, Félix, quoted, 232–33
Nollet, Abbé, 212
Norman conquest, 288
Normandy, 120, 143, 158, 159, 164,
316
Normannus Americanus, pamphlet
on growing potatoes, 160. *See also*
Crèvecoeur
North Pole, 213
Nouvelle Héloise, La, Rousseau, 154,
195
Nouvelles Eaux de Passy, Les, 141–42

Oberkirch, Baroness d', 203
O'Gorman, Chevalier, 237
Ohio River, BF offers land on to
Mme. Helvétius, 332
Orange County, N.Y., 166
Ostend, 159

Pagin (violinist), 30, 34, 73, 77, 83,
102, 108, 111, 117
Paine, Thomas, 186
Parabole contre la Persécution. See
under *Bagatelles*
Paris, 48, 115, 148, 149, 152, 153, 154,
192, 194, 195, 244, 253, 257, 276,
286, 322; Opéra, 37, 192, fire at,
102; "libertine" ladies of, 105;
weather, 108; Brillons winter in,
117; welcome for BF, 124, 189;
drinking water, 141; acceptance of
Crèvecoeur, 160–62; friends of
Crèvecoeur given "freedom of the

Paris—*cont.*
    city" of New Haven, 166–67;
    debate over Mesmer, 168, 171,
    173–75; Mayor of, 171; Ameri-
    cans in, 194, 200; visit of Rous-
    seau's Persian cousin to, 197;
    excitement over balloons in, 215,
    218; first air view of, 218; BF
    likeness as status symbol in, 229,
    232–34; residence of Helvétius,
    246, 247; suburbs, 298; goods
    desired by Americans, 327 ff.
Paris Academy of Sciences. *See*
    Royal Academy of Sciences
Pâris d'Illins, Col. Marie-Antoine,
    96, 97, 100, 117, 313–20 passim
Pâris d'Illins, Cunégonde Brillon de
    Jouy: BF proposes marriage of
    Temple to, 91–96, 156, 313; BF's
    opinion of, 92; marriage to
    Frenchman, 96, 100, 117, 313, 320;
    first daughter, 96, 313, 317; as
    mother, 97; other children, 316,
    319, 320
Paris Faculty of Medicine, 171, 226,
    274
Parmentier, Antoine, champions
    potato, 161
Pascal, *Provinciales*, 276
Passy, 281; BF describes, 12; BF's
    friends and neighbors in, 18, 22,
    33, 71, 100, 123–49, 244, 310, 311,
    322 (*see also* Brillon; Chaumont;
    Le Veillard); BF's printing press
    at, 27, 70, 203, 229; aquatint of by
    Mme. Brillon, *37*; ladies, BF
    accuses of lack of neighborliness,
    79, BF given permission to kiss,
    105–06; garden sketched by BF,
    86; Brillon residence in, 104, 317,

    319 (*see also* Brillon de Jouy,
    Anne-Louise); distance from
    Paris, Versailles, 117, 124; shop-
    keepers left unpaid by BF's
    majordomo, 133; mineral waters
    and spas at, 141–42; Le Veillard
    becomes Mayor of, 148; residence
    of Mme. Filleul, 228; Chau-
    monts' house in, 324
Passy, BF's residence at, 12, 52, 103,
    195, 282, 297, 299; open door
    policy, 8, 9, 123; described, 124;
    rent, 124, 126; dining fare, 131,
    132, cost of, 132; household staff,
    131–32, 281 (*see also* Finck;
    Chaumont, Mlle. "mère Bobie");
    wine cellar, 132, 236, 296; BF's
    alterations to, 135, 137; meetings
    of Mesmer Commission at, 172,
    174; eagle falls in garden of, 176–
    77; Fourth of July celebration at,
    200
Passy, Mlle. de, 129
Paté de foie gras, 236
Paulze, Jacques, 207–08, 211
Payan de l'Etang, Marie-Anne Hen-
    riette. *See* Bourdic, Baronesse de
Pennsylvania, 305; Voltaire's view
    of, 15; BF elected President of the
    Supreme Executive Council of,
    304, 323
Pennsylvania, University of, BF's
    papers given to, 342
Pennsylvania Gazette, 50
Perno, Abbé, 23
Persia, Persian, relations of Rous-
    seau, 196–97
Peru, 161
Petition of the Cats, by Morellet,
    296–97

Petition of the Flies. See *Bagatelles, Mouches à Mme. He[lvétius]*

"Petits Oiseaux" (song), 117

Philadelphia, 145, 157, 284, 289; BF's return to, 26, 133, 134, 140; customs, 158; newspapers, 196; BF's friends in, 253; young BF arrives in, 276; BF in, 277; welcomes back BF, 304; demand for Parisian items, 327 ff.

Physiocrats, support of U.S., 15–16

Pianoforte, 9, 30; BF's use of, 133

Piccinni, 22, 49; BF refers to, 51

Pierre, M., 234

Pinel, Philippe, 287

Pitt, the younger, 202

Plutarch, 276

Polignac, Diane, Comtesse de, receives "portrait" of BF from Louis XVI, 184

Poor Richard Almanack, 277; cited, 41, 253, 288; quoted, 64; style, 83

Potato, development in France, 160–61, 186

Princeton, N.J., 209

Pringle, Sir John, 226

Prussia: U.S. Treaty of Amity and Commerce with, 4; King of, 114

Puritanism, 281

Quaker: as symbol, 15, 16; BF as, 131, 195

Quesnay, François, 15

Ray, Cathy, 19

Raynal, 246

Réaumur, René Antoine Ferchault de, 50

"La Religieuse" (music), 323

Remarks on the Politeness of Savages, 278

Remarks Concerning the Savages of North America. See under *Bagatelles*

Reprisal, 1

Réveillon, M., 216

Rhone, 103

Richardson, *Pamela,* 245

Rivers, Milady (widow of Earl of Chatham), party at Nice, 111–12

Rochambeau, 109, 135; Expeditionary Corps in America, 196

Rohan, Prince-Cardinal Louis-René de, 244, 286–87

Roman building, 212

Rouen, 322

Rousseau, Jean-Jacques, 225; relation to BF, 16–17, 127, 279–80; in Passy, 141; affair with Comtesse d'Houdetot, 153–56, drawn upon in *La Nouvelle Héloïse, Confessions,* 154–56; advice on hygiene, 195; *Romances,* 196; Persian cousin of, 196–97; *Confessions,* relation to BF's *Autobiography,* 279–80

Royal Academy, London, 212

Royal Academy of Sciences (Paris), 15, 169, 171, 213; influence of La Rochefoucaulds in, 187–88; BF's friends in, 207, 208 (*see also* Lavoisier, Antoine-Laurent; Le Roy); in French Revolution, 211

Royal Society, London, President of, 216. *See also* Banks

Rozier, Pilâtre de, 218, 221

Rumford, Count von. *See* Thompson

Saar, 190

Sage et la Goutte, Le. See under *Bagatelles*

Sainte-Beuve, analysis of *Elysian Fields*, 265, 268

St. Germain, 298, 314 n.; fair (*1784*), 225

Saint John, Hector. *See* Crèvecoeur

Saint-Lambert, Chevalier Jean-François de, 153–54, 155, 162, 166

Saint Non, Abbé de, aquatint of BF by, *iii*

St. Paul, 295

Salons, eighteenth-century, 20, 21, 261; of Mme. Helvétius, 246–47. *See also* Auteuil Academy

Salpêtrière, La (insane asylum), 287

Sannois (estate), 167–68; fête at, 156–58

Saratoga, 36

Sardinia, King of, 106

Sarsefield, Count, 254

Saxe dinner service, 236

Schobert, 30–31

Schubert, 31

Schweitzers (physicians), 245–46

Scotland, Scotch, music, BF's fondness for, 22, 34–35, 68, 290

Seine, 49, 124, 138; pollution, 141; BF swims, 281

Sequeville, de (King's secretary), quoted, 182

Sèvres china: medallion of BF, 114; chamberpots, 184; porcelain, 236

Shaftesbury, 276

Shelburne, Lord, 247, 284, 288; pro-Americanism, 111, 115; opinion of BF, 115; BF's letter to, quoted, 115–16

Shipley, Georgiana, 19

Short, William, quoted, 155

Silkworm industry, 186

Small, Alexander, 275

Smith, Adam, 186

Smith, William, 188

Smollett, Tobias, cited on Nice, 106–07

Sociétés de l'Harmonie, 173–74 n.

Socrates, 266, 276

Sorbonne, 247, 249

Southampton, England, 139; BF leaves from, 300

Spain, Ambassador to France, 192

Spectator, The, 276

Staël, Mme. de, 249

Stanislas of Lorraine, King of Poland, 153

Steak pommes frites, origin of, 161

Stevens, Henry, 342

Stevenson, Margaret, 123, 226

Stevenson, Mary (Polly). *See* Hewson

Stiles, Ezra, 94; *Journal* cited, 166–67

Stormont, Lord, 180, 184, 185

Story of a French Louse, or the Spy of a New Species, slanderous tale about BF, 238–39

Story of the Whistle, The. See under *Bagatelles*

Strasbourg, installation of lightning rods on, 213

"Such merry as we have been" (Scotch song), 34–35

Sweden: U.S. Treaty of Amity and Commerce with, 4; Ambassador to France, 192

Swift, Jonathan, 296

Switzerland, 161; Benny Bache educated in, 12, 233

Tartini, 30

Tell, William, 157, 189

Third Estate, 307. *See also* Bourgeoisie

Thompson, Benjamin, 211
Thuillerie, La, 60
Timothy, 295
Tinker, Chauncey, quoted, 25
Tippet, Mehetabel, 159
Tocqueville, Alexis Charles Henri
   Maurice Clerel de, *La Démocratie
   en Amérique*, 197
Tonneins, 116
Tonnerre (Burgundy), 237
Tonnerre, Marquis de, 129
Tories (U.S.), 1, 211
To the Royal Academy of ——
   [*Brussels*]. See under *Bagatelles*
Toulon, 193
Toulouse, Archbishop of, 307
Tours, 270
Treatises upon Morals, 297
Trenton, 189
Tressan, Comte de, 157
Trumbull, 192
Tuileries, 13
Turgot, Anne-Robert, 160, 185, 246,
   256, *269*, 285; pro-Americanism,
   16; epigram quoted, 67; courtship
   of Mme. Helvétius, 245, 249–50,
   264; friendship with Mme. Hel-
   vétius, 249–51; role in BF's court-
   ship of Mme. Helvétius, 263–64,
   267, 270–71, quoted on, 264, 270
Turgot, Marquis Robert, interest in
   Crèvecoeur and his knowledge of
   growing potatoes, 160–61
Turkey, 106, 114
Turkey, American, 177
Tussaud, Curtius, 225
Tussaud, Mme., wax sculptures of
   BF and royal family, 225
Twain, Mark: quoted, 278; cited,
   279

United States: Commissioners to
   France, 3, 124 (*see also* Adams;
   Deane; Franklin; Lee); economic
   situation (*1776*), 3; relations and
   treaties with France, 3–4 (*see*
   France; Franklin, Benjamin, mission in France); Treaty of Peace
   with Britain, 4, 145, negotiations
   for, 6, 114–16, 117, 253; Treaties
   of Amity and Commerce with
   France, Sweden, and Prussia, 4;
   negotiations with France and
   Spain, 12; French views of, 13–
   16, 164; European view of
   climate, 14; victory at Yorktown,
   109–10, 115; commercial agreement with Bavaria, 191; Capitol
   Rotunda, 192; Ambassador to
   Paris, 197, 304; social equality
   in, 205; press, BF's letters to,
   221; bankruptcy of paper money,
   270; postrevolutionary, 304, 306;
   BF's defense of to French friends,
   304–07; import duties and taxes,
   305, 325. *See also* American
   Revolution; Congress; Continental Army

Valentinois, Hôtel de (BF's Passy
   residence), 124, 126, 233, 326. *See
   also* Passy, BF's residence in
Vanloo, Charles-Amédée, 284
Vanloo, Louis-Michel, *284*; portrait
   of Mme. Helvétius, *242*, 284
Vanloo, Philippe-Amédée, portrait
   of BF, *272*
Vaughan, Benjamin, 145, 146
Vergennes, Comte de, 4, 126, 135,
   180, 181
Vermont, 159

Vernet, Claude-Joseph, 227

Vernet, Emilie, 227, 228–29

Versailles, French court at, 151, 165, 192, 227, 240; BF and ladies at, *xv*; acceptance of BF, 5, 124, 179–85, 353; mores, 66; painters, 127, 183–84, 227; interest in mesmerism, 173; BF's first reception at (*1778*), 179–81; magnificence and decay of, 181; BF as ambassador to, 182–84, 234, quoted on, 183; deaths and births at, 182–83; etiquette, 182–83, 253; fashions, 203; banquet at, *204*; BF's fascination with, 228; physicians, 246. *See also* Louis XVI; Marie-Antoinette

Vichy, mineral waters, 141

Vicomte de Barjac, quoted, 14

Vienna, 168

Vigée-Lebrun, Elisabeth, artist at court of Louis XVI, 227, 228; quoted, 49; description of BF quoted, 184; cited, 314 n.

Villefranche, Bay of, 107

Villers-sur-Mer (château), 120

Virginia, 189; locust, 157; Lafayette daughter named for, 199; hams and cardinals desired by French friends, 331

Volney, Constantin, cited, 273

Volta, 220

Voltaire, 7, 37, 185, 186, 225; pro-Americanism in *Lettres philosophiques*, 15; quoted, 153, 245; in l'Académie d'Auteuil, 249, 265

Voyage en Amérique septentrionale, by Chastellux, 197

Walpole, Horace, 179, 180, 184

Warville, Jean-Pierre Brissot de, *Mémoires* quoted, 164

Washington, George, 109, 190, 288; Long Island campaign (*1776*), 3–4; BF's bequest of walking stick to, quoted, 189; Lafayette's son named for, 200; portrait, 200; letter from BF quoted, 324–25; letter to Lafayette quoted, 331

Watelet, Claude-Henry, 49

Watson, Elkanah, 225; quoted, 27

Wax sculpture, 224–25

West Indies, 3

Whistle, The Story of the. See under *Bagatelles*

William the Bastard (Conqueror), 160, 282

Williams, Jonathan, as BF's assistant, 12

Wines, French, 237; BF's love for as cause of the American Revolution, 291–92; BF's letter on, 294–96

Wright, Patience, 225

Wycombe, England, 284

Xenophon, 276

Xeres (Spanish wine), BF's predilection for, 132, 296

Yale College, 94

Yale University: volume of BF's *Bagatelles*, 119 n., 344; publication of BF's papers, 343–44

Yonkers, N.Y., 159

Yorktown, British defeat at, 109–10, 115, 192

Zweibrücken. *See* Deux-Ponts